Leo Paul Dana, PhD

When Economies Change Hands
A Survey of Entrepreneurship
in the Emerging Markets of Europe
from the Balkans to the Baltic States

More pre-publication
REVIEWS, COMMENTARIES, EVALUATIONS . . .

"*When Economies Change Hands* is an insightful combination of foundation, blueprint, and roadmap. In the years immediately preceding and following the collapse of the Soviet Union, the world witnessed remarkable events. Leo Paul Dana has compiled a country-by-country account of the transitions that occurred in the former Soviet Republics and satellite nations. These transitions are not merely economic, but also political, legal, social, and even technological.

Dana conducted an exhaustive literature review, bringing together information and concepts from a variety of perspectives. This work will benefit scholars, public policymakers, economic development specialists, and business leaders. The author demonstrates how influential cultural differences have proved to be in the emergence of nations from planned economies. There is clearly no one way to convert to a free enterprise system. Similarly, there is no one way to succeed as an entrepreneur or investor in the new economies. This book gives the reader a basis for understanding current circumstances, which will aid in making future decisions. In addition, Dana points the way for researchers so that they can collect and analyze information to help practitioners."

Frank Hoy, PhD
*Director, Centers for Entrepreneurial Development, Advancement, Research and Support (CEDARS),
University of Texas at El Paso*

"*T*his book covers development paths and future challenges of entrepreneurship in all European transitional economies. Readers will find information essential to understanding specific features of transition processes in different countries and their implications for entrepreneurship. The author has done impressive fieldwork, via interviews with politicians, officials, entrepreneurs, consultants, and trainers, and by observing the business realities in countries from the Balkans to the Baltic States. That fieldwork has produced valuable insights of successful entrepreneurship modes and small-business sector development measures in different countries.

When Economies Change Hands benefits readers interested in understanding links between history of a nation, privatization policy, the role of cross-cultural cooperation and national minorities in business, and different patterns of entrepreneurship and economic growth. It is useful reading for politicians and entrepreneurship support system developers interested in benchmarking their efforts and results with entrepreneurship development practices in other countries."

Tiit Elenurm, PhD
*Professor and Head,
Entrepreneurship Department,
Estonian Business School*

International Business Press®
An Imprint of The Haworth Press, Inc.
New York • London • Oxford

When Economies Change Hands

*A Survey of Entrepreneurship
in the Emerging Markets of Europe
from the Balkans to the Baltic States*

INTERNATIONAL BUSINESS PRESS®
Erdener Kaynak, PhD
Executive Editor

When Economies Change Hands
A Survey of Entrepreneurship in the Emerging Markets of Europe from the Balkans to the Baltic States

Leo Paul Dana, PhD

International Business Press®
An Imprint of The Haworth Press, Inc.
New York • London • Oxford

For more information on this book or to order, visit
http://www.haworthpress.com/store/product.asp?sku=5292

or call 1-800-HAWORTH (800-429-6784) in the United States and Canada
or (607) 722-5857 outside the United States and Canada

or contact orders@HaworthPress.com

Published by

International Business Press®, an imprint of The Haworth Press, Inc., 10 Alice Street, Binghamton, NY 13904-1580.

Cover design by Marylouise E. Doyle.

Library of Congress Cataloging-in-Publication Data

Dana, Leo Paul.
    When economies change hands : a survey of entrepreneurship in the emerging markets of Europe from the Balkans to the Baltic states / Leo Paul Dana.
        p. cm.
    Includes bibliographical references and index.
    ISBN-13: 978-0-7890-1646-1 (hc. : alk. paper)
    ISBN-10: 0-7890-1646-X (hc. : alk. paper)
    ISBN-13: 978-0-7890-1647-8 (pbk. : alk. paper)
    ISBN-10: 0-7890-1647-8 (pbk. : alk. paper)
    1. Europe, Eastern—Economic policy—1989—Case studies. 2. Privatization—Europe, Eastern—Case studies. 3. Entrepreneurship—Europe, Eastern—Case studies. I. Title.

HC244.D334 2005
330.94'0559'091717—dc22
                                                                                2004027924

To spread knowledge is to spread well-being.

Alfred Nobel

This book is dedicated to N. J. Dana

ABOUT THE AUTHOR

Leo Paul Dana, MBA, PhD, serves as the Senior Advisor to the World Association for Small and Medium Enterprises, and as an editorial board member of several journals. He is the founding editor of the *Journal of International Entrepreneurship.* He is the author of 100 articles in refereed journals and 15 books, including the best-selling text *Entrepreneurship in Pacific Asia* (1999), as well as *Economies of the Eastern Mediterranean Region* (2000), and *When Economies Change Paths: Models of Transition in China, the Central Asian Republics, Myanmar, and the Nations of Former Indochine Française* (2002). Professor Dana was formerly Deputy Director of the International Business MBA Programme at Singapore's Nanyang Business School. He also served on the faculties of McGill University and INSEAD.

CONTENTS

Foreword

Today, more than ever before, interest is increasing in the area of entrepreneurship among businesspeople, consumers, educators, and government officials. The number of courses and seminars on the topic, entrepreneurship professors, journals devoted to the field, new ventures and existing organizations establishing an intrapreneurial climate, and coverage of entrepreneurs and their ventures by the media are all increasing.

The most interest is focused on the role of entrepreneurship in economic development. It involves more than just increasing per capita output and income; it involves initiating and constituting change in the structure of business and society. This change is accompanied by growth and increased output, which allow more wealth to be divided by the participants in the economic unit. The result is an entrepreneurial culture in which individuals are willing to accept all the risks and put forth the necessary effort to create something new of value.

Having many similar characteristics regardless of culture, this individual may be a man or woman, someone from a lower-class or upper-class background, a technologist or someone with minimal or no technology capability, a person with a graduate degree or a high school dropout, a twenty-year-old or someone over sixty. The person may be a doctor, lawyer, nurse, farmer, engineer, student, professor, salesperson, businessperson, inventor, or even unemployed. He or she is someone who is able to work in his or her culture, and juggle work, family, and civic responsibilities while creating something new that has value to the particular marketplace.

No area is more important to understanding and adopting this process than the transitional economies, and Professor Leo Paul Dana, one of the world's experts on entrepreneurship, is quite capable of looking at this process. His understanding and insights are a result of working in a variety of nations too numerous to count. This knowledge through personal exploration is evident in each of his previous books and is at the heart of this book as well.

In *When Economies Change Hands: A Survey of Entrepreneurship in the Emerging Markets of Europe from the Balkans to the Baltic States,* Professor Dana discusses the state of entrepreneurship in each transitional economy from a historical perspective, its present situation, and future evolution. Each of the countries presented has been carefully researched and the resulting contents verified by country experts.

You will find this book meticulous, yet easy to read. The ideas presented will stimulate your own thinking and give you insights on the similarities and differences among the cultures and the people involved. Professor Dana clearly evaluates each of these transitional economies in a way that is meaningful to everyone. You will truly enjoy this reading experience.

Robert D. Hisrich
Mixon Chair of Entrepreneurship and Professor
Weatherhead School of Management
Case Western Reserve University

Preface

My intrigue with Eastern Europe dates back to Expo '67, the 1967 World's Fair, where I was fascinated by the pavilion of the Union of Soviet Socialist Republics and those of Soviet satellites. At the time, these nations seemed worlds away, and it was not until 1979 that I had the opportunity to personally explore communist lands.

One day at East Berlin's Schöenefeld International Airport, I watched a Soviet-built Ilyushin Il-18, operated by the East German flag carrier Interflug. As the turboprop advanced, I flirted with the question, "If the German Democratic Republic were to reunite with the Federal Republic of Germany, what would be the impact on the economy?" Shortly thereafter, *National Geographic* reported on East and West Germany, "Unity no longer seems plausible" (Vesilind, 1982, p. 13).

Within a decade, however, a domino effect was about to take place. In Poland, the Solidarity trade union emerged from eight years underground and swept the Polish elections. Independent parties also sprung up in Hungary. The East German economy was fused into that of the Federal Republic of Germany, and communist governments fell one after another.

How would these nations transform their economies? In December 1991, the United Nations Resolution on the Development of Entrepreneurship recommended the promotion of entrepreneurship, by supporting national efforts and market-oriented approaches to further entrepreneurship development. In April 2002, Bulgaria, the Czech Republic, Estonia, Hungary, Latvia, Lithuania, Poland, Romania, Slovakia, and Slovenia signed the Maribor Declaration, acknowledging the principles of the European Charter for Small Enterprises as the basis for their support for small enterprises.

Entrepreneurs have since developed their firms, and these have been crucial in increasing supplies of goods and services, thereby transforming Eastern Europe from a region of shortages to a region with great economic potential. Yet theories and policies from the West do not necessarily apply without first being adapted to the environment; this is what prompted me to write this book. Enjoy it!

Acknowledgments

Research for this book was conducted on location, in the transitional economies of Eastern Europe. For travel to the region, I received funding from the Canadian MBA Program in Romania, the Ecole de Management EM Lyon (France), Nanyang Business School (Singapore), and the University of Pittsburgh. In addition, secondary research was conducted at various university libraries, including the University of Ottawa, the University of Oxford, the University of Richmond, and the University of Southern California. I would like to express gratitude to these universities, all of which provided substantial funding.

In the process of preparing the manuscript, each chapter was sent to experts for review. The following individuals kindly volunteered their time, providing inspiration, encouragement, and constructive comments:

- Gregor Bauman, Journalist, *Slovenia Times,* Ljubljana
- Rasa Brickiene, Senior Specialist, Public Relations Division, Bank of Lithuania, Vilnius
- Robertas Bruzilas, Lithuanian Development Agency for Small and Medium Enterprises, Vilnius
- Steve Cook, Department of Geosciences, Oregon State University, Corvallis
- Teresa E. Dana, Senior Lecturer, Christchurch College of Education, New Zealand
- John Dawson, Professor of Marketing, University of Edinburgh, Scotland
- Erzsébet Dobos, The Hungarian Investment and Trade Development Agency, Budapest
- Juris Dzenis, Deputy Director of Entrepreneur Department, Head of Entrepreneur Environment and Small and Medium Enterprise Development Policy Division of the Ministry of Economy of the Republic of Latvia, Riga

- Tiit Elenurm, Chairman of the Council, Estonian Business School Executive Training Center, Tallinn
- Radu Enescu, Academy of Economic Studies, Bucharest, Romania
- Michael Frese, President of the International Association of Applied Psychology, London Business School
- Allan A. Gibb, Former Chairman, University of Durham Foundation for Small and Medium Enterprise Development, England, United Kingdom
- Jerzy Gierusz, Professor of Accounting, University of Gdansk, Poland
- Eglantina Gjermeni, Professor of Social Work, Tirana University, Albania
- Jolanta Gladys-Jakobik, Professor of Sociology, Warsaw School of Economics, Poland
- Miroslav Glas, Professor of Economics, University of Ljubljana, Slovenia
- Nahum Goldmann, ARRAY Development and School of Management, University of Ottawa, Canada
- Adrian Grycuk, Senior Research Specialist, Polish Agency for Foreign Investment, Warsaw, Poland
- Ceslavs Grzibovskis, Economic Analyst, Economic Policy Department, Ministry of Economics, Riga, Latvia
- Inese Gûtmane, Administrator, The Latvian Chamber of Commerce and Industry, Riga
- Katrin Hille, Department of Psychology, University of Canterbury, Christchurch, New Zealand
- Petar Ivanovic, Executive Director, Institute for Strategic Studies and Prognoses, Podgorica, Serbia and Montenegro
- Renata Januszewska, Department of Agricultural Economics, Gent University, Belgium
- Andreas Kaju, Marketing Project Manager, Estonian Chamber of Commerce and Industry, Tallinn, Estonia
- Anhelita Kamenska, Latvian Center for Human Rights and Ethnic Studies, Riga
- Jerome A. Katz, Mary Louise Endowed Professor of Management, Saint Louis University, Missouri
- Kristine Kizika, Attaché of the Information Division, Ministry of Foreign Affairs, Riga, Latvia

- Kostadin Kolarov, Entrepreneurship Development Center, University of National and World Economy, Sofia, Bulgaria
- Katarzyna Kosmala-MacLullich, Heriot-Watt University, Riccarton, Edinburgh, Scotland
- Margit Kottise, Specialist of the Information and Marketing Section Statistical Office of Estonia, Tallinn
- Tadej Krošlin, Assistant, Institute for Entrepreneurship and Small Business Management, Faculty of Economics and Business, University of Maribor, Slovenia
- Kállay László, Economic Analyst, Institute for Economic Analysis, Budapest, Hungary
- V. Lescheva, Statistician, Department of Work with Statistics Users, Ministry of Statistics and Analysis, Minsk, Belarus
- Lelo Liive, Deputy Director, Financial Services Department, Ministry of Finance of Estonia, Tallinn
- Nikola Manzelov, Legal Adviser, Foreign Investment Agency, Sofia, Bulgaria
- Audrone Mishkiniene, Statistical Information Division, Lithuanian Department of Statistics, Vilnius
- Silviu Neget, Vice Dean, Faculty of International Economic Relations, Academy of Economic Studies, Bucharest, Romania
- Eve Nurk, National Library of Estonia, Tallinn
- John Oliver, Ambassador to Serbia and Montenegro, Australian Department of Foreign Affairs and Trade, Belgrade, Serbia and Montenegro
- Sarmite Ozolina, Press Secretary, Latvian Development Agency, Riga
- Steven Paulikas, Vilnius Bureau Chief, *The Baltic Times,* Lithuania
- Igor Pavlin, Head, Management and Entrepreneurship, International Center for Promotion of Enterprises, Ljubljana, Slovenia
- Rok Petric, Publisher, *The Slovenia Times,* Ljubljana
- Larissa Piskunova, Assistant Public Information Officer and Webmaster, United States Agency for International Development, Kiev, Ukraine
- Andreas Polkowski, Hamburg Institute of International Business, Germany
- Inese Pommere, Public Relations Officer, Bank of Latvia, Riga

- Joan Popa, Dean, Faculty of International Economic Relations, Academy of Economic Studies, Bucharest, Romania
- Miroslav Rebernik, Director, Institute for Entrepreneurship and Small Business Management, Faculty of Economics and Business, University of Maribor, Slovenia
- Julius Riaubunas, Infostructura, Vilnius, Lithuania
- Karin Rits, Head of European Union and International Cooperation Division, Ministry of Economic Affairs and Communications of Estonia, Tallinn
- Kadri-Mai Rosenfeld, Press and Information Department, Estonian Ministry of Foreign Affairs, Tallinn
- Elzira Sagynbaeva, Deputy Resident Representative, United Nations Development Program (UNDP), Tirana, Albania
- Helena Schlamberger, Adviser, Slovenian Trade and Investment Promotion Agency, Ljubljana
- Maria Strykowska, Professor, Adam Mickiewicz University, Poznan, Poland
- Antal Szabo, Regional Adviser, United Nations Economic Commission for Europe, Geneva, Switzerland
- Krista Taurins, Executive Director, American Chamber of Commerce in Latvia, Riga
- Erik Terk, Director, Estonian Institute for Futures Studies, Tallinn
- Jaka Terpinc, Editor-in-Chief, *Slovenia Times,* Ljubljana
- Kiril Todorov, Director, Entrepreneurship Development Center, University of National and World Economy, Sofia, Bulgaria
- Merike Traat, Executive Director, American Chamber of Commerce Estonia, Tallinn
- Maaja Vadi, Professor of Economics and Business Administration, University of Tartu, Estonia
- Momanu Valeriu, Senator, Parliament of Romania, Bucharest
- Karmo Velling, Public Relations Officer, Estonian Ministry of Finance, Tallinn
- Tiia Vissak, Chair of International Economy, Faculty of Economics and Business Administration, University of Tartu, Estonia
- Tihomir Vranešević, Professor of Economics, Faculty of Economics, Zagreb, Croatia

- Richard W. Wright, The E. Claiborne Robins Distinguished University Chair, University of Richmond, Virginia
- Eremic Zoran, Business and Information Advisor, Regional Agency for Development of Small and Medium Enterprises and Entrepreneurship—Banat, Zrenjanin, Serbia and Montenegro

Chapter 1

Introduction

THE CONTEXT FOR ENTREPRENEURSHIP

Opportunities for entrepreneurship, and constraints as well, are often a function of the environment. As discussed by Hakansson (1982), enterprise does not take place in a vacuum, but rather involves interactions among members of society. Herbig and McCarty elaborate, "Culture is a primary determinant of innovation but is strongly moderated by the structural aspects of a society" (1995, p. 62). Huntington (1993, 1996) showed that globalization has neither standardized societies, nor produced a homogeneous world culture. Comparing different cultures in Eastern Europe, Jerschina and Górniak (1997) suggested that people from some cultures have a different achievement orientation and a higher *n ach* (need for achievement) (McClelland, 1961) than people from others.

Around the world, different styles of entrepreneurship have evolved, reflecting a variety of macroeconomic, political, sociocultural, and technological characteristics. In North America, for example, mainstream entrepreneurs thrive independently in a prosperous environment that features economic and political stability, while fostering innovation. There are, however, subgroups of people there, such as the Eskimos in Alaska, who do not value the "independent" nature of business ownership; influenced by the characteristics of their own culture, they exhibit a less individualistic form of entrepreneurship (Dana, 1995). In Japan, business also occurs along less-independent lines, as the makeup of society encourages entrepreneurs to work for larger firms, rather than to compete with them (Dana, 1998b). In advanced industrial societies, there are few barriers to entrepreneurs wishing to set up and manage formal businesses; elsewhere, external forces are quite different and have, as a result, prompted individuals to pursue alternate forms of entrepreneurship.

Transitional economies provide a particularly fascinating back-drop for the development of entrepreneurship. In the words of Birzulis, "MBA courses teach their pupils that business is a dicey, dynamic world where anything can happen. But no amount of seminars and lectures can prepare the budding entrepreneur for the surprises awaiting them in the postcommunist environment" (2002, p. 20).

In transitional economies, two principal schools of thought have given rise to two streams of public policy. One approach is that reform must take place gradually, at a cautious pace, in order to avoid side effects. In contrast, the big-bang approach prescribes the closure of money-losing state-owned industries (see Photo 1.1) and proclaims immediate transition to capitalism.

China and Vietnam (see Photo 1.2) are examples of countries that have implemented models of gradual transition, tolerating private enterprise as a complement to the centrally planned state sector, but not as a replacement (Dana, 1999d, 2002). Kruft and Sofrova (1997) emphasized the gradualism. In China, the government allows some en-

PHOTO 1.1. Obsolete factories shut down.

PHOTO 1.2. Merchants crossing between China and Vietnam.

trepreneurs to function outside the planned sector, while other aspects of the economy remain under state control. The rich literature on this topic includes Beamish (1993); Chau (1995); Chow and Tsang (1995); Dana (1998a, 1999c); Dandridge and Flynn (1988); Fan, Chen, and Kirby (1996); Lombardo (1995); McMillan and Naughton (1992); Overholt (1993); Peng (2000); Shirk (1993); Siu and Kirby (1995); Wei (2001); and Williams and Li (1993). Similarly, Vietnam introduced some free-enterprise policies without rejecting socialism, as discussed by Dana (1994a,b); Litvack and Rondinelli (1999); Peng (2000); Ronnås (1996); and Tan and Lim (1993). The result is a gradual transition involving a complementarity between state firms operating under a system of centralization and the small-business sector operating independently. Cuba has also clung to its socialist policies while tolerating some forms of entrepreneurship (Dana, 1996b).

In contrast to the gradual approach of transition, several countries have opted for the expedient liberalization of prices and privatization of state firms, with the expectation that this will lead to rapid transition to a healthy market-oriented economy in which entrepreneurs usher in capitalism. The conviction here is that although private ownership is not a sufficient condition to ensure the efficient operation of a market economy, it is a prerequisite. Variants of this model have been adopted in some countries of Africa (Dana, 1996c; Gray and Allison, 1997) and Central Asia (Dana, 1997a, 2000a, 2002), as well as in Eastern Europe (Arendarski, Mroczkowski, and Sood, 1994; Sachs, 1993) and Russia (Boycko, Shleifer, and Vishny, 1995; Hisrich and Gratchev, 1993). It should be emphasized, however, that the rate of new venture formation may be slower than the rate of unemployment generated during privatization (Thomas, 1993). Engholm (1994) noted a relationship between the pace of reform and the potential for rising unemployment; experience has shown that an economy cannot be instantly transformed without social problems.

Much has been written about privatization[1] and about how its pace affects unemployment (Bolton and Roland, 1992; Estrin, 1994a,b; Frydman, Rapaczynski, and Earle, 1993; Hughes and Hare, 1992; Ivy, 1996; Murrell, 1993; Seibert, 1992; Simoneti, 1993; Wilson, 1992). Where privatization has taken place rapidly, many have been pushed to self-employment (Meager, 1992). Where privatization and downsizing of state-owned enterprises cause mass unemployment, there is often a mismatch between market demand and skills available in the workforce. The workforce needs retraining in skills that are in demand. Certain skills that are not deemed necessary in the West can be very useful in a postcommunist economy (see Photo 1.3).

Although privatization gave rise to opportunities, unemployment was allowed to surge and as a result, some people were pushed to become self-employed due to the lack of alternatives. In other instances, individuals became rent-collecting capitalists by chance, simply because restitution laws restored property to them. Others simply tried to profit from arbitrage, as described by Hayek (1948). By being alert to opportunities, it was possible to identify them (Kirzner, 1973, 1979, 1982, 1985). None of these were Schumpeterian innovators (1912, 1928, 1934, 1939, 1942, 1947, 1949) causing disequilibrium.

For those who opted to exercise outside the formal sector, the parallel market provided opportunities; activities could be informal, internal, or even covert. In some countries, liberalization allowed entrepreneurs to shift their unofficial pretransition activities into the formal sector.

This book discusses results obtained through the implementation of differing policy approaches to transition. Although some governments sought rapid transition, others adopted a policy of slow reform.

PHOTO 1.3. Learning skills on the job.

Each model has its advantages and its problems, and the nature of entrepreneurship is very much a function of the environment.

The Czech Republic[2] and Hungary[3] have been particularly aggressive in their pursuit of market-driven philosophies, supporting earlier findings (Carroll and Green, 1995; Geib and Pfaff, 1999; Moskowitz and Rabino, 2001). The German Democratic Republic, Estonia, and Hungary privatized by means of agencies; most countries did otherwise. To improve access to finance for small firms, some countries established public-guarantee funds.

Estonia, Latvia, and Lithuania took very significant actions in reducing taxes; Lithuania introduced a 13 percent tax rate for microenterprises. Slovenia attracted foreign investment by providing a neutral tax base. In contrast, Slovakia assessed relatively high tax rates but offered preferential treatment to some investors; this model appears to have had less success than the former.

This book looks at differences among countries in transition, but some common trends may also be observed. As discussed by Kruft and Sofrova (1997), the private sector in transitional economies often lacks intermediate support structures that are available in the West.

METHODOLOGY

Although countless country-specific publications have been written on transition from centrally planned to market economies, the purpose of this book is to provide a single-volume overview of transition in Europe, from the Balkans to the Baltics. This work is the result of inductive, ethnographic research with an emic design, coupled with over 300 secondary sources that are listed in the reference section at the end of this book.

Primary sources of information included archival research, participant observation, unobtrusive measures, and open-ended interviews with consultants, entrepreneurs, and government officials. Interviews typically lasted between two and three hours. Some respondents asked to be paid.

Challenges included difficulties with infrastructure. MacIntyre (1991) reported that of 786 long-distance calls attempted by *The Economist*'s Moscow correspondent between June 21 and July 17, 1991, 754 resulted in no connection, and of the thirty-two completed calls, two were wrong numbers and six were cut off in the middle. Writing over a decade later, telecommunications have improved, but interviews are interrupted for other reasons.

Special care was taken to not be misled by socially desirable responding, as discussed by Adair (1984); Arnold, Feldman, and Purbhoo (1985); Crowne and Marlowe (1960); Rahim (1983); and Zerbe and Paulhus (1987). Numerous studies have raised concerns about the contamination of research findings by such socially desirable responding (Arnold and Feldman, 1981; Golembiewski and Munzenrider, 1975; Rosenkrantz, Luthans, and Hennessey, 1983; Stone et al., 1979; Thomas and Kilmann, 1975).

Content validity was enhanced with triangulation (Patton, 1982, 1987, 1990). This was especially useful when investigating the unofficial economy. Supporting earlier findings (Johnson et al., 2000), numerous entrepreneurs were found to hire much of their labor, and sell much of their output, through unofficial channels; this is true, even among registered firms. As suggested by Johnson, Kaufmann, and

Shleifer (1997) and by Johnson et al. (2000), official gross domestic product (GDP) figures may be significantly underestimated.

THE FORMAL ECONOMY:
THE FIRM-TYPE SECTOR AND THE BAZAAR

Readers are likely to be most familiar with the firm-type sector, an economic institution that involves a mode of commercial activity such that industry and trade take place primarily within a set of impersonally defined institutions. In this sector of the economy, the decision space is occupied by product attributes; the buyer and seller are secondary, if not trivial, to the transaction decision. The interaction between the buyer and the product is deemed more important than that between the buyer and the seller. It is assumed that profit-maximizing transactions will occur based on rational decision making, rather than the nature of personal relationships. The focus is on impersonal considerations, as described in Weber's (1924) thesis. Competition takes place between sellers, who engage in segmentation, in order to partition the market into like groups of predictable consumers. Prices are tagged, reflecting market forces. Although Western marketing principles (Gronroos, 1989) apply to this sector, market orientation is linked to the maturity of the industrialization process.

In contrast, the bazaar is a social and cultural system, a way of life, and a general mode of commercial activity in which interpersonal relationships are central to recruitment, retention, promotion, and purchasing decisions; nepotism often takes priority over merit. The price and the level of service quality reflect the relationship between the buyer and the seller. In this scenario, consumers do not necessarily seek the lowest price or the best quality. An individual gives business to another with whom a relationship has been established, to ensure that this person will reciprocate. Reciprocal preferential treatment reduces transaction costs.[4] The multiplicity of small-scale transactions in the bazaar results in a fractionalization of risks and therefore of profit margins; the complex balance of credit relationships is carefully managed, as described by Geertz (1963).

Prices in the bazaar are negotiated, as opposed to being specified by the seller. In contrast to the firm-type sector, in which the primary competitive stress is between sellers, the sliding-price system of the bazaar results in the primary competitive stress being between buyer and seller (Parsons and Smelzer, 1956). The lack of information results in an imperfect market and with few exceptions, such as basic food staples, retail prices are not indicated; rather, these are determined by negotiations. The customer tests price levels informally, before bargaining begins. It is often the buyer who proposes a price, which is eventually raised. As discussed by Geertz, the "relatively high percentage of wholesale transactions (i.e., transactions in which goods are bought with the express intention to resell them) means that in most cases both buyer and seller are professional traders and the contest is one between experts" (1963, p. 33). Once a mutually satisfactory transaction has taken place, the establishment of a long-term relationship makes future purchases more pleasurable and profitable. As noted by Webster (1992), building long-term relationships can be viewed as a social and economic process. Unlike Western relationship marketing, which is customer centered, whereby a seller seeks long-term business relationships with clients (Evans and Laskin, 1994; Zineldin, 1998), the focus in the bazaar is on the relationship itself. In the bazaar, *both* the buyer and the seller seek a personal relationship. Firms in the bazaar are not perceived as rivals of one another. There is minimal—if any—brand differentiation among merchants (see Photo 1.4). Table 1.1 compares features of the firm-type sector with those of the traditional bazaar.

THE PARALLEL ECONOMY:
INFORMAL, INTERNAL, AND COVERT

Under central planning, the lack of a legal market economy led to permanent shortages (see Photo 1.5). Survival strategies often involved the emergence of entrepreneurs in the parallel economy, where inefficient regulations could be circumvented. According to Grossman (1977), this underground activity increased the overall efficiency of resource allocation under central planning. The problem is that a mind-set evolved which equated efficiency with the evasion of regulation.

Recent years have been characterized by economic and regulatory reform, but change in mind-set has not kept up with changes in regulatory framework (North, 1990). Since these have not evolved at the same pace, new problems have become associated with transition. As

PHOTO 1.4. Selling the same products as the neighbors.

TABLE 1.1. Contrasting sectors of the formal economy.

	The firm-type sector	The bazaar
Focus	Product and impersonal transaction	Personal relationships
Segmentation	By target market—demographic, geographic, etc.	By producer and the type of good being sold
Prices	Indicated by the vendor, with the view of covering expenses, making a desired profit, and providing the desired image for the product	Negotiated, often starting off from an unreasonable price, either unusually high from the vendor's side or low from the buyer's side
Competition	An activity that takes place among sellers, competing for clients	Tension between buyer and seller competing to influence price

a consequence of their experience under central planning, many people equated entrepreneurship with the avoidance of communist law. When new regulations were introduced to usher in market economics, people continued to circumvent business law. As noted by Feige and Ott (1999), during transition, evasion and noncompliance with new rules renders them ineffective. Thus, where economic reform has been more rapid than the ability of people to adapt, inertia has de-

PHOTO 1.5. Sparsely stocked shelves.

layed actual transition. Štulhofer (1999) used the term *cultural inertia* to describe a collectivist legacy that has survived from the past. Especially among the elderly (see Photo 1.6), there is still a distrust of the state, of banks, and of legal institutions. Conditions in transitional economies thus make the parallel sector very popular, avoiding all forms of taxation. In transitional economies that lack developed market institutions, it is common to have a high proportion of underground activities. This is no surprise, considering the low initial role of legitimate private enterprise, coupled with a high degree of liberalization, hindered by the lack of macrostability in the absence of a sufficiently developed legal framework.

The size of the parallel economy and the level of corruption[5] vary greatly across Eastern Europe. Johnson, Kaufmann, and Shleifer (1997) estimated that the unofficial economy was 15 percent in Poland, compared with 50 percent in Russia and the Ukraine. Johnson et al. (2000) reported that Russia and the Ukraine had higher levels of unofficial business and corruption than was visible in Poland, Romania, and Slovakia. Johnson et al. (2000) reported that 90 percent of their Russian and Ukrainian respondents said it was normal to pay bribes, while in Slovakia only 40 percent said the same; in Poland and Romania, the percentage was 20 percent. As illustrated in Table 1.2, forms of entrepreneurship in the parallel economy may be informal, internal, or covert.

PHOTO 1.6. Affected by personal experience.

TABLE 1.2. Entrepreneurship in the parallel economy.

Sector	Exchange	Focus	Examples
Informal	Legal transaction	Informality	Street vending, unrecorded sales
Internal	No transaction	Subsistence	Subsistence agriculture, hunting, fishing
Covert	Illegal transaction	Illegal cash	Prostitution, drug dealing

Informal economic activity[6] can take the form of an impromptu stall (see Photo 1.7) or itinerant vending (see Photo 1.8). Unrecorded cash sales circumvent taxation as well as regulation. The law is often bent, but authorities generally tolerate the sector. A relevant discussion from Dana (1992) is presented concisely by Chamard and Christie (1996). Johnson, Kaufmann, and Zoido-Lobaton (1998) discuss discretion in the sector.

PHOTO 1.7. Impromptu stall.

PHOTO 1.8. Itinerant vendor.

Internal subsistence activity[7] is often necessary as a means to adapt to rapid reform. Whereas McClelland defined the word *entrepreneur* as an individual who has "some control over the means of production and produces more than he can consume in order to sell (or exchange) it" (1961, p. 65), internal subsistence activity refers to that which is consumed internally rather than sold (see Photo 1.9). Thus, this category of economic activity is described as internal, because it does not involve an external exchange; no business transaction takes place. Wealth is created, but nothing is sold for profit; that which is created is consumed or saved for personal use.

Internal subsistence activity includes subsistence agriculture and subsistence fishing (see Photo 1.10). Both are legal but involve no market transaction external to the producer. Although internal economic activity exists—as an activity of choice—even amid the most advanced and industrialized backdrop (Dana, 1995), for some people in transitional economies this is the only strategy for survival. In Moldova, for example, where prices have escalated while pensions

PHOTO 1.9. Not for sale.

PHOTO 1.10. Fishing for dinner.

have not, retired professionals have been growing food that they otherwise could not afford.

Covert economic activity[8] involves business transactions that are illegal and therefore conducted in a covert way, in order to avoid punitive measures from law-enforcing authorities (Haskell and Yablonsky, 1974; Henry, 1978). Because the liberalization of the marketplace has facilitated organized crime, many entrepreneurs have set up businesses that sell children into the sex trade.[9] This is a growing issue in Eastern Europe, as young women are being enticed into prostitution as a means to a "better future." In the case of Albania, prostitutes are considered to be the nation's most profitable exports. Although Cantillon (1755) referred to self-employed prostitutes as entrepreneurs, today's covert activities include large-scale transnational trafficking of human beings. Officials estimate that each year 100,000 people become enslaved prostitutes against their will. In Moldova, observers report that 400,000 women have been sold into prostitution since the country's independence. Ethnic Albanian entrepreneurs in Kosovo, Macedonia, and Serbia use the flesh trade to finance their separatist movements. In Macedonia, Ljube Boshkovski, the Minister for Interior Affairs, publicly announced that police are on the payroll lists of covert smugglers (see Photo 1.11).

PHOTO 1.11. Police on payroll.

Chapter 2

Land of the *Perseritje* Model

THE REPUBLIC OF ALBANIA

Albania covers 11,101 square miles, bordering the Adriatic Sea, the Former Yugoslav Republic of Macedonia, Greece, and Serbia and Montenegro.[1] Albanians are divided into two dialect groups; Gheg is prevalent in the north and Tosk, the official dialect, in the south. After several decades of centralized planning and a policy of isolationism, Albania adopted the *Perseritje* model of transition. The nation was soon described by the Bretton Woods institutions[2] as being among the most successful transforming countries of Eastern Europe. Yet, Albania also remains among Europe's poorest, as crime is a major player (see Photo 2.1).

PHOTO 2.1. Public phones have been vandalized and copper wiring sold as scrap metal.

Historical Overview

In ancient Roman times, the land currently known as Albania was part of the provinces of Epirus and Illyria. When the Roman Empire was split during the fourth century, the territory was assigned to the Byzantine Empire. Then came invasions by Goths and Slavs. During the ninth century, Bulgaria absorbed Albania.

The Albanians first became independent during the fifteenth century, under a Gheg known as Gjergi Kastrioti Skanderbeg. However, independence did not last long, as the country soon fell under Ottoman rule, which lasted until 1912 when Albania became a principality under Prince William of Wied. The Albanian State Bank was founded in 1925 with Italian aid. The national leader, named that year, became King Zog I in 1928. During his rule, a trade agreement with Italy encouraged foreign investment, but illiteracy in Albania remained at 85 percent.

In 1939 Benito Mussolini seized control of Albania, and the country was occupied by the Italians. The Nazis arrived in 1943, asking for a list of Jews, but the government refused to cooperate. The Albanian resistance announced that anyone refusing to give sanctuary to Jews would be subject to execution, "for the crime of dishonoring the Albanian people." Thus, the entire community escaped the Holocaust. Nazi occupation ended in 1944.

When the Albanian People's Republic was proclaimed, the country became communist under the totalitarian rule of Enver Hoxha, perhaps the most eccentric dictator in Eastern Europe. Hoxha banned bananas, beards, bright colors, foreign journalists, most imports, and even religion. He denounced the communist parties of Yugoslavia in 1948 and the Union of Soviet Socialist Republics in 1961. Albania continued importing from China (see Photo 2.2) until Hoxha denounced the Chinese Communist Party in 1978. Paranoid of invasion, he built concrete bunkers across the country.

Promoting Entrepreneurship

After the death of Hoxha in 1985, Ramiz Alia became president. Alia proposed more scope for small business and introduced some liberal reforms. Yet in 1987 there were only forty automobiles in Albania. As Albania entered the 1990s, main roads had truck traffic but relatively few cars (see Photo 2.3).

PHOTO 2.2. Chinese import.

PHOTO 2.3. Bicycle and truck on main road.

In November 1990, foreign investment was legalized. Although opposition parties were permitted in December 1990, a communist government was elected in March 1991. A noncommunist government was elected in March 1992. Doder (1996) reported that the average weekly wage was equivalent to to about US$5 in 1992; the rate of urban unemployment was about 50 percent that year. Recovery began in 1993, and by 1994 unemployment had fallen and inflation was reduced to an annual rate of 30 percent. Self-employment became widespread. In recognition of progress, in 1994 the International Monetary Fund (IMF)[3] approved a further extended arrangement with Albania. By the mid-1990s, output was growing by more than 10 percent per year, and an entrepreneurial mind-set was replacing communist ideology. Pages from Hoxha's books were being used to package roasted almonds or sausages (see Photo 2.4).

In 1995 a privatization program for large enterprises was initiated, under the aegis of the National Privatization Agency. The collapse of pyramid investment schemes in 1997 led to a brief crisis. Although the economic situation stabilized in 1998, those who lost money were still unhappy (see Photo 2.5).

In November 1998, a popular referendum endorsed the new constitution. In 1999, 450,000 refugees arrived in Albania, escaping conflict in Kosovo. This put stress on the infrastructure (see Photos 2.6

PHOTO 2.4. Using Hoxha's book to serve sausages.

PHOTO 2.5. Happier before the crisis.

PHOTO 2.6. Hoping to get on the bus.

and 2.7) while increasing the demand for food (see Photo 2.8) and housing (see Photos 2.9 and 2.10).

The inflow of 20,000 North Atlantic Treaty Organization (NATO) soldiers was an unexpected boost for the Albanian economy. This put an end to rampant crime. Journalists and aid workers from 180 differ-

PHOTO 2.7. Lines at the telephone office.

PHOTO 2.8. The dairy shop.

ent organizations provided business for hotels and guesthouses (see Photos 2.11 and 2.12).

In accordance with Decision 463 of the Council of Ministers on October 6, 1999, amended by Decision 123 on March 18, 2000, the Ministry of Public Economy and Privatization announced the privatization of four leading enterprises in Albania: Ajka, the largest dairy and producer of cheese and yogurt in the country; Birra Malto, Alba-

PHOTO 2.9. Housing for the rich.

PHOTO 2.10. And for the not so rich.

PHOTO 2.11. Mrs. Papa's family welcomes visitors who rent a room in her house.

PHOTO 2.12. In the kitchen, the drain for the shower serves as the toilet.

nia's largest brewery; Kantina, the nation's largest producer of wines and spirits; and Profarma, the largest producer of pharmaceuticals. The four consumer-oriented firms were transformed into joint-stock companies, and it was decided that employees be allowed to partici- pate in the privatization. In the case of Birra Malto, 6 percent of the shares were reserved for individuals related to the company, and the remaining 94 percent were offered to the public. The Council of Min- isters decided to sell each of the previously mentioned businesses by tender, awarding them based on five criteria:

1. the price offered for the shares;
2. the level of proposed investment;
3. the business plan and technical quality of the proposal;
4. the previous achievements of the investor; and
5. the plan for retraining and employment.

Each tender required a guarantee deposit of $30,000, blocked in a bank account of the National Agency of Privatization at the Savings Bank of Albania in Tirana. A Bid Evaluation Committee, including representatives from the Ministry of Public Economy and Privatiza- tion and the National Agency for Privatization, was responsible for ranking the bidders. The recommendations of the committee would be implemented only if and when approved by the Council of Minis- ters. Albania introduced its Law on Small and Medium Enterprises in 2002. This formalized the state's support for the sector.

The Women's Center in Tirana is an important organization that encourages the participation of women in entrepreneurship (see Photo 2.13). Recognizing the need for networking (Aldrich, Rosen, and Woodward, 1987; Aldrich and Zimmer, 1986; Birley, 1985), the center provides these opportunities, as well as providing documenta- tion, information, assistance, training, and access to experts and spe- cialists. Courses offered include "Start Your Business" and "Improve Your Business."

Foreign Entrepreneurs

In November 1993 a new and liberal Foreign Investment Law per- mitted foreign investments without prior authorization or licensing

PHOTO 2.13. Preparing for a new venture.

requirements. Since then, Albanian law has treated local and foreign entrepreneurs alike. Capital exits Albania without difficulty.

The Albanian Economic Development Agency (AEDA), a joint-stock company, was created by the Albanian government in August 1998. Its purpose is to encourage and facilitate domestic and foreign investment in order to stimulate economic growth in Albania. The agency consists of three departments, allowing for the efficient management of several activities: the preparation, publishing, and distribution of economic promotional materials (by the Department of Information and Publishing); the identification of opportunities, the promotion of international trade, and the promotion of Albania as an attractive environment for investment and assistance to investors (by the Department of Promotion and Consultancy); and assistance to the government in the formulation of promotion policies and strategies, and in reforming the legal framework for investment (by the Department of Personnel, Administration and Finance).

The AEDA provides potential investors with details of firms about to be privatized, and it offers consulting services to potential investors. In addition, it assists small, local companies wishing to expand or to participate in joint ventures. The agency prepares company profiles and serves as a matchmaker. It also hosts trade fairs, seminars, conferences, and roundtables on various economic issues. It provides training in business, economic issues, and business law as well.

The Albanian Guarantee Agency (AGA) administers the Political Risks Guarantee Facility, involving World Bank[4] funds, to increase investor confidence in Albania. This program provides insurance from political risks, war, civil unrest, tax increases, and trade bans.

The State of Entrepreneurship and the Small-Business Sector

The *Perseritje* model of transition has increased the scope for small business while introducing liberal reforms. In 1992, huge prairie fields of the Albanian agricultural system were privatized. By 1994, there were 420,000 self-employed farmers, with private holdings averaging 1.4 hectares. Since 1995, the sale and purchase of agricultural land has been permitted. In 1996, 60 percent of the population depended on agriculture. Today, over half of Albania's GDP is derived from agricultural activities, a sector employing about half of the working population directly (on the farm) or indirectly (at the markets) (see Photo 2.14).

In addition to using their own property, farmers also graze their animals along the roadside. It is common to see a Muslim woman, with her head covered, walking her sheep on a rope. Cows, goats, and

PHOTO 2.14. Farmers' market.

sheep are raised not only for their meat, but also for their milk, cheese, and wool. The hides are also an economically important by-product. Poultry is common, not only among farmers; even urbanites often have a few chickens and a rooster by their homes. Honey is harvested, and a Riesling wine is locally produced. Agricultural produce includes barley, beans, corn, figs, grapes, honey, lemons, oats, olives, pomegranates, rice, rye, tobacco, tomatoes, and watermelons (see Photo 2.15).

Since the privatization of farmland, Albanian farmers are obtaining intrinsic job satisfaction that was previously nonexistent. This motivates them considerably. In contrast to the constant shortages experienced during communist rule, local agricultural products are now plentiful (see Photo 2.16). At the indoor-market stalls of Durres, it is possible to purchase a variety of produce, including fresh cantaloupe, eggs, garlic, green peppers, okra, potatoes, and watermelon. Peaches are available, either canned or fresh. It is also possible to buy tomatoes, which are grown in local greenhouses. Local and imported wheat is available in abundance. The food shortages of recent years seem to have been forgotten.

A new problem is that the division of farms into privatized plots has eliminated economies of scale. On many farms, oxen have replaced tractors to plow. Donkeys are used for transport (see Photo 2.17). Privatization has created incentives that did not exist under

PHOTO 2.15. Selling watermelons along the sidewalk.

PHOTO 2.16. Agriculural produce has become plentiful.

PHOTO 2.17. Donkey transport.

communist rule, but at the same time, the redistribution of land to small-scale farmers has resulted in a return to less mechanization.

Albania has privatized over 500 small and medium enterprises, and new ventures are sprouting (see Photo 2.18). However, few are substantial, and many of the new firms are subsistence enterprises.

PHOTO 2.18. New venture, open part-time.

In the past, everyone in Albania was guaranteed a job. Officially, there was no unemployment and there were no beggars. Today, there are both. When state-owned factories were rationalized, workers were laid off. The solution for many has been to create a subsistence-level microenterprise. Some sell newspapers in the streets as "newsies" did in America at the turn of the twentieth century. Others exchange dollars in the streets, in a corner of a local post office, or on a bench by the seafront (see Photo 2.19).

In big cities, independent banana dealers are numerous. Each has a minuscule inventory (see Photo 2.20).

In Durres, a man sells packages of Camel cigarettes, which he carries around town in a duffel bag. Another, in Tirana, sits down with a cardboard box that serves as an impromptu stall; he sells chocolate bars imported from Greece. In other words, microenterprise is widespread but not innovative entrepreneurship in the Schumpeterian sense (1912, 1928, 1934, 1939, 1942, 1947, 1949). Doder writes,

PHOTO 2.19. Change money?

PHOTO 2.20. Banana dealer.

"For entrepreneurs, freedom equals goods from Greece, where they swap livestock for electronics and appliances" (1996, p. 71).

In 1998, the Women's Center in Tirana conducted a study (personal communication from Eglantina Gjermeni, Executive Director, Women's Center, Tirana, Albania) with the participation of 606 women-led firms, eighty-five potential women entrepreneurs, and 100 defunct enterprises. Almost 80 percent of the women were over twenty-nine years old, but fewer than 40 percent had a bank account; only 8 percent obtained bank credit. Respondents stated that they would like access to financial support to expand business operations, as well as technical assistance in accounting, administration, and planning.

Toward the Future

The government's attitude during the 1999 Kosovo Crisis launched a new image of Albania. Since NATO used Albania as a supply base, the international community welcomed it as a partner.

Albania's growth-oriented reform program, based on free-market economic principles, law, and order, is being implemented with the cooperation of the IMF. In March 2000, Albania approached the international donor community in Brussels with plans to modernize the Durres port (see Photo 2.21).

PHOTO 2.21. Durres port.

Tirana, a quiet town during my first visit in 1994, is now bustling with fashionable shoppers, eager to display their newly acquired spending power. Rising disposable incomes have boosted consumer demand. Underdeveloped until the 1990s, the service sector is booming.

A concern is the growth of the covert sector in Albania. An important industry has been the smuggling of Albanian citizens into Italy. Although as many as 35,000 are sent back to Albania in any one year, the authorities do not send back minors, and so impoverished families pay to have their children smuggled to the West with the hope of facing a better future.

Chapter 3

The Former Yugoslav Republics

In 1929, Yugoslavia was the name given to the Kingdom of Serbs, Croats, and Slovenes. As the name implies, this was a multicultural country. The state was created in 1918 with the fusion of lands that were on opposing sides during World War I. The nature of pluralism in Yugoslavia eventually led to the demise of the federation, resulting in the independence of Bosnia-Hercegovina, Croatia, the Former Yugoslav Republic of Macedonia (FYROM), and Slovenia. Montenegro remained united with Serbia, together forming the Federal Republic of Yugoslavia. Of all the Yugoslav republics, only Slovenia was selected for the expansion wave of the European Union in May 2004.

PLURALISM AND THE YUGOPLURALIST MODEL

Where groups with unlike spheres of values coexist, the result is a pluralistic society.[1] Anthropologist Frederik Barth (1963, 1966, 1967a,b, 1981) placed great emphasis on the existence of different spheres of values. Central to his discussion is the concept of the entrepreneur as an essential broker, mediating boundary transfers in this situation of contacts between cultures. By being active in the transformation of a community, entrepreneurs are social agents of change.

The nature of pluralism affects entrepreneurship. It is, therefore, important to distinguish among (1) *melting-pot* pluralism; (2) *structural* pluralism; and (3) *fragmented* pluralism.

1. When people from different cultures share activities in a secular mainstream arena, the expression of cultural differences is limited to private life. Often, employment is shared in a common sphere of life, while cuisine, customs, languages, and religion are a domestic concern. This form of socioeconomic pluralism

is referred to as melting-pot pluralism. This is descriptive of the situation in the United States.

2. In contrast, structural pluralism involves a society with different cultures that do not share a secular mainstream arena. In such a case, there is minimal interaction across cultures. Rather, each ethnic group has its distinct institutions, and members of a given community have a lifestyle that is incompatible with that of people from other backgrounds. This type of pluralism is prevalent in Xinjiang (Dana, 1998a) and in the Central-Asian republics (Dana, 2002).

3. Fragmented pluralism is an unstable state of socioeconomic pluralism from which a society can shift (sometimes by force) to another form of pluralism, or even away from pluralism altogether and toward "ethnic cleansing." With fragmented pluralism, distinct societies are *loosely* held together by a *weak* political unit, and each ethnic group lives a separate life. Despite a federal government, there is minimal interaction between competing ethnic groups.

After Josip Tito's death, loosely federated Yugoslavia became an example of fragmented pluralism. Had ethnocultural differences been eroded and cultures interacted in a mainstream arena, then fragmented pluralism in Yugoslavia would have shifted toward melting-pot pluralism. If the ethnic groups had accepted the authority of a strong political unit, then the result would have been structural pluralism. In contrast, the yugopluralist model decentralized power to the communes, and the authority of the federal government faded. The lack of a common interest resulted in a fragmented economy, and cultural differences contributed to regional disparities, leading to the collapse of Yugoslavia.

AN INTRODUCTION TO YUGOSLAVIA

The former Yugoslav federation consisted of six culturally different republics and two autonomous provinces. The republics were Bosnia-Hercegovina, Croatia, Macedonia, Montenegro, Serbia, and Slovenia. The provinces were Kosovo and Vojvodina.

In the past, Bosnia, Macedonia, Montenegro, and Serbia were part of the Ottoman Empire. Bosnia came under Turkish rule in 1463, and in 1482, Hercegovina was attached to Bosnia, forming Bosnia-Hercegovina. Whereas Montenegro and Serbia both obtained independence in 1878 with the Treaty of Berlin, Bosnia-Hercegovina was occupied by the Austro-Hungarian Empire. In 1908, Bosnia-Hercegovina was annexed to the Austro-Hungarian Empire and remained so until the collapse of the empire.

In 1914, the assassination of the Austrian archduke Franz Ferdinand in Sarajevo, triggered the Great War that came to be known as World War I. After the surrender of the Austro-Hungarian empire, "Slovenia, Croatia, Slavonia, Bosnia, Herzegovina, Dalmatia, part of Banat, and the Kingdom of Montenegro were added to Serbia" (Chater, 1930, p. 264), to form the Kingdom of the Serbs, Croats, and Slovenes. It consisted of formerly Turkish Serbia, Montenegro and Macedonia, and Bosnia-Hercegovina (which chose to join victorious Serbia), and Croatia and Slovenia (which had long histories of Austro-Hungarian rule).

In 1921, a member of the former Serbian royal family became king. Not surprisingly, Croats resented this. Because of Serb-Croatian rivalry, in 1929 King Alexander I Karadjordjević instituted direct rule (i.e., a royal dictatorship). The country's name was changed to Kingdom of Yugoslavia (*Jugoslavia* in Serbo-Croatian, meaning "Land of the southern Slavs"). In 1934, King Alexander I was assassinated in Marseilles by a terrorist.

Chandler gave a breakdown of ethnic communities shortly before the outbreak of World War II: "Serbian Orthodox (49 percent of the population), Roman Catholic (37 percent), Moslem (11 percent), followed in fractional percentages by some half a dozen others" (1939, p. 692).

The monarchy joined the Axis in 1941, and the Nazis occupied most of Yugoslavia until 1943. Montenegro was occupied by the Italians. Croatia became independent during the war, under a Nazi and Italian protectorate. During World War II, Porter wrote, "Foes for centuries, Moslems and Christians are good neighbors in Yugoslavia" (1944, p. 510).

After the war, the Socialist Federative Republic of Yugoslavia was forged under the leadership of Josip Broz, who had adopted the code name Marshal Tito. The federation artificially united Slovenia, Croatia, Serbia, Bosnia-Hercegovina, Macedonia, and Montenegro along with two autonomous provinces. In honor of Tito, Montenegro's capital Podgoritsa changed its name to Titograd.

Nationalization began with the agricultural sector, as postwar legislation put a ceiling on the area of land that could be owned by an individual. Soon, entrepreneurship was limited to artisans, independent professions, and small landholdings.

Although Yugoslavia opted for a policy of industrialization and self-management with a shade of capitalism, Moscow preferred for the former to be dependent on Soviet exports and proposed a merger of Yugoslavia with Bulgaria. Because of such disagreements, Stalin expelled Yugoslavia from the Soviet bloc in 1948. Henceforth, Tito led the republics along the road of what he called *self-managing socialism* or nonaligned Marxism.

Unified under the control of the Communist Party in Belgrade, and not being a member of the Warsaw Pact, Yugoslavia followed a distinct route of its own. For administrative purposes, the six republics and two autonomous provinces of the federation were divided into about 500 communes. It was at the commune level that the people's committees planned economic development. The means of production were managed by basic organizations of associated labor.

In 1962, Grosvenor observed "the government permits limited private ownership of small businesses employing up to five workers. However, the private employer is harassed by such high taxes and compulsory employee benefits that many private businesses fail" (1962, p. 241).

Nevertheless, in the absence of constraints by Moscow, Yugoslavia was among the first in Eastern Europe to move toward a market economy. Until 1964, artisans were allowed to employ a maximum of three craftspersons. This increased to five in 1965 and to ten in 1983.

Jordan wrote: "Yugoslavs use two alphabets, embrace three religious faiths, speak three main languages and numerous other tongues" (1970, p. 592). Photo 3.1 illustrates a typical sign showing two alphabets.

Until 1980, the different nations of Yugoslavia were held together under the strong central government of Tito in Belgrade. After his death on May 4, 1980, the federal government became Serb-led. The Croatian minority consequently felt a diminution of social status. According to Hagen (1962), such social grievances may stimulate a desire to excel in the economic realm via entrepreneurial activity.

PHOTO 3.1. Cyrillic and Latin.

Without Tito's leadership, the Communist Party's control over the Yugoslav federation decreased, and some republics embarked on their own paths toward pluralistic democracy and a market economy. Others did not, demonstrating that greater independence for republics does not necessarily imply greater freedom within them.

During the late 1980s, the gross social product (Eastern European version of gross domestic product) of Yugoslavia stagnated at best. Entrepreneurship was often viewed as a phenomenon intertwined with the capitalist greed for material gains through the exploitation of others (Glas, 1998).

The Enterprise Law permitted the private ownership of firms. Although the pace of privatization was slow, many managers opted to create their own spin-off firms. Unemployed people became self- employed. Yet entrepreneurs faced numerous problems, including exponential inflation that began escalating that year. In 1989, despite weak demand and soaring unemployment, inflation reached 2,700 percent (Anonymous, 1990). Photo 3.2 illustrates a now worthless 50,000- dinar banknote.

PHOTO 3.2. A lot of money before inflation.

By 1990, after a decade of evolution under decentralized federalism of the yugopluralist model, Yugoslavia had a benignly weak central government. The economy was still planned, but firms were doing most of their planning with their local party leader rather than with Belgrade. Trade among the Yugoslav republics decreased, and few firms had branches outside the republics in which they were based. Although Serbia still wanted a federation, the economic reality of the yugopluralist model was that the Yugoslav republics were behaving as separate countries.

In contrast to reform in Council for Mutual Economic Assistance (COMECON) nations, Yugoslavia initiated reform at the local level. As suggested by Weber (1904-1905) who linked entrepreneurship to cultural values such as asceticism, frugality, and thrift, some cultures had a naturally higher propensity for entrepreneurial behavior than others. In each republic, culture was an important factor. Not surprisingly, due to the multicultural nature of Yugoslavia, some of its republics achieved considerably more reform than others. As Yugoslavia entered the last decade of the twentieth century, Slovenia had five noncommunist movements and Croatia had one. It appeared that the republics of northern Yugoslavia were more tolerant of political pluralism than were their southern neighbors. Also, the republics of the north made visible progress toward free enterprise. Croatia and Slovenia were the most developed of the Yugoslav constituents (Glas, Drnovšek, and Mirtic, 2000). Of Yugoslavia's 24 million people, it was evident that the Croats and the Slovenes could best adapt to

Western values and entrepreneurship. Although entrepreneurial activity was generally limited to craftspeople, repairpeople, and eating establishments, the spirit of entrepreneurship was already visible in Croatia and Slovenia. In Slovenia, for example, reforms increased advertising, and as the government relaxed restrictions, almost two dozen independent advertising agencies formed in the republic. The standard of living in Slovenia rose far higher than in other republics. Slovenia had a concentration of factories, and in the stores, shelves were stocked.

Yugoslavia, under communist rule, had traditionally limited local consumption in order to boost exports. Entering the 1990s with a current account surplus, Yugoslavia no longer needed to stifle domestic demand. Augmented wages in 1990 gave Yugoslav consumers unprecedented purchasing power, creating opportunities for entrepreneurs identifying consumer needs and catering to incipient demand.

The introduction of the "new dinar" (worth 10,000 dinars) was central to the restructuring of the economy in 1990. The new dinar resulted in stable prices for the first time in several years. This made a fundamental difference in entrepreneurs' abilities to plan. Furthermore, whereas exchange control under the traditional communist regime made the dinar nonconvertible, the new dinar was made convertible and pegged to the German currency, which reached an all-time high relative to the U.S. dollar in 1990.

Until 1989, Austrians had shopped for bargains in Yugoslavia. In 1990, Yugoslavs crossed into Austria for less-expensive products. Most relevant for entrepreneurs was the fact that they could easily import sophisticated machinery for automation.

Another significant reform taking place under the yugopluralist model was that of having a formal debt-swap program, something absent in all other Eastern European countries except Poland. Hard currency was raised abroad and leveraged into favorable terms in Yugoslavia, using debt-for-equity swaps and countertrade as well as cash. The ContiTrade Services Corporation, for example, packaged investments for the emerging Eastern Europe fund consisting of capital ($75 million in 1990) that was raised in England and administered by Tyndall Holdings PLC. This allowed returns on a modernized factory to be significant. The first Yugoslavian debt-equity swap was engineered by the First National Bank of Chicago. Conversion of a thrice-restructured Yugoslavian debt, held by the bank, resulted in the construction of a luxury Hyatt hotel in Belgrade.

Inviting foreign investment resulted in good import/export and joint-venture opportunities for entrepreneurs both in and outside Yugoslavia. By late 1990, there were already forty joint ventures in Yugoslavia. Most of these were in the beer industry.

Acceptance of entrepreneurial values, however, was not evenly distributed. With cultural heterogeneity among six republics, five ethnic groups, Catholics, Serbian Orthodox, Greek Orthodox, and different groups of Muslims, one cannot expect them to think alike or to agree on a common policy for entrepreneurship. Danforth wrote, "Civil war is discussed daily in every republic" (1990, p. 103).

The weak central government of the Yugoslavian federation did not implement a federal policy on entrepreneurship. Members of the federation gained substantial autonomy as decentralization of the federal system enabled each one to implement change at its own pace. Culture was an important determinant of differences in economic policy, which in turn contributed to regional disparity. Under the yugopluralist model, each republic decided for itself according to its prevailing cultural values. Decentralization and cultural pluralism led to economic pluralism, resulting in entrepreneurship in Croatia and Slovenia.

The federal government redistributed wealth from the entrepreneurial to the less entrepreneurial. Given that one-third of Yugoslavia's exports were produced in Slovenia and 50 percent of Slovenia's GNP (gross national product) was being taken by the central government for redistribution to less-developed republics, Slovenia's industrial base and infrastructure tumbled.

Yugoslavia's economy became increasingly fragmented, and federal redistribution of wealth encouraged inefficiency. The authoritarianism of Tito was gone, and the discipline of a market-driven economy was lacking. There was neither an integrated national market, nor a reason to maintain the federation.

The combination of regional, historical, ideological, and cultural factors resulted in entrepreneurship gaining considerably more acceptance in both Croatia and Slovenia than in the other constituents of the former Yugoslav federation. With their industrious, methodological, and reserved attitude, both Croats and Slovenes progressed rapidly toward market economies. By 1990, Slovenia (with 8 percent of Yugoslavia's population) produced 29 percent of the country's exports (see Table 3.1).

Given the new dinar's strength, the Slovenes imported modern machinery to increase the efficiency of their factories. This was not sur-

TABLE 3.1. Regional disparity in 1990.

Yugoslav constituent	Capital city	Per capita GNP (USD$)	Average salary (USD$)	Percentage of Yugoslavia's exports
Bosnia-Hercegovina	Sarajevo	3,590	4,380	14
Croatia	Zagreb	7,110	6,144	21
Macedonia	Skopje	3,330	3,600	4
Montenegro	Titograd	3,970	4,452	2
Serbia	Belgrade	4,950	5,076	21
Slovenia	Ljubljana	12,520	6,396	29
Kosovo Province	Pristina	1,520	3,048	1
Vojvodina Province	Novi Sad	6,790	5,280	8

Source: Dana, 1994d, p. 178.

prising, considering their industrious, methodological, and thrifty values. Workers' councils in Croatia and Slovenia wanted reform, and the yugopluralist model allowed it to happen. In contrast, workers' councils in other republics preferred to maintain status quo.

As with all federations, the rich subsidized the poor. As the gap widened, Slovenes and Croats were no longer interested in working to support a less-entrepreneurial Serb-dominated Yugoslavia.

In December 1990, a parliamentary blueprint was proposed by the Yugoslav parliament's constitutional commission, suggesting that republics should have the right to secede. On June 25, 1991, Croatia and Slovenia declared independence. Meanwhile, Serbia democratically elected a communist government.

When Croatia and Slovenia declared their independence, Yugoslavia was concerned about losing its wealthiest, most productive industrious republics. Military intervention resulted in civil war.

Macedonia declared its sovereignty in September 1991. Following an October referendum, Bosnia-Hercegovina declared sovereignty on October 15, 1991. On December 19, 1991, Macedonia requested international recognition, despite strong objections from Greece.

Meanwhile, Serbia began resettling Serbs into Croatian homes occupied during the war. Broadcasts announced that at least 100 Croatian stores were available to Serb settlers for gratis, as well as 4,000 comfortable homes where Croatian occupants had fled Serbian forces. Farms, crops, livestock, and firms had no proprietors.

The Serbo-Croatian War lasted until January 1992, when a cease-fire came into effect. On January 15, 1992, Croatia and Slovenia were both given international recognition. The war killed 10,000 people and created 50,000 refugees.

On May 30, 1992, economic sanctions were imposed on Montenegro and Serbia. This resulted in massive gasoline smuggling. In October of that year, the United States removed these remaining Yugoslav republics from Column 1 customs treatment.

In summary, the yugopluralist model led to increased regional disparities. For those welcoming entrepreneurship, the ability to express cultural pluralism resulted in economic pluralism. In other words, the yugopluralist model allowed cultural pluralism to result in vast regional disparities. In 1990, the private sector in Yugoslavia, excluding agriculture, produced about 7 percent of the GDP. This entrepreneurial activity was concentrated in Croatia and Slovenia. Bosnians and Serbs flocked to Slovenia for jobs, not even speaking the language. Meanwhile, in Macedonia, horse-drawn carts continued to pass by shops with empty shelves, and those vehicles carrying produce most likely obtained it on farms rather than in stores. Yugoslavia was among the first socialist countries to welcome reform, but only some Yugoslav republics accepted genuine change. Historical and cultural factors are the causal variables. Successful republics resented demands by the federal government to subsidize the less-entrepreneurial republics. The result was war and the demise of the former federation. A lesson to be learned from the yugopluralist model is that the importance of such regional differences must not be underestimated.

THE FEDERATION OF BOSNIA-HERCEGOVINA

Bosnia-Hercegovina is 19,781 square miles, bordering Croatia and Serbia and Montenegro.[3] Here, a free-enterprise system is not so much the result of the transfer of ownership of existing firms; instead, entrepreneurs are rebuilding the economy by identifying niches, and the flexible structures of new ventures make these dynamic.

Civil war interrupted the process of privatization in Bosnia-Hercegovina, and most of the formerly state-owned industry was damaged during interethnic fighting. At the end of the war, the Dayton Agreement created a federal Bosnia-Hercegovina, consisting of two political entities, and the Brcko District as a separate unit. One of these is the Bosnian Federation, which welcomed the postwar reconstruction boom and is headed for a market economy. However, the other constituent of Bosnia-Hercegovina, namely Republika Srpska, encountered a further struggle with postwar politics, and entrepreneurship is less visible there. Bosnia-Hercegovina operates as three economies, each of which has issued its own regional currency. When coins are scarce, retailers give chewing gum and tram tickets in lieu of change. O'Driscoll, Holmes, and Kirkpatrick (2001) reported that estimates place the level of black-market activity at 40 to 60 percent. Covert activities include the trafficking of stolen cars and export of prostitutes.

Historical Overview

The Bosniaks trace their origins to Slavs who converted to Islam in order to obtain tax advantages. Slavs settled in this region during the seventh century, and medieval Bosnia was the strongest power among the southern Slavic nations. In 1463, however, Bosnia was taken over by the Ottomans. In 1482, the fertile farmland of Hercegovina was attached to the vast forests of Bosnia. Thus came into existence the entity called Bosnia-Hercegovina. Under Ottoman rule, this region was primarily agricultural, and the imperial agrarian system influenced many residents to convert to Islam. This contributed to the decline of the Bosnian Church.

A multicultural society developed and religious affiliations became the basis of "national" identities within Bosnia-Hercegovina. The Serbs preserved their Byzantine and Slavic traditions. The Muslims—later known as Bosniaks—adopted a Turkish-Islamic culture along with the values of the bazaar economy. The Croats observed Catholicism with its influences from Western Europe. Beginning in the 1500s, Ladino-speaking Sephardic Jews, tracing their origins to Spain and Portugal, became prominent in the business realm of Bosnia-Hercegovina. They pioneered in the medical, pharmaceutical, and metalsmith trades.

In 1878, the Austro-Hungarian Empire occupied Bosnia-Hercegovina and, at the Berlin Congress, received a thirty-year mandate to govern it, even though the area remained formally under the sovereignty of the Ottoman sultan. German-speaking Ashkenazi Jews came from the Austro-Hungarian Empire in large numbers, encouraging and financing the industrial development of Bosnia-Hercegovina. This trend was accelerated in 1908, when Bosnia-Hercegovina was annexed to the Austro-Hungarian Empire. Jews served as a middleman minority between Christians and Muslims.[4] For a discussion of middleman minorities, see Bonacich (1973) and Cherry (1990).

Created in 1918, the Kingdom of Serbs, Croats, and Slovenes included the area that is today Bosnia-Hercegovina. Under Italian and German dictatorship during World War II, Bosnia-Hercegovina became part of the independent state of Croatia. After the war, the region was integrated into the Socialist Federative Republic of Yugoslavia, under the strong leadership of Marshal Tito, a Croat who ruled from Belgrade. He favored industrialization, and considerable industry was concentrated in Bosnia-Hercegovina. Given the availability of iron ore and coal, much steel was produced in Bosnia-Hercegovina, where Yugoslavia's largest steelmill was set up eighty miles from Sarajevo. Bosnia-Hercegovina also became home to a major oil refinery on the Sava River, and an aircraft industry in Mostar.

Tito tried to create a Yugoslav nationalism that would melt cultural differences. Although urbanization encouraged secular life, ethnic consciousness emerged when cultural beliefs were incompatible with one another. In a Muslim family, it was more important for women to stay home than to receive higher education; this contributed to a substantial income differential between Muslims and non-Muslims. Also, the population growth of Muslims increased, becoming twice that of Croats and Serbs. In 1968, Tito recognized Bosnian Muslims—Bosniaks—as having their own nationality.

Following similar moves by other Yugoslav republics, Bosnia-Hercegovina adopted a declaration of independence on October 14, 1991. Never before had this country been an independent entity. In a February 29, 1992, referendum, the nation voted in favor of independence, which was declared on April 5, 1992. The new country was recognized by both the European Union and the United States. Perhaps even more significant was Bosnia-Hercegovina's membership in the United Nations (UN) on May 5, 1992.

On April 6, 1992, Bosnian Serbs joined Serbia in a war against Bosnian Croats and Bosniaks (see Photo 3.3). The following year, a separate conflict arose between Bosnian Croats and Bosniaks.

Repeatedly, mortar attacks killed civilians in Sarajevo's Central Market. Some were waiting in line for bread; others were in the queue for water. Bridges were blown up (see Photo 3.4).

Blockades interrupted manufacturing. Factories were looted (see Photo 3.5). Fighting stopped production at Volkswagen's passenger-car assembly line in Sarajevo. The Holiday Inn was among the many hotels that were bombed. Most enterprises were paralyzed. Marlboro and Pall Mall cigarettes were a common currency.

A few entrepreneurs prospered during the war. Among these were Mirsad Delimustafic and his brothers—owners of the BH Banka and of Cenex, a food-processing and trading conglomerate. Cenex also operated a luxury hotel in Sarajevo. Political connections helped this commercial empire flourish; one of the brothers was minister of interior during the war. Other entrepreneurs thrived in black-market activities arising from wartime shortages. Even water was rationed and could be sold to desperate buyers who were willing to pay a premium. Additional clandestine opportunities arose when Serbia and Montenegro cut economic ties with Bosnian Serbs. Individuals made money smuggling guns (see Photo 3.6). Others exported drugs or

PHOTO 3.3. Bomb shelters to the right and to the left.

PHOTO 3.4. Fallen bridge.

PHOTO 3.5. After the looters.

profited by selling orphans whose parents had been killed during the war. Some children were sold to people who wished to adopt them; many were sold into sex slavery. Interviewees who classified themselves as Croatian intellectuals told me that particularly ethnic Croats in Bosnia-Hercegovina profiteered during the war.

PHOTO 3.6. Arms for sale.

Although much wartime entrepreneurial activity was opportunistic, the situation also gave rise to legitimate value-adding activities. Houses needed roofs (see Photo 3.7), collapsed walls needed to be rebuilt (see Photo 3.8), shattered windows had to be replaced (see Photo 3.9), and balconies needed reinforcing (see Photo 3.10). Opportunities arose in building reconstruction (see Photo 3.11).

Civil war interrupted the privatization of the media. Fighting damaged existing print shops as well as capacities for radio and television production and broadcasting. Although government and military personnel controlled the state-owned media, some entrepreneurs identified an opportunity to create new ventures. Hence, a variety of media outlets were launched. Among those that pioneered alternative journalism in Bosnia-Hercegovina—with no political or military censorship—were *Dani* (an independent monthly launched in 1992); *Slobodna Bosna* (a biweekly subsidized by the Soros Foundation and first published in September 1995); Studio 99; Radio ZID; and TV Zetel.

PHOTO 3.7. Needing a roof.

PHOTO 3.8. Tumbled walls.

PHOTO 3.9. Paneless windows.

PHOTO 3.10. Missing a piece.

PHOTO 3.11. Crane at work.

TV Zetel, founded by entrepreneur Zeljko Lincner, began broad-casting in Zenica in 1992. That same year, ten entrepreneurs jointly created independent television *Hayat* in Sarajevo. Croat television Mostar, employing only two journalists, was launched in July 1994. Independent Radio-Television 99 Sarajevo, owned by a group of journalists and technicians, had twenty-two employees; its NTV 99 television station began broadcasting February 1, 1995. That same year, entrepreneur Zoran Udovicic founded Media Plan, Bosnia-Hercegovina's first private firm specializing in media development. Through this organization, he started the first wartime school for television reporting in Sarajevo (see Photo 3.12).

Even in areas controlled by Bosnian Serbs—where media pro-duced propaganda for the authorities—independent newspapers emerged in 1995. Examples were *Nezavisne Novine* and *Novi Prelom* in Banja Luka, *Panorama* in Bijeljina, and *Alternativa* in Doboj. The *Nezavisne Novine* called for interethnic cooperation, and the *Novi Prelom* focused efforts on promoting a market economy.

In early 1995, a UN protection force, numbering over 35,000, was sent to encourage peace in the former Yugoslavia. Approximately 22,000 of these UN peacekeepers were stationed in Bosnia-Herce-govina (see Photo 3.13). However, on May 26, Bosnian Serbs bombed Sarajevo and took 350 UN peacekeepers hostage.

PHOTO 3.12. Sarajevo, home of the wartime school.

PHOTO 3.13. Peacekeeping forces.

Finally, the Bosnia-Hercegovina Peace Agreement (also known as the Dayton Peace Accord) was initialed in Dayton, Ohio, on November 21, 1995, and signed in Paris, France, on December 14, 1995. This document became the blueprint for a single sovereign state with a clearly defined international boundary and an internationally recognized central government, one central bank, a single currency, and a collective head of state made up of Bosniak, Croat, and Serb members. However, that same agreement legitimated two entities (i.e., the Bosnian Federation and Republika Srpska). The Bosnian Federation, shared by Bosnian Croats and Bosniaks, corresponds to 51.4 percent of the area of Bosnia-Hercegovina.

The new constitution of Bosnia-Hercegovina put trade, customs, monetary policy, banking, financial agreements, and financing under the jurisdiction of the central government. Peacemakers thought that economic interests would overcome ethnic differences, thus making partition irrelevant. For instance, the production of aluminum in Mostar (see Photo 3.14) is dependent on cooperation between Bosnian Croats who have bauxite and Bosniaks who control the power, yet neither group was eager to cooperate with the other.

Unlike the Bosnian Federation, which welcomed the postwar reconstruction boom, Republika Srpska encountered further struggle with postwar politics. A feud between President Biljana Plavsic and

PHOTO 3.14. Mostar.

wartime leader Radovan Karadzic contributed to economic stagnation in Republika Srpska.

Promoting Entrepreneurship

The entrepreneurs I interviewed suggested that the state is not doing as much as other countries to promote entrepreneurship. In fact, much entrepreneurship is organized and paid for by external sources.

A women's action group, operating as VIDRA, is a nongovernmental organization in the Banja Luka region. Since 1997, VIDRA has promoted entrepreneurship among women. The group includes thirty women who assist others in starting businesses.

In 2002, the United Nations Development Program (UNDP),[5] made possible a Youth Enterprise Program in the Brcko District. This focuses on encouraging entrepreneurship among people who are between the ages of eighteen and thirty. Three components provide

1. training;
2. business mentoring and advisory services; and
3. microcredit finance.

The training and business advisory services are free of charge. The mentoring and financing operate on a cost-recovery basis. As of this writing, in 2005, thirteen local youths have created ninety-two jobs in the district.

In December 2002, the Canadian Center for Entrepreneurship and Development cohosted a ten-day entrepreneur training course for women to become entrepreneurship trainers. The Swiss Development Corporation contributed funding. A second component was organized to tech additional trainers in 2003, initiated by a multidonor initiative managed by the Small and Medium Enterprise Department of the World Bank Group and the International Finance Corporation. CARE International also supports self-employment and job creation by small and medium enterprises through financial assistance.

The State of Entrepreneurship and the Small-Business Sector

Although multinationals were hesitant to invest in a country lacking privatization laws and a commercial code, entrepreneurs identified a variety of opportunities in Bosnia-Hercegovina. This is most visible in the Bosnian Federation. However, entrepreneurship is largely limited to reconstruction (see Photo 3.15) and small-scale retail trade (see Photo 3.16).

To get around expensive bank loans and the lack of private investment, local entrepreneurs obtain capital from foreign sources, including a U.S. government loan fund and a venture capital loan fund launched jointly by Austrian investors and the European Bank for Reconstruction and Development. Arab entrepreneurs have also invested, but very selectively. According to Catholic and Christian-Orthodox respondents, Arabs have financed only Muslim entrepreneurs, to create a greater solidarity among followers of Islam.

It is not difficult to launch a new venture in Bosnia-Hercegovina. However, start-up fees exceed the cash reserves of many would-be entrepreneurs and there is little start-up assistance. Furthermore, survival is a challenge. Interviewees expressed to me that the government does little to support small businesses. Taxes were cited as crippling enterprises that would otherwise be economically viable. Until

PHOTO 3.15. Reconstructed without the second floor.

PHOTO 3.16. Retailer in Sarajevo.

1997, an entrepreneur was required to pay to the government 140 percent of total wages paid to employees; a typical wage, at the time, was 26,000 Bosnian dinars monthly, the equivalent of 260 German marks. Effectively, this meant that the entrepreneur's cost of creating jobs was more than doubled. Although the tax was reduced to 86 percent of wages paid, taxes are still collected on a weekly basis, and this is perceived as a burden on the time of owner-managers.

Another factor that interviewees described as crushing entrepreneurial spirit is the deficient infrastructure. Although Bosnia-Hercegovina is legally divided into two entities, it operates as if it were three countries, each with a separate (but inadequate) banking, electricity, telephone, and transportation system (see Photo 3.17).

In August 1994, the Narodna Banka (People's Bank) issued Bosnian dinars, but these were not accepted as a national currency. Even within the Bosnian Federation, entrepreneurs in the self-proclaimed "Croat-Republic of Herzeg-Bosnia" have dealt in Croatian kuna.

Although the Dayton Agreement did not recognize the self-proclaimed state of Bosnian Croats within the Bosnian Federation, the situation took time to stabilize. Croats in the region suggested that since it was acceptable to divide Bosnia-Hercegovina into two components, then they wished to have a third entity (independent from the Bosnian Federation) to represent the interests of Bosnian Croats.

PHOTO 3.17. Damaged by war.

They proposed a Swiss-style canton-type confederation consisting of the Bosnian Federation, the Croat-Republic of Herzeg-Bosna, and Republika Srpska. To complicate matters, there is a general distrust between Croats in Croatia and Bosnian Croats in the Bosnian Federation.

Less entrepreneurial activity takes place in Republika Srpska than in the Bosnian Federation. According to unpublished records at the Economics Institute of Republika Srpska, 1.3 million people live there, and almost one-fourth are refugees. Communist-era policies have perpetuated a nonentrepreneurial frame of mind in this part of Bosnia-Hercegovina. During the 1990s, unemployment in Republika Srpska exceeded 60 percent and typical wages were the equivalent of US$20 monthly.

New-venture creation in Republika Srpska is stifled by political elites who have privatized formerly state-owned firms and created barriers to entry in order to deter competition. Unlike the situation in the Bosnian Federation where there is light at the end of the tunnel, the economic forecast is grim in Republika Srpska. Individuals stand outside gutted factories and try to sell inexpensive local cigarettes in recycled Marlboro packages (see Photo 3.18). Nevertheless, some areas demonstrate a strong entrepreneurial spirit, such as the municipality of Laktaši near Banja Luka.

PHOTO 3.18. Cigarettes for sale near a gutted factory.

Rich farmlands of this region used to provide food for the rest of Bosnia-Hercegovina and for Croatia. However, much fertile land has become idle as the economy is too poor to provide a local market. Weeds have taken root in fields that once yielded cabbage, corn, and green peppers. Pomegranates hang from trees near abandoned homes that are scarred with bullet holes (see Photo 3.19).

Today, the Srpska Seljacka Partija (Serb Peasants Party) is a lonely supporter of agricultural development. Industrial production is a fraction of its prewar figure. There is almost no trade between Republika Srpska (which uses unconvertible Bosnian-Serb dinars) and the Bosnian Federation (where Bosnian dinars were pegged at the rate of one Bosnian dinar to one German pfennig). Republika Srpska remains cut off from its traditional markets, and new markets are unlikely as long as Republika Srpska retains its image of political pariah. Serbia, its only friend, is too impoverished to help.

The boundary between the Bosnian Federation and Republika Srpska was intended to be similar to the boundaries within former Yugoslavia; this is equivalent to a state line in the United States. Yet Republika Srpska, acting as a separate country, treats the boundary as an actual partition, with different currencies and policies on both sides. Pale, a community in Republika Srpska, is about ten miles from Sarajevo, and according to Dayton, both are in the same country, yet a

PHOTO 3.19. Abandoned home scarred with bullet holes.

phone call would have to pass through Serbia. Economically, this does not make sense. Most entrepreneurs I interviewed agreed that the small-business sector and the national economy of Bosnia-Herce-govina would prosper the most if both constituents (the Bosnian Federation and Republika Srpska) were to function as one economic unit. A unified banking system, for example, would be desirable. Yet, until recently, entrepreneurs in Republika Srpska preferred to deal in Yugoslav dinars rather than in Bosnian dinars; today, the convertible euro has gained acceptance.

Another issue is that almost like Pakistan before the independence of Bangladesh, Republika Srpska is in turn divided into two geographic regions, both Bosnian-Serb areas. Although the Posavina corridor, around Brcko, physically connects both of these Serb-controlled entities, each has its own economic leaning. The eastern strip maintains economic ties with Serbia, but entrepreneurs in the Banja Luka region express a greater affinity toward the economy of Croatia. This affinity is supported by the fact that many people from the northwest part of Bosnia were formerly employed in Croatia and Slovenia, currently important trading partners.

The Koalicija Demokratski Patriotski Blok RS (Democratic Patriotic Block of Republika Srpska), which was established in Banja Luka during 1996, supports strong ties with Montenegro as well as

Serbia. Also based in Banja Luka are the Srpska Radikalma Stranka (Radical Party of the Serb Republic), which demands unification of Republika Srpska with Serbia, and Narodna Stranka RS (the Peoples' Party of Republika Srpska), which supports this idea. This could lead to a political as well as economic split within Republika Srpska. Few entrepreneurs are willing to undertake risks in such an environment of uncertainty.

Toward the Future

To date, foreign aid has been Bosnia's largest source of capital. The United States Agency for International Development (USAID) made available $70 million to entrepreneurs. Entrepreneurs have made money by restoring basic services, using donated funds. What will happen when the physical infrastructure is restored or when donations run out? In the future, it would be preferable for a self-sustaining private sector to lead the country to value-adding prosperity.

Much entrepreneurship in Bosnia-Hercegovina is short-term in scope, with the hope of making money quickly. Most entrepreneurs I surveyed had not even prepared a business plan. Furthermore, their focus is on themselves rather than on the customer or on market needs. Can this be sustainable? A prerequisite to sustainability is a transformation of the dependence-context economy. One long-term way to attract capital investment is through tax incentives and the establishment of a stable and integrated banking infrastructure and legal system. Then, multinationals will be in a position to subcontract to local entrepreneurs.

The Stranka Privrednog Prosperiteta BiH (Party of Economic Prosperity of Bosnia-Hercegovina), composed mainly of businessmen from Sarajevo, Tuzla, and Zenica, suggests that only economic ties can reintegrate Bosnia-Hercegovina. In April 1997, Republika Srpska agreed to have a customs union with what remained of Yugoslavia, namely Montenegro and Serbia. However, the 1999 war in Serbia over Kosovo further disrupted value-adding entrepreneurship in the region.

Serbs trade with Bosniaks at the Trznica-Virginia market open-air bazaar in Memici, between Tuzla and Zvornik. Items include cigarettes, fabrics, hardware apparatus, household items, and shoes. This same phenomenon became strong in the Arizona marketplace in

Brcko. It would be encouraging to see more trade that is interethnic. Given the low wage structure in Bosnia-Hercegovina, tremendous potential in light manufacturing exists, especially with the technical and financial assistance of foreign partners. Some municipalities, including Vitez and Zepce, have supported new ventures, while the dominance of the trade sector is still strong.

THE REPUBLIC OF CROATIA

Croatia covers 21,829 square miles, bordering the Adriatic Sea (see Photo 3.20), Bosnia-Hercegovina, Hungary, Serbia and Montenegro, and Slovenia.[6] Following a referendum that endorsed secession from Yugoslavia, Croatia declared its independence on June 25, 1991. This prompted civil war (see Photo 3.21) and led to a period of substantial impoverishment. Until 1993, inflation and high taxes contributed to growth of the unofficial economy. The reduction of taxes in 1994 prompted a shift from the parallel sector to the firm-type economy. Privatization was concluded faster in Croatia than elsewhere among the former Yugoslav republics. However, as discussed by Glas, Drnovšek, and Mirtic (2000), Croatia's privatization model enabled a few Croats to take over important firms without the needed

PHOTO 3.20. Cavtat, along the Adriatic Sea.

PHOTO 3.21. Ready for attack.

resources and managerial knowledge; this was referred to by the Strategic Planning Office as tycoon-based privatization.

Historical Overview

As a result of a personal union of thrones, in 1091 Croatia came under Hungarian administration. This lasted until World War I, after which Croatia become a part of the Kingdom of Serbs, Croats, and Slovenes. Dalmatia, which had been under Venetian rule from 1420 to 1797, and under Austrian rule since 1813, was annexed to Croatia in 1919. Under the rule of the Kingdom of Serbs, Croats, and Slovenes and later Yugoslavia, Croatians were treated unfairly by the central government (Pozzi, 1935), and this led to a nationalist separatist movement.

After the defeat of Yugoslavia in 1941, regions of Croatia were annexed by Hungary and others by Italy. The rest of Croatia, occupied by Germany and Italy, became the Nezavisna država Hrvatska (NDH), translated as the Independent State of Croatia. During the war, hundreds of thousands of gypsies, Jews, and Serbs were executed. Yad Vashem presented certificates of honor and the Medal of the Righteous to over eighty persons who helped save Jews in Croatia during World War II.

In the 1980s, 10 percent of Yugoslavia's hard-currency earnings came from tourism, and this sector earned Croatia $2 billion in 1990 (see Photo 3.22). In May 1991, a referendum endorsed independence from Yugoslavia, and forecasts predicted that tourism would yield an independent Croatia $5 billion that year. However, predominantly Serb areas of Croatia, including the Krajina, leaned toward union with Serbia.

As Belgrade refused to accept Croatia's statehood, Croatian civilians spent the summer of 1991 armed to protect their crops from Serbian forces, and Croatia's tourism industry was crippled (see Photo 3.23). The state of war prompted inflation that escalated to 2,000 percent in 1993 (Martin and Grbac, 1998). Yet, during the period from 1996 to 1998, Croatia had a lower rate of inflation than any other country in Eastern Europe (*Ostwirtschaftsreport,* cited in *International Herald Tribune,* Wednesday, June 24, 1998, p. 12).

In 1999, Croatia experienced negative growth and an unemployment rate that exceeded twenty percent. For elderly people, the job search was a challenge (see Photo 3.24). The following year, a coalition led by the Social Democrats and the Social Liberals left Franjo Tudjman's Croatian Democratic Union as Opposition. The new leader was Ivica Racan, a former communist who believed the government should have a strong hand in the economy. A high level of state intervention in the economy still exists.

PHOTO 3.22. Dubrovnik, a popular tourist destination.

PHOTO 3.23. Public bus damaged during the war.

PHOTO 3.24. Looking for work.

Promoting Entrepreneurship

The promotion of entrepreneurship has intensified. In 1997, the state granted a concession for the establishment of a free zone at Osijek (see Photo 3.25). Two phases were planned within the eastern industrial sector of the city. The first is at the western portion of the "Tranzit" River Port and MIO complex; the second, twice the area of the former, is at Saponia, Niveta, and Osijek-Klisa Airport. The retail sector in Osijek has since flourished (see Photo 3.26).

In November 2001, the Strategic Planning Office in Zagreb included extensive support to entrepreneurship as a developmental priority of the republic. The government announced favorable conditions for craftspeople, as well as the establishment of technological incubators and a system of financial stimulation to encourage small and medium entrepreneurship.

Croatia's Law on Small Business Development Encouragement was accepted in 2002, as prepared by the Ministry for Crafts, Small and Medium Enterprises. The Department of Entrepreneurship Promotion at this ministry has been headed by former television commentator and journalist Dragica Karaic. She has defined long-term measures aimed at encouraging the activities of craftspeople, cooperatives, and small firms. With the assistance of the Dutch government, an operational model has been developed to train advisors and to pro-

PHOTO 3.25. Osijek.

PHOTO 3.26. Retail district in Osijek.

mote entrepreneurs. A credit line was established for small and medium enterprises in international business. However, some entrepreneurs say that not enough is being done. Glas, Drnovšek, and Mirtic (2000) showed that entrepreneurs in Croatia demand tax incentives, as well as better access to premises and infrastructure (see Photo 3.27).

Foreign Entrepreneurs

Recognizing the administrative barriers to foreign investment, the Ministry of Economy decided to organize workshops (the first in June 2001) to remove existing barriers. Also, a real estate fund was planned to facilitate the allocation of land for lease by foreign investors.

In November 2001, the Strategic Planning Office announced that the Ministry of Economy would establish a "one-stop shop" to pro-

PHOTO 3.27. High demand for premises.

vide necessary information to potential investors and to protect Croatia from investments that would be contrary to the national interest.

Generally, Croatia is open to foreign entrepreneurs. As foreign enterprises seek local partners, consultants, subcontractors, and suppliers, this translates into new opportunities for Croatian entrepreneurs (see Photo 3.28).

The State of Entrepreneurship and the Small-Business Sector

Biljan and Lovric (1995) noted that from 1991 to 1994 the number of small firms in Croatia increased by 211 percent, while the number of large firms decreased by almost two-fifths. More recently, small business (representing 44 percent of total employment in Croatia) was the only sector of the national economy to record positive results as well as increased employment. This suggests the success of entre-

PHOTO 3.28. Opportunity for local advertising firm.

preneurship. However, entrepreneurs reported to me that they perceived corruption to be a very big problem and that law avoidance is the "most intelligent means by which to cope with authorities." In addition, taxes are problematic, and some interviewees told me that they admired entrepreneurs who evaded them. Further investigation prompted interviewees to explain that the privatization process involved nepotism, as sales reflected political loyalty.

Entrepreneurs in Croatia also complained about government regulations and about the lack of access to finance. Likewise, Glas, Drnovšek, and Mirtic (2000) found that finance is a problem in Croatia. That same study found that the general opinion of entrepreneurship is higher in Slovenia than in Croatia. However, the study points out that than when compared with those in Slovenia, Croatian municipalities display more support for entrepreneurs, perhaps finding it the only real force to exercise an economic change.

Finally, a trait particular to many small firms in the coastal regions of Croatia is the fact that they experience a strong seasonal variation in sales. Turnover is very high during summer months and much lower in the winter (see Photo 3.29).

PHOTO 3.29. Busier in summer.

Toward the Future

Martin and Grbac (1998) suggested that small firms in Croatia appeared to be making more progress toward a free market economy than was the case with large companies. However, Franičević (1999) noted the problems of the parallel economy in Croatia. Entrepreneurs sometimes avoid the formal sector because of regulation and high taxation. More entrepreneurship-based employment would be desirable.

Croatia has huge resources available in tourism, a sector in which small and medium enterprises could become the key to improved service quality. Small-scale home-based entrepreneurs already provide seasonal facilities for tourists (see Photo 3.30).

Viducić and Brcić (2001) recommended the franchise option as a means toward development of the formal sector in Croatia. "The overall business operation of the average Croatian entrepreneur can only benefit from the capital commitments franchisers bring" (2001, p. 221).

The Faculty of Economics in Zagreb appears to be very strong in corporate topics, with emphasis on large firms. Perhaps more focus on entrepreneurship across Croatian universities could be helpful (see Photo 3.31).

PHOTO 3.30. Bed-and-breakfast.

PHOTO 3.31. Faculty at Osijek.

THE FORMER YUGOSLAV REPUBLIC
OF MACEDONIA (FYROM)

FYROM covers 9,928 square miles, bordering Albania, Bulgaria, Greece, and Serbia and Montenegro.[7] During an embargo against this newly independent state, some entrepreneurs opted for the covert sector and made fortunes by smuggling. Other Macedonians went abroad where they acquired entrepreneurial skills pertinent to legitimate business; upon their return home, they became quite successful in the firm-type sector. Encouraging more Macedonians to sojourn abroad may increase legitimate entrepreneurship in FYROM.[8]

Historical Overview

Although the Ottoman Empire lost Serbia as well as Montenegro in 1878, the sultan kept his hold on Macedonia, a region that had been Turkish since 1371. Unlike Slovenia, Croatia, and Bosnia-Hercegovina, which had been governed by the Austro-Hungarian Empire, Macedonia did not experience Occidental rule until the Balkan Wars (1912-1913), when Macedonia was partitioned into three separate territories. Aegean Macedonia would be henceforth governed by Greece; Pirin Macedonia would come under the authority of Bulgaria; and Vardar Macedonia would join the Kingdom of Serbs,

Croats, and Slovenes. Although the monarchy officially joined the Axis in 1941, much of the population resisted such an alliance. In response to this resistance, the Nazis occupied most of Yugoslavia until 1943.

Macedonia declared its independence on November 20, 1991, and obtained international recognition on December 19. On February 6, 1992, Turkey recognized the independence of the Republic of Macedonia. Greece strongly opposed recognition of Macedonia's independence, angered by the use of the name Macedonia, which also refers to a region in northern Greece. In addition, Greece protested that the new republic should not be allowed to include the sixteen-point sun on its flag, as this symbol is Greek in origin. The reaction of Greece was to impose an embargo on Macedonia in 1992, and the Macedonian economy slowed down (Photo 3.32). Nevertheless, the Macedonians continued to have access to a wide variety of Greek products, as smuggling by entrepreneurs helped many items find their way into Macedonian shops. Empty Pepsi cans and wrappers from "Kiss" brand chocolate bars, both from Greece, littered the streets of Skopje, the Macedonian capital. Finally, in September 1995, the United States brokered an end to the embargo when Macedonia accepted changes to its flag as well as to its name, such as to exclude possible symbolism for territorial expansion.

PHOTO 3.32. The nation's capital during the embargo.

Once the Republic of Macedonia agreed to change its name to FYROM, the embargo was lifted. This change of name legalized international trade, thereby increasing opportunities for entrepreneurship. Those who exhibit entrepreneurial behavior are often Macedonians who have worked abroad. Meanwhile, at home in FYROM, once-subsidized prices have skyrocketed, as has unemployment. The elderly have suffered the most (see Photo 3.33).

Especially among retired people who cannot compete in the new system, there is still nostalgia for the "good old days" of unity under Tito, whose portrait is admired across the country. His name comes up often in discussions (see Photo 3.34).

To prevent the spread of hostilities, the UN set up several bases surrounding the republic (see Photo 3.35), yet interethnic tension between Christians and Muslims remains.

Promoting Entrepreneurship

In 1997, the state established its National Enterprise Promotion Agency, a trading company with the mission to support the develop-

PHOTO 3.33. No longer employed.

PHOTO 3.34. Nostalgic for Tito.

PHOTO 3.35. UN forces.

ment of small and medium enterprises. However, its success was very limited, as it failed to obtain support from various institutions and ministries.

In December 2002, the Ministry of Economy stated that despite the consensus on the importance of entrepreneurship and the development of small and medium enterprises, insufficient efforts had been made to promote the sector. Consequently, the ministry introduced its Program of Measures and Activities for Entrepreneurship Promotion and Creation of Competitiveness of the Small and Medium Enterprises in the Republic of Macedonia.

Citing the fact that the National Enterprise Promotion Agency failed to obtain support from various institutions and ministries, the ministry proposed the establishment of an Entrepreneurship Support Coordinative Council, consisting of representatives from a variety of relevant ministries, agencies, banks, and trade unions. The ministry also suggested that a central Entrepreneurship Agency would be more effective than was the National Enterprise Promotion Agency. The new program involves financial and other support. It focuses on four areas:

1. the creation of institutional infrastructure for the promotion of entrepreneurship;
2. the establishment of an economic environment favorable for the start-ups of new ventures;
3. entrepreneurship promotion; and
4. financial support.

The State of Entrepreneurship and the Small-Business Sector

It used to be that Macedonians were told what to do. They did what was expected, and nobody starved. Workers were often apathetic, product quality was often low, and service was usually poor; however, everyone had a job. Free enterprise was a step in the right direction, but for many Macedonians it was a leap for which they were unprepared. Still, workers are often apathetic, product quality is quite low, and service is usually poor. The big difference is that not everyone has a job anymore.

Because jobs are fewer in number, a reasonable solution might be for more people to become self-employed. However, given major infrastructure problems (see Photos 3.36 and 3.37), inadequacies in technical knowledge, and a lack of entrepreneurial expertise, the environment in FYROM is not conducive to new-venture creation.

A simpler path to accumulate capital is by working abroad. For those who work in Austria, Germany, Kuwait, Sweden, or Switzerland, a return to FYROM from sojourning allows splurging on overpriced consumer items, as well as the possibility of investing in new ventures. In fact, these are the Macedonians who tend to have both the capital and the willingness to invest in FYROM. Those with incomes from these savings are willing to pay high prices in FYROM. For most who do not sojourn, freedom from Yugoslavia is also freedom from a job, and consequently a shortage of money. The result has been a new two-class society, and the gap is growing (see Photos 3.38 and 3.39).

Currently, much self-employment in FYROM takes place in the agricultural sector. Principal produce includes citrus fruit, corn, cotton, millet, mulberry leaves, opium poppy (for pharmaceuticals), rice, sesame, tobacco, and a variety of vegetables. The raising of livestock is also widespread. Even in the capital city, Skopje, goats graze by the river and poultry feed freely. Just outside the city limits, peasants try to sell watermelons and other produce along the highway, but prices are high. Yet producers are reluctant to reduce prices because

PHOTO 3.36. Retailers sometimes offer phone service when they are open for business, but little privacy is available.

PHOTO 3.37. As home telephones are few in number, people make calls from telephone offices; however, this can be expensive.

PHOTO 3.38. Well-off.

PHOTO 3.39. Not so well-off.

their expenses are high. Since horse-drawn carts have been banned from major urban centers (see Photo 3.40), farmers pay dearly for the use of public transportation.

Meanwhile, cows stroll across the major motorway linking Skopje and Ohrid Airport. In the fancy resort town of Struga, peasants wash laundry in the river (see Photo 3.41) and goats graze outside the central bus station. Suddenly, a stray donkey blocks traffic. Inside the Struga bus terminal hangs a photo of Marshal Tito. Although he was a Croat who ruled Macedonia from Serbia, his portrait is common in FYROM. Life under Tito may have been difficult, but for many it was better than it is now.

Perhaps most noticeable are the infrastructure deficiencies that impede entrepreneurship. Before the Yugoslav civil war, there was regular train service from Greece, across Macedonia, to Belgrade and beyond. Within Macedonia, there was frequent rail service between Gevgelija, Skopje, Titov Veles, and the Serbian border. In recent years, rail service has deteriorated noticeably.

Bus schedules are unreliable in FYROM, and public transportation is relatively expensive considering the local income levels (see Photo 3.42). At some ticket booths, agents also expect a "gift" from passengers for selling them a ticket. A bicycle is often the best mode of travel (see Photo 3.43).

PHOTO 3.40. New traffic regulations.

PHOTO 3.41. Doing the laundry in the river.

PHOTO 3.42. "Do we have enough money?"

PHOTO 3.43. Reliable and affordable.

The banking system in FYROM is still developing. The most efficient money exchanges are conducted in the black market, for instance at a camera shop (which sells few, if any, cameras). In contrast to the situation existing in neighboring Albania, where U.S. dollars are preferred, informal money changers deal primarily in euro.

Local governments in FYROM are responsible for a variety of services, including water supply; sewage; construction and maintenance of streets, bridges, public cemeteries; garbage collection; fire protection; and local public transport. In this sense, municipalities have a decisive influence upon the choice of service providers. A serious problem here is that nepotism is as common as bidding by tender. Procedures continue to follow the old schemes, ignoring the need for more efficient management. Furthermore, any reform is slowed due to mandatory membership of each local government in a bureaucratic organization known as the Macedonian Association of Municipalities and the City of Skopje.

After years of socialist conditioning, people should not be expected to transform themselves into capitalists without a painful adjustment period. Employees were apathetic under socialism. Even now, clerks and shopkeepers still lack consumer orientation. Buying an item or service is still perceived as a privilege. Tellers think they have the right to short-change customers. Consumers would almost certainly prefer establishments with less-hostile attitudes.

Macedonians who sojourn abroad bring back entrepreneurial skills; however, sojourners are relatively few and both entrepreneurial and managerial skills are generally lacking in FYROM. A lack of marketing expertise also exists. Under the socialist regime, demand for goods was higher than supply, and since prices were heavily subsidized and competition lacking, marketing and advertising were not very necessary. Now that the system has changed, it will be useful for the Macedonians to acquire the skills necessary in a postsocialist society.

On the technological side, FYROM does not appear to be in a rush to improve its levels of automation. Cabbage heads are harvested one by one and manually placed on a donkey-drawn cart, as was done centuries ago. Hay carts are pulled by horses (see Photo 3.44). In the town of Gostivar, horse-drawn carriages contribute to rush-hour traffic jams. On intercity buses, rubbish bins consist of baskets tied to seats with coat hangers. In shops, weighing of produce is approxi-

PHOTO 3.44. Hay cart.

mate, and in the absence of cash registers or calculating devices, prices are quite subjective.

Most consumer goods in FYROM are imported. Bananas come from Ecuador, Wrigley's chewing gum is imported from Austria, and Pepsi (in cans) is imported from both Greece and Jordan. Sprite is also imported (in cans) from Jordan. Coke and Fanta (in plastic bottles) are imported from Bulgaria. Afri-Cola is also available, but domestic industry is still in need of considerable development (see Photo 3.45).

Toward the Future

With the exception of those who have sojourned abroad, Macedonians generally do not have the capital or the skills to set up new ventures. Many are waiting for direction (see Photo 3.46). As noted by the Ministry of Economy in 2002, the promotion of entrepreneurship has been less than adequate. Those who have lived abroad often become successful entrepreneurs, but these represent a minority of Macedonians. Therefore, it could be beneficial to establish large-scale work abroad/sojourn programs in FYROM, as have been organized by Israeli organizations in Romania. Encouraging more Macedonians to sojourn abroad could thus enable more individuals to

PHOTO 3.45. Advertisement for Afri-Cola.

PHOTO 3.46. A long wait.

accumulate working capital, and more important, to experience a free-enterprise market-oriented economy. This may facilitate the acquisition of the skills necessary in a small business. Also, a service-orientation might be adopted.

Creating a program to encourage joint ventures or partnerships with foreigners who have experience running a small business in an open economy would be useful. This may facilitate the learning curve involved in becoming an entrepreneur.

A few Macedonians developed a taste for free enterprise, usually while working abroad, as well as capital from such employment. However, to date this wealth has contributed to higher prices. Future research might include empirical studies of Macedonia sojourners, their duration of work abroad, values adopted from host societies, and their propensity for self-employment. In addition, further research might compare individuals who have worked in some countries with others who have worked elsewhere. Finally, it could be useful to research the causal variables influencing people to leave FYROM, work abroad, and return to set up new ventures. This might make it easier to encourage more entrepreneurship in this slowly emerging economy.

THE STATE UNION OF SERBIA AND MONTENEGRO

Following the secession of Bosnia-Hercegovina, Croatia, Macedonia, and Slovenia from the former Socialist Federative Republic of Yugoslavia, Montenegro and Serbia announced on April 27, 1992, the formation of a new Federal Republic of Yugoslavia.[9] In February 2003, this federation was restructured into a loosely linked confederation, officially called Serbia and Montenegro. Despite the existence of a federal-level government, each constituent has considerable autonomy. Serbia uses the dinar, issued in Belgrade; in Montenegro, both the dinar and the euro are legal tender. The union covers 39,517 square miles, bordering the Adriatic Sea, Albania, Bosnia-Hercegovina, Bulgaria, Croatia, FYROM, Hungary, and Romania.

Historical Overview

Serbia

The Serbian state was created in 1170, and a monarchy was established in 1180. The Kingdom of Serbia reached its zenith under Stefan Dusan, self-proclaimed emperor of Serbs and Greeks, from 1346 to 1355.

At the Battle of Kosovo in 1389, Serbia was defeated by the Turks, and the Serbs remained under Ottoman rule until 1815. In 1830, Serbia became a principality, and in 1878, the Treaty of Berlin broke Serbia's last ties with the Ottomans. In 1882, the Serbian monarchy was reestablished as the country reverted to being a kingdom.

In 1912, the European powers declared the independence of Albania from the Ottoman Empire; landlocked Serbia was greatly angered, eying Albania for its seaports. The Serbian kingdom nevertheless gained territory in 1913, when as a result of the First Balkan War, Turkey lost its last remaining Balkan possessions. Bulgaria also being the recipient of considerable land with that war, Serbia demanded a large section of Macedonia from Bulgaria. In October 1915, the Austro-Hungarian Empire, Bulgaria, and Germany invaded Serbia; Serbia was then occupied by German-Bulgarian forces from 1915 to 1918. Within the Kingdom of Serbs, Croats, and Slovenes, Serbia was the leading nation, and its capital city, Belgrade, served as the national capital of Yugoslavia (see Photos 3.47 and 3.48).

During World War II, the Nazis invaded Serbia and made it a puppet state. At the time, Belgrade had an important community of Jewish people, many of whom were entrepreneurs. Although the Nazis took a toll, the Jewish community in Belgrade was rekindled after the war (see Photo 3.49).

During the era of central planning, Belgrade was Yugoslavia's capital and home of the central government. Policies and standards for Yugoslavia were set in Serbia. Major state-owned enterprises were based here, as was the flag-carrier airline (see Photo 3.50).

In 2000, democracy was reestablished in Serbia. Since February 2003, the Republic of Montenegro has been united with the Republic of Serbia, in a loose confederation, the federal capital of which is Belgrade. In March 2003, Serbia's prime minister, Zoran Djindjic, was assassinated.

Montenegro

Ruled by bishop princes until 1851, Montenegro was never fully subdued by the Ottomans (Hodgson, 1977). In 1878, the Congress of Berlin gave Montenegro full independence from Ottoman rule. Montenegro was a principality until 1910, when it followed the Serbian example and became a monarchy. Cetinje was the capital of the

PHOTO 3.47. Belgrade, then.

PHOTO 3.48. Belgrade, now.

PHOTO 3.49. Synagogue in Belgrade.

PHOTO 3.50. Douglas DC-6 airliner with flag of Yugoslavia.

Montenegrin kingdom. In 1916, the Austro-Hungarian Empire occupied Montenegro. In 1918, Montenegro was united with Serbia.

A mountainous region nestled between the Adriatic Sea and the Dinaric Alps, Montenegro escaped conquest by the Germans and the Italians in World War II. After the war, Montenegro reemerged as a political entity, a constituent republic of Tito's Socialist Federative Republic of Yugoslavia. Podgorica became the communist-era capital of the Yugoslav republic of Montenegro.

The 2003 Privatization Plan emphasized the protection of ownership rights, economic freedom, and the national treatment of the foreigners (see Photo 3.51). This has had an amazing impact. The privatization process has already brought significant foreign investments to Montenegro, and the benefits are not limited to inflow of new capital; investors are introducing new technologies, implementing training programs for employees, and contributing to the creation of a new business environment. A large portion of the revenues from privatization is used for financing loan programs for new businesses.

Promoting Entrepreneurship

Serbia

Serbia has taken recent steps toward fostering a healthy entrepreneurship sector. In 2002, the Serbian Law on Private Entrepreneurs was amended, as was the federal Enterprise Law.

Among the current priorities of the Republic of Serbia are economic recovery and development by means of a strong private sector, with entrepreneurs and small and medium enterprises creating a majority of new jobs. The strategic plan for the period 2003 to 2008 calls for the creation of an environment favorable to entrepreneurs and to small and medium enterprises. Specifically, steps have been taken to

1. remove administrative and legal obstacles to entrepreneurship;
2. establish institutions to assist the development of small and medium enterprises; and
3. assist with problems of small and medium enterprises pertaining to financing.

The body in charge of economic policy for the development of small and medium enterprises is the Ministry of Economy and Privatiza-

PHOTO 3.51. Foreigner.

tion. This ministry has two sectors; one is for the development of small and medium enterprises and the other for private entrepreneurship. Among the goals of the ministry is the creation of conditions for faster development of internationally competitive, export-oriented small and medium enterprises.

The primary player in implementing the strategy for the development of small and medium enterprises and entrepreneurship during the period from 2003 to 2008 is the Agency for the Development of Small and Medium Enterprises and Entrepreneurship in Belgrade. Founded in 2001, the mission of this agency is to aid, advise, assist, and protect the development and interests of small and medium enterprises in

1. invigorating the regional economic development and changing the economic structure;
2. solving unemployment problems more efficiently;
3. locally producing otherwise imported goods;
4. intensifying competitiveness of small and medium enterprises;
5. stimulating various forms of cooperation with big enterprises;
6. introducing modern technologies and enhancing innovations; and
7. utilizing business premises and equipment more economically.

Other participants in the strategy for the development of small and medium enterprises and entrepreneurship during the period from 2003 to 2008 include the Ministry of Agriculture and Waterpower Engineering; the Ministry of Economic Relations with Foreign Countries; the Ministry of Education and Sport; the Ministry of Finance and Economy; the Ministry of Labor and Employment; the Ministry of Science, Technology, and Development; the Ministry of State Administration and Local Self-Government; and the Ministry of Trade, Tourism, and Services. Working together, their goals are to

1. develop small and medium enterprises and entrepreneurship in agricultural processing, e-commerce, manufacturing, and tourism;
2. strengthen the competitiveness of the sector through the development of management, quality, innovations, and technology;
3. transfer new skills by strengthening ties between research, education, and the business sector; and

4. increase symbiosis between small and large firms (as discussed by Dana, 2000c; Dana, Etemad, and Wright, 1999, 2000).

Montenegro

Changes to the federal Enterprise Law in 2002 simplified the registration procedure of new ventures across the union. Simultaneously, the Republic of Montenegro embarked on a mass-privatization scheme, involving the mass distribution of vouchers. The Act of Modifications of and Supplements to the Act of Privatization of the Economy provided every adult Montenegrin with two vouchers. This accelerated the pace of privatization and stimulated development. In 2003, more than half of the state-owned capital in Montenegro was privatized; more than 90 percent of firms had been privatized or were about to be. In 2003, some 350,000 Montenegrin citizens held the shares of companies or privatization funds.

One of the institutions that support entrepreneurship in Montenegro is the Center for Entrepreneurship and Economic Development, the first consulting center established in Montenegro. This center has been one of the key supporters of entrepreneurship and the development of small and medium enterprises. Through its network of offices, it assists start-ups as well as existing firms.

Another important player is the Montenegro Business Alliance (MBA), an association of domestic and foreign business and entrepreneurs. The MBA is the leading voice of business in Montenegro, articulating the benefits of a private competitive market system. With the cooperation of the Center for Entrepreneurship and Economic Development, the MBA launched a program called Business-to-Business (B2B), to promote free trade and to establish new links and renew old ones among the former constituents of Yugoslavia.

The State of Entrepreneurship and the Small-Business Sector

A great deal has been done toward transforming the Montenegrin economy into a market-driven, private-sector economy attractive for development of small and medium enterprises. Already, the Montenegrin economy is dominated by small and medium enterprises that represent more then 95 percent of the whole economy.

A problem across Serbia and Montenegro, however, is that entrepreneurs wishing to launch a new venture in the formal sector are burdened by heavy paperwork requirements and complex procedures. Obstacles are many, and once established, their small and medium enterprises must face burdensome regulations.

Entrepreneurs also complained to me about corruption. This is not surprising, as the monthly salaries of state officials were as low as 100 euro in 2003.

Toward the Future

Although vouchers have resulted in 350,000 Montenegrins owning shares, the lack of access to affordable financing is still an important problem for Montenegrin entrepreneurs. Although Montenegrin commercial banks provide loans to small and medium enterprises, this is still not enough to accelerate economic development. Nevertheless, conditions for entrepreneurship in Serbia and Montenegro are improving. The Labor Institute has a program of self-employment already providing credits to entrepreneurs. Establishment of investment funds for financing small and medium enterprises is expected in the near future.

More important, a new entrepreneurial mind-set is emerging. The Serbian Ministry of Education and Sport is developing and adapting educational programs to the emerging market economy and the development of entrepreneurship and small and medium enterprises.

The future of the confederation, however, is not certain. *The Economist* (Anonymous, 2001) suggested that Montenegrin independence might be inevitable.

THE REPUBLIC OF SLOVENIA

Located between the Alps and the Adriatic Sea, Slovenia covers 7,827 square miles.[10] The country borders Austria, Croatia, Hungary, Italy, and the Gulf of Trieste. Slovenia was the wealthiest of Yugoslavia's constituent republics. A vanguard of reform, Slovenia declared its independence on June 25, 1991. Article 11 of the constitution makes Hungarian and Italian official languages along with Slovene, within a limited geographic area. Article 64 grants special rights to

Hungarian and Italian communities in Slovenia. This country ranks among the most successful transitional economies. Glas, Drnovšek, and Mirtic (2000) noted that Slovenia had the highest per capita GDP of all Eastern Europe. As discussed by Pavlin (2001), Slovenia has a relatively strong infrastructure, a well-trained labor force, low corporate taxes, and a relatively stable currency.

Historical Overview

Slavs came to dominate the land, which is today's Slovenia, in the sixth century, and the first independent Slovenian state (the Duchy of Carantania) was established in this area during the seventh century. Christianity arrived during the eighth century, and the Frankish feudal system soon began to spread.

During the fourteenth century, the Hapsburgs took control of Slovenia; the last of the feudal Slovene dynasties disappeared in 1456. In 1774, compulsory education was introduced in the Slovene language. When Napoleon conquered parts of Slovenia, he created the Illyrian Provinces of the French state, and Ljubljana (see Photo 3.52), on the Ljubljanica River (see Photo 3.53), became the capital of these provinces. Although Macedonia, Montenegro, and Serbia did not experience Occidental rule, the French Empire thus stretched into Slovene lands. French rule reformed taxation policies, but feu-

PHOTO 3.52. Ljubljana castle overlooking Ljubljana.

PHOTO 3.53. The Ljubljanica River.

dalism survived. Following a brief French presence, Austrian rule resumed.

Slovenia's National House was built between 1893 and 1896; it has since been converted to serve as a national gallery (see Photo 3.54). Impressive buildings were erected in the following years (see Photo 3.55). In 1918, Slovenia became a part of the Kingdom of Serbs, Croats, and Slovenes, and it was more Westernized than were its Slavic neighbors (Danforth, 1990).

As a constituent republic of the Yugoslav federation, Slovenia was wealthier than the others (see Photo 3.56). Jordan reported, at the time, "Slovenia's sister republics envy her affluence as the most industrially advanced of the country's six republics. Her workers take home about $120 a month—about 50 percent more than the national average" (1970, p. 603).

Since the mid-1980s, referendums existed in Slovenia and opposition groups obtained permission to collect signatures for petitions. At the Congress of Slovene Journalists in October 1986, the clause prescribing allegiance to Marxist-Leninism was dropped from the statutes of the journalists' union. By late 1986, a political opposition was emerging in Slovenia, inevitably leading to political pluralism in Ljubljana.

PHOTO 3.54. The National Gallery in Ljubljana.

PHOTO 3.55. Presernov Trg.

PHOTO 3.56. Wealthy living in Ljubljana.

Each year the federal government redistributed wealth from Slovenia to the poorer republics. One third of Yugoslavia's exports were produced in Slovenia, and half of Slovenia's GNP was taken by the central government, in Serbia, for redistribution to less-developed republics. Slovenia's industrial base and infrastructure declined.

On December 23, 1990, by a 90 percent majority, the Slovene people voted for independence from Yugoslavia. The Serbian government responded by confiscating properties held in Serbia by firms based in Slovenia. In addition, Belgrade put into effect a boycott on all Slovenian industrial products. Fearing Serbian dominance, Slovenia declared independence on June 25, 1991. The Yugoslav army attacked Slovenia, but the war was over in ten days (see Photo 3.57).

In 1991, the Yugoslav currency tumbled as hyperinflation and civil war crippled the economy of the federation. Slovenia's solution was to issue its own currency. Slovenes were given seventy-two hours to change Yugoslav new dinars into convertible Slovenian tolars at the

PHOTO 3.57. The Ministry of Culture of the newly independent republic.

rate of 1 to 1. Slovenia adopted its constitution on December 23, 1991. Article 33 guarantees the Right to Private Property and Inheritance, and Article 74 guarantees Free Enterprise. By January 1992, when Slovenia's sovereignty was recognized by world powers, the tolar was worth almost double the new dinar. Slovenia became a permanent member of the UN on May 22, 1992.

In 1993, Slovenia's Company Law raised the minimum capital required in order to launch a company. Coupled with complex accounting requirements, this decreased the appeal for companies. The following year, the Law on Crafts abolished the status of part-time artisans and reclassified full-time crafts into the category of sole proprietorship.

A 1994 study used the following terms to describe the fundamental personal attributes of the Slovene national character: introverted, inward-looking, correlated with individualistic behavior, unstable emotions, pessimistic, psychotic behavior, discipline, diligence, ambition, and envy (Glas, 1998).

Slovenia signed the European Union Association Agreement in 1996, and it came into effect in 1999. Value-added tax (VAT) was introduced in 1999.

Slovenia did not develop a scheme for the privatization of small firms, since these were already in private hands. However, the general privatization scheme, as noted by Glas (1998), did not serve as a real opportunity for entrepreneurs to take over existing companies. It favored internal privatization, with existing employees becoming owners under privileged terms. Meanwhile, entrepreneurs focused more on launching and growing new small-scale ventures, which demanded considerably more time to capture strong market positions (see Photo 3.58).

Promoting Entrepreneurship

As pointed out by Glas (1998), the development of small and medium enterprises in Slovenia is synonymous with entrepreneurship promotion. Early attempts to promote entrepreneurship in Slovenia included the establishment of a Small Business Development Fund that provided loan guarantees and subsidized interest rates. A problem, however, was that the fund was soon depleted. Although well-endowed, the Ministry of Finance had its limits (see Photo 3.59).

In 1990, the National Employment Office introduced its Program of Self-Employment, which encouraged many skilled workers to become self-employed from 1991 to 1996. Glas, Cerar, and Hazl (1996) evaluated the program and found that it played a significant role. Glas and Cerar (1997) explained how the National Employment Office Program of Self-Employment adapted policies of the West to local conditions, including the scarcity of equity resources for new ventures, the lack of business skills, shortcomings in business support networks, and the low mobility of Slovenes who were unwilling to relocate.

The National Employment Office developed two streams of entrepreneurship assistance. One option involved a program of training, coaching, and financial assistance. The alternative was limited to financial assistance only.

In 1996, a Small Business Development Center was established to coordinate a Small Business Development Network. This plan missed the expected results when the center did not received adequate funding. Only after 2000, with substantial funding and staff, did the center exercise some impact on the development of small and medium enterprises.

Established in 1997, the Ministry for Small Business and Tourism finally allocated financial resources to small business. When govern-

PHOTO 3.58. Open twenty-four hours and trying to capture a strong market position.

PHOTO 3.59. The Ministry of Finance in Ljubljana.

ment support dwindled, however, the small-enterprise sector failed to become the core of government support. Entrepreneurs expected the state to do more for the promotion and facilitation of entrepreneurship than was the case. Glas (1998) reported that 38.8 percent of the respondents in his research cited the acquisition of permits as being the most important barrier to becoming an entrepreneur. The study suggested that the most important gap in the development of an entrepreneurial culture in Slovenia was the hesitation of the state to support small and medium enterprises and to push the restructuring of larger companies. In this way, any form of support has not been consistently executed, and financial assistance to entrepreneurs has been consistently inadequate. Although attempts to grow incubators have failed, the state has provided funding for technological parks in Ljubljana and Maribor, but Rebernik (2003) found that the effectiveness of these parks is poor.

Special economic zones are areas where entrepreneurs were expected to benefit from special tax treatment, if at least 51 percent of production would be exported. Entrepreneurs who qualify have their corporate income tax rate reduced from 25 to 10 percent. They can also deduct 50 percent of their investment from their tax base. Yet these zones are considered to have had little success.

Foreign Entrepreneurs

In 1999, Slovenia eliminated the requirement that the managing director of a business be a Slovenian national. The investment process was liberalized as well. Since January 2000, the government has implemented a program to encourage foreign investment. Foreign entrepreneurs now enjoy the same incentives offered to Slovenian nationals. Hotels (see Photo 3.60) and restaurants (see Photo 3.61) have prepared for an increase in business travelers. English is widely spoken in Slovenia and is often used in advertising and in business dealings (see Photo 3.62).

O'Driscoll, Holmes, and Kirkpatrick reported, "Latent hostility against foreign investment and a privatisation programme that preferred management/employee buy-outs over international tenders has held back foreign direct investment (FDI) in Slovenia" (2001, p. 332). Nevertheless, FDI inflows surged from $136 million in 2000, to

PHOTO 3.60. Grand Hotel Union.

PHOTO 3.61. The well-known Europa Restaurant.

PHOTO 3.62. French firm advertising in English.

$500 million in 2001, and almost $2 billion in 2002 (Slovenian Trade and Investment Promotion Agency, Ljubljana).

Foreigners now have the right to own real estate in Slovenia, but this does not mean that the citizens of the European Union will have the right of ownership without restrictions. The constitutional amendment means only that such ownership is possible. The state can still impose restrictions on foreigners, as it can for Slovenians.

The State of Entrepreneurship and the Small-Business Sector

Slovenia's macroeconomic environment was traditionally inconducive to entrepreneurship. Inhibitors included the limited access to capital, the shortage of special skills, and the lack of incentives.

Rebernik (2003) estimated that there were about 58,000 nascent and new entrepreneurs in Slovenia in 2002. Today, 99 percent of firms are small and medium enterprises. Rebernik et al. (2003) further distinguished among microenterprises with no employees, those with nine or fewer employees, small enterprises with between ten and forty-nine employees, and medium-sized firms with between 50 and 249 employees. That study found that microenterprises represented 94 percent of firms in Slovenia, providing 28 percent of the nation's jobs; only 0.3 percent of all enterprises in Slovenia had 250 or more employees. The authors pointed out that most enterprises in the local market are owner managed, financially weak, and lack bargaining power.

Examining business ethics, Glas (1997) found that, although ethical standards in Slovenia were relatively low, entrepreneurs cared more about their customers than did managers. Glas and Petrin (1998) found that entrepreneurs in Slovenia lacked high levels of formal education; perhaps for this reason, entrepreneurship tends not to be very innovative or high-tech in nature. Furthermore, most firms in this country lack a strong growth orientation.

Nevertheless, it is noteworthy that high-tech skills do exist in Slovenia. In July 2002, Canada's Bombardier Aerospace selected Slovenia as the first location in Europe to be authorized to carry out major modernization and other modifications to the Canadair series of regional jets (see Photo 3.63); this includes the fifty-seat CRJ-100, the seventy-seat CRJ-700, and the newer eighty-six-seat CRJ-900.

PHOTO 3.63. Canadair CRJ-700.

Among the Slovenian entrepreneurs interviewed, a reoccurring concern was that fact that growth was limited or "very difficult" because the small domestic market effectively limited growth within Slovenia. Although a small national market may impede growth within the country, this could lead to opportunities abroad. Glas et al. (1999) observed that the internationalization of Slovenian enterprises follows a stage model (as described by Johanson and Wiedersheim-Paul, 1975). They noted that the export performance of small businesses depends on the location of a firm relative to international boundaries. Rebernik (2003) pointed out that 18 percent of Slovenian entrepreneurs expect to export more than half of their production.

Slovenia still has a significant black market, estimated to be one-fifth of GDP, according to the Ministry of the Economy.

Toward the Future

Glas (1998) suggested that entrepreneurship in Slovenia has a long road ahead to catch up with the developed market economies of Western Europe. This was confirmed by the findings of the Global Entrepreneurship Monitor (GEM) study, in which Slovenia participated for the first time in 2002. The government has an important role in enabling this process to run smoothly by providing appropriate support to entrepreneurs.

It is currently the government's policy to support the clustering of small and medium enterprises at the national level, in order to develop increasingly sophisticated products and to improve local and international competitiveness. Through a voucher system, the government is providing soft support to new-venture start-ups. In particular, the state is supporting technology-oriented entrepreneurs. However, a problem facing entrepreneurs in Slovenia is the lack of venture capital. Although banks are many, first-time entrepreneurs have limited access to capital (see Photo 3.64).

The anti-bureaucracy program is progressing slowly. Rebernik et al. reported:

> The majority of time is wasted in order to take out various licenses and permissions. We cannot be content with the fact that Slovenian enterprises have to be involved in six procedures when recruiting their first employee, and four procedures when recruiting a subsequent employee. (2003, p. viii)

PHOTO 3.64. One of the many established banks in Ljubljana.

In the future, less paperwork would be appreciated. As well, cooperation with large firms could be very beneficial to small ones (Dana,
2000c; Dana, Etemad, and Wright, 1999, 2000). This appears to be
lacking in Slovenia, although subcontracting is taking place, as well
as franchising (see Photo 3.65).

Slovenians may be described as forward-looking people. Wagstyl
(2002) reported that of Slovenia's 2 million people in December
2002, 31.1 percent were Internet users (compared with 3.1 percent in
Turkey, 3.6 percent in Romania, and 33.6 percent in the United
Kingdom).

Slovenians can be very successful entrepreneurs. Kmecl described
the lifestyle of Slovenians as combining Germanic discipline, Bohe-
mianism, Slavic melancholy and "the Balkan zest for life" (1993,
p. 14). With the appropriate mix of incentives, entrepreneurship can
gain substantial importance in Slovenia.

PHOTO 3.65. McDonald's franchise at the Ljubljana train station.

Chapter 4

The East Bloc of COMECON

In January 1949, Bulgaria, Czechoslovakia, Hungary, Poland, Romania, and the Union of Soviet Socialist Republics reached the decision to create the Council for Mutual Economic Assistance (COMECON). Albania joined in February 1949, followed by the German Democratic Republic in 1950. In 1961, Albania ceased to participate, although it did not revoke its membership. Mongolia joined in 1962, Cuba in 1972, and Vietnam in 1978. COMECON was disbanded in 1991.

Bulgaria, Czechoslovakia, the German Democratic Republic, Hungary, Poland, and Romania are referred to as the East Bloc of COMECON. This chapter will discuss the East Bloc.

THE REPUBLIC OF BULGARIA

Bulgaria is 42,855 square miles, bordering the Black Sea, FYROM, Greece, Romania, Serbia and Montenegro, and Turkey.[1] Medieval Bulgaria was an important economic power, and the nation has great potential, although it has its share of challenges. Bulgaria was the first nation in the region to adopt a new constitution (on July 12, 1991), but the leap to democracy was not equaled by economic reform; instead, the state continued subsidizing inefficient state firms. Privatization finally took place following a model similar to that implemented in the Czech Republic and in Poland. Today, networks and long-term business relationships are central to entrepreneurship in Bulgaria.

Historical Overview

At the crossroads of Europe and the Near East, Bulgaria was often on the path of advancing armies. Romans passed by on their way to

Asia, and later the Turks crossed Bulgaria on their way to Europe. In times of peace, Bulgaria became central to burgeoning intercontinental trade.

Bulgaria got its name from the Bulgars; Williams wrote that Bulgar means "a man with a plow" (1932, p. 185). These people were nomads who, during the seventh century, migrated from the lands between the Caspian Sea and the Caucasus. They joined the Slavic tribes who dwelled on the land that would become the first Bulgarian kingdom in 681. The monarchy adopted Orthodox Christianity during the ninth century. Subsequently, Bulgaria expanded to include most of the Balkan Peninsula under the rule of Tsar Simeon I, who reigned from 893 to 927.

A brutal occupation by Byzantium began in 1014, when the Byzantine Empire conquered Bulgaria and the invading emperor ordered 14,000 prisoners of war to be blinded. Byzantine rule ended in the late twelfth century, when the Bulgars revolted and the second Bulgarian kingdom was established, but the Ottomans seized Bulgaria in 1393.

Nineteenth-century nationalism, under Ottoman occupation, led to the establishment of a Bulgarian school system in 1835. After the Russo-Turkish War of 1877-1878, northern Bulgaria became an autonomous principality, enlarged with the annexation of Eastern Rumelia in 1885. Ferdinand I of Saxe-Coburg-Gotha, a German prince who became the Bulgarian monarch in 1887, assumed the title of tsar in 1908. He formed an alliance with Greece, Montenegro, and Serbia. Times were relatively prosperous. In 1912, the First Balkan War forced Turkey to withdraw from its Balkan lands. The following year, during the Second Balkan War, Bulgaria was defeated by the Greeks, the Romanians, the Serbs, and the Turks.

In 1918, Ferdinand abdicated in favor of his son Boris III. After World War I, at the postwar negotiations in Neuilly, Bulgaria lost territory to Greece and Serbia. The subsequent years were difficult for Bulgaria, and repatriation payments contributed to severe economic problems. Unemployment rose due to the huge influx of numerous Bulgarian refugees from territories lost during the war. Although the need for housing contributed to a housing boom, construction lacked the ornate glamour of more prosperous times (see Photo 4.1). Williams (1932) gave an account of this constitutional monarchy during

PHOTO 4.1. Residential building constructed in Varna in 1926.

the early 1930s. An interviewee stated at the time, "The young folk are living beyond their means" (Williams, 1932, p. 186).

In 1934, the monarch and the army jointly imposed dictatorship. Boris III reigned until 1943. Given that Bulgaria sided with Germany during World War II, in September 1944 the Soviets declared war on Bulgaria and occupied it. On September 15, 1946, Bulgaria was declared a republic; eight-year-old King Simeon II (Simeon Borisov Saxe-Coburggotski) was exiled.

The Bulgarian communists seized power and, in 1947, imposed a one-party communist dictatorship. Under the communist regime, Bulgaria's economy was centrally planned, with the state setting economic goals and directing the processes of production. Land was collectivized, and in a series of sequential administrative steps, land became de facto state property even if it was de jure referred to as co-operative property. Homes remained in the private domain, with four out of five Bulgarian families owning their domiciles. Although production was state owned and managed, rural households had small plots of land that could be used for subsistence agriculture. Thus, a small degree of self-employment survived. The state subsidized the arts (see Photo 4.2) and transportation (see Photo 4.3), but entrepreneurs received no assistance.

PHOTO 4.2. The opera received considerable funding.

PHOTO 4.3. State employee cleaning the track for electric streetcar.

For the first time, much emphasis was placed on educating the Bulgarian people. With universal, compulsory education being free, the literacy rate among adults rose to 95 percent. The state went as far as to support those who qualified for higher education, either at the University of Sofia or abroad, particularly within the Soviet bloc.

The Politburo—the ruling council of the Bulgarian Communist Party—was instrumental in industrializing Bulgaria, a nation that had almost no modern industry up to the communist takeover. With communist rule, the industrial sector became the principal component of the Bulgarian economy. Almost half the jobs in Bulgaria were found in the production of chemicals, machinery, metal products, processed foods, wine, etc. Bulgaria was the leading country within COMECON, in terms of production and export of electronics.

The communist government was highly interventionist, controlling every aspect of society, from the price of bread to education. Although government intervention may have been effective in the early stages of industrialization, the system eventually collapsed. As of 1986, new regulations allowed many service providers to operate independently from the state. However, central management of all sectors inhibited the development of that which is generally considered normal commercial relationships.

In 1989, the dictatorship fell and the small-business sector became legal as Bulgaria began to move toward a free-market system. However, communists here retained greater power than did their counterparts in other transitional economies of Eastern Europe. Bulgaria relied on the COMECON system for 80 percent of its trade.

After three-and-a-half decades in power, on November 10, 1989, the leader of the Bulgarian Communist Party and of the Government of Bulgaria was forced to step down. The nation was headed for change. However, due to opposition to reform, the rate of reform was much slower than that in other COMECON countries.

Several new political parties were created, some of which formed the Union of Democratic Forces (UDF), which pledged to transform Bulgaria into a parliamentary democracy. The UDF had the support of many, including the church, entrepreneurs, and trade unions. However, the reality was that Bulgaria was still quite intimate with Moscow. In 1989, while Poland and Hungary sent out 25 percent of their exports to the Union of Soviet Socialist Republics, Bulgaria relied on Moscow for two-thirds of its exports. Furthermore, over 50 percent of

Bulgaria's imports came from the Soviet superpower, while only 20 percent of Poland's imports came from there.

There was lengthy debate in Bulgaria as to whether the nation should adopt a gradual transition model or a rapid shock-therapy approach. Those who thought they had nothing to lose supported shock therapy. The elderly with their pensions or savings were weary of social difficulties and expressed preference for gradual transition.

Finally, the Bulgarian Socialist Party opted for gradual transition. Bulgaria became the last of the former Soviet satellite states to make the change toward a free-market economy. The pace of both economic and political reform in Bulgaria was especially slow, as most means of production remained under state ownership years after privatization was announced.

Bulgaria entered the 1990s with promises of reform, but none promulgated. Meanwhile, there were shortages of meat, milk, and sugar. Inflation rose from 6 percent in 1989 to 23 percent in 1990.

Bulgaria held its first postcommunist elections in June 1990. Those elected would comprise a Grand National Assembly whose main purpose was to write a new constitution for Bulgaria. A surprise to many, the Bulgarian Socialist Party (formerly the communists) obtained 47 percent of the popular vote and won 211 out of 400 seats.

In September 1990, Bulgaria obtained membership to the IMF. In December 1990, the Government of the Republic of Bulgaria received its official mandate to begin radical economic reform. Yet conditions in Bulgaria at the time were unique. More than was the case anywhere else in Eastern Europe, Bulgarian industry had been molded for the convenience of the Soviet economy. The industrial complex of Bulgaria included 5,500 large firms employing hundreds of thousands of employees. Ninety-eight percent of production was under state ownership. Bulgaria had adopted the Soviet model, and even its cities showed Soviet influence (see Photo 4.4).

During 1991, several important developments occurred as Bulgaria opted for radical economic reform. The new constitution was adopted, the small-privatization bill was passed, Bulgaria obtained most favored nation preferential tariff treatment by the United States, and the rate of inflation was controlled from 220 percent in February to 46 percent in March, 2.7 percent in April, and 0.8 percent in May. The value of the lev (plural is leva) rose from 35 per dollar in January to 18 per dollar during the summer. However, the army, the civil ser-

PHOTO 4.4. Urban scene.

vice, the foreign ministry, and the police remained under the control of the Bulgarian Socialist Party. Managers of state firms abused their power and there was widespread asset stripping. State-owned property was allowed to deteriorate (see Photo 4.5).

Controlled liberalization of some prices, along with the relaxation of petty-trade regulations, led to the creation of a highly visible street market. Whereas state shops offered low prices but had almost nothing to sell, the street market had an abundance of merchandise at expensive prices. I remember the window of a government store in which toothpaste, shoes, shampoo, clothing, and cosmetics were displayed all together, with little if any regard for aesthetic value. Outside, vendors were sitting at impromptu stalls—a common sight in Bulgaria. Near a closed restaurant, one woman sold juice and marzipan with expiration dates long-past. Nearby, an old man tried to sell pens to supplement his meager income. Yet the quality of service was usually poor. A vendor might be more interested in writing a letter than in serving customers (see Photo 4.6).

Despite the poor level of service quality, the lack of confidence in the public sector caused an inflation psychosis as people scrambled to buy anything and everything. They waited in line with little concern as to what was being sold (see Photo 4.7). Although entrepreneurship and small business had been legalized, no significant level of small-

PHOTO 4.5. No longer well-maintained.

PHOTO 4.6. Customers can wait.

PHOTO 4.7. Keen to buy.

business activity was taking place (information provided by the Agency for Small and Medium-Sized Enterprises, Sofia).

A change for the better was possible with the general elections of October 1991, resulting in a noncommunist government. This was followed by Bulgaria's first presidential elections in January 1992. At the time, 95 percent of firms were owned by the state. In December 1992, Bulgaria obtained conventional debt rescheduling. Inflation for 1992 was controlled at 79.4 percent (information provided by the Bulgarian Foreign Investment Agency, Sofia). However, unemployment increased from 1 percent in 1990 to 12 percent in 1992, due to cutbacks and closures of state-owned firms (information provided by the Ministry of Labor and Social Policy, Sofia). Former employees of the state tried to make ends meet by selling pistachios and sunflowers at impromptu stalls.

The Law on Transformation and Privatization of State-Owned and Municipality-Owned Enterprises was adopted in May 1992. In 1993, a plan to privatize 500 firms was introduced. However, current account deficits as well as trade deficits pushed foreign debt beyond serviceable levels. Interest payments were suspended, and by 1994, foreign credits were almost unavailable. Inflation exceeded 63 percent in 1993 and 121 percent in 1994 (information provided by the Bulgarian Foreign Investment Agency, Sofia). Senior citizens despaired as the purchasing power of their lifelong savings dwindled. I recall several elderly men, each with a household scale, hoping that a passerby would stop to weigh himself (see Photo 4.8). During the exchange-rate crisis of March 1994, the lev-per-dollar exchange rate jumped from 26.8 per dollar to 64.9 per dollar.

According to data I obtained from the Vienna Institute for Comparative Economic Studies, in 1994 Bulgaria lost about 30 percent of the value of goods and services produced before the reforms. Unemployment reached 16.4 percent (information provided by private communication with Economic Committee of the Senate, Bucharest). A 2.9 percent growth rate in 1995 brought false hopes, while the annual inflation rate fell to 32.9 percent in 1995, before soaring to 310.8 percent in 1996.

Although the Center for Mass Privatization was established in 1994, mass privatization did not begin until January 1996, when every citizen eighteen and older was permitted to buy a privatization ledger for 500 leva (interview conducted at the Privatization Agency, Sofia). Privatization proceeded following a model similar to that implemented in the Czech Republic and in Poland. The first auction took place in November 1996.

Meanwhile, inflation, coupled with devaluation, crippled the economy. The situation was aggravated on July 1, 1996, when value-added tax (VAT) was increased. This prompted entrepreneurs to dive

PHOTO 4.8. Desperate for business.

deeper into the informal sector in order to evade paying such taxes (see Photo 4.9). Inflation requires price adjustments, and lag time can blur the information embodied in relative prices. Combined with excessive taxation, hyperinflation diverted entrepreneurial efforts from long-term industrial development to short-term financial gains.

Despite a bumper crop in 1996, GDP fell by more than 10 percent that year, and a flour shortage struck the following year. The economic situation worsened, and the currency collapsed as prices were changing by the hour. Shelves of stores stayed empty for days at a time. Prime Minister Zhan Videnov's government was accused of being corrupt, and demonstrations led to its fall.

Severe depreciation of the national currency in 1997 fueled the annual rate of inflation, which surpassed 569 percent (Bulgarian Foreign Investment Agency, Sofia). For entrepreneurs, this impeded the accuracy of pro forma statements and financial planning. A pensioner's monthly income was reduced to the equivalent of $2, and many simply could not afford to pay liberalized prices (see Photo 4.10). This stifled consumer demand. Simultaneously, the lack of an indexation allowance on fixed assets became a problem for manufacturers. That year, GDP fell by 7.4 percent.

Following an agreement with the IMF, a currency board was established in July 1997. In December 1999, the Bulgarian lev was pegged to the German mark and the economy began a recovery. Bulgaria was

PHOTO 4.9. Informal sales.

PHOTO 4.10. "How much bread can I afford?"

invited to begin official negotiations for accession to the European Union, and these began the following February. In 2000, the lev was pegged to the euro at the rate of 0.51129 euro per lev. By December 2000, 99 percent of agricultural lands had been restituted, and 51 percent of the long-term assets of the state were privatized.

In June 2001, Bulgarian voters gave a big victory to Simeon Saxe-Coburg Gotha (their former King Simeon II) and his National Movement. He became the world's first dethroned monarch to win back power at the ballot box. Successful Bulgarian firms looked to expand, and many enterprises turned to franchising as an expansion option (Nedialkova, 2001).

A new Privatization Law came into effect on March 23, 2002. Between January 1, 1993, and February 28 2003, 158 privatization deals involved foreign investors (Privatization Agency, Sofia).

Promoting Entrepreneurship

Since the early 1990s, the Government Reform Program has seen the development of small and medium enterprises as crucial. The Union of Private Economic Enterprises, a nonprofit organization with several thousand members from the business community, lobbied for the postcommunist government to look at entrepreneurship as the fast lane to recovery. The Bulgarian Investment Fund, an affiliate of the First Private Bank, provided venture capital to young enterprises. The First Private Bank—created by the same group of entrepreneurs who established the Union of Private Economic Enterprises—collapsed with its 650 employees working in over seventy branches.

Further to Decree 110, of June 13, 1991, the unemployed were encouraged to propose a business plan in order to receive seed capital. Since then, a variety of schemes have come and gone. In 1997, a pilot loan guarantee scheme was created to assist women requesting loans for the start-up of micro-enterprises.

In 1999, an incubator project was launched in Vidin. This was funded by USAID and managed by the UNDP. With the Bulgarian Ministry of Labor and Social Policy, the UNDP also launched a joint microenterprise project that targeted unemployed people. Activities included entrepreneurship promotion and local support of micro-enterprise, along with facilitated access to credit. In 2001, the European Union funded a project for the accelerated growth of small and medium enterprises.

The Agency for Small and Medium Enterprises (ASME) promotes entrepreneurship in Bulgaria. At the ministerial level, ASME encourages the reduction of bureaucratic hurdles and restrictions that impede entrepreneurship. At the firm level, the agency has developed a statute of a guarantee fund to assist entrepreneurs seeking finance. A training program has been organized as well.

It may be said that free-trade agreements are also facilitating entrepreneurship. Bulgaria joined the World Trade Organization (WTO) on December 1, 1996. Since January 1, 1998, Bulgaria's industrial exports have entered the European Union with no duties. In July 1998, Bulgaria became a member of the Central European Free Trade Agreement.[2] A free-trade agreement between Bulgaria and Turkey came into force on January 1, 1999. Another with FYROM came into effect on January 1, 2000. Free-trade agreements with Croatia, Estonia, and Israel became effective on January 1, 2002. Free trade with Lithuania came into effect on March 1, 2002, and with Latvia on April 1, 2003.

In 2003, a corporate tax rate of 23.5 percent served as a positive force in the promotion of new ventures in Bulgaria. Beginning January 1, 2003, manufacturers located in regions of high unemployment were granted corporate tax exemptions for a period of five years. For individual taxpayers, the highest tax rate was dropped to 29 percent.

Foreign Entrepreneurs

Bulgaria has one of the most liberal foreign investment climates in the region. The 1992 Law on the Transformation and Privatization of State and Municipal-Owned Enterprises permits foreigners to purchase state firms. Since April 1995, the Bulgarian Foreign Investment Agency serves as the state's coordinating body for investment; it serves as a one-stop shop for foreign investors, providing information, advice, and support. In March 1998, the Bulgaria Economic Forum was established as a nongovernment organization with the objective to promote Bulgaria to foreign investors.

Although Bulgarian entrepreneurs complain of difficulties obtaining finance, it is relatively easy for foreign entrepreneurs to obtain financing for a new venture. For instance, the Chicago-based Bulgarian-American Enterprise Fund offers entrepreneurs loans and equity in amounts ranging from a couple of thousand dollars to several million. An affiliate of the Small Enterprise Assistance Fund (based in Washington, DC), CARESBAC Bulgaria, provides equity for firms with less than $1 million in assets. The EuroMerchant Balkan Fund and Raiffeisen Investment also provide foreign entrepreneurs with financing.

The Bulgarian International Business Association represents foreign investors in Bulgaria. It is a nonprofit organization, established in April 1992.

Trans-Mediterranean Entrepreneurship

A culture encouraging entrepreneurship in Bulgaria is that of the Ladino-speaking Sephardic Jews, and although most of these have emigrated, many commute to Bulgaria, where they still own firms.[3] This minority traces its origins to Roman times and records indicate the founding of a congregation in Sofia immediately after the Byzantine conquest. During the fourteenth century rule of Bulgarian Tsar Ivan Alexander, his Jewish wife became Queen Theodora. At the end of the fifteenth century, more than 30,000 Sephardic Jews arrived in Bulgaria from Spain (interview with Mr. Asher Danon in Pazardzik).

During the centuries of Ottoman rule, the native Bulgarians pre-ferred to work the land. Their population was spread across rural ar-eas, physically segregated from the ethic minorities, which were con-centrated in urban areas. Notably, the Turkish Muslims had political and economic power and the Sephardis concentrated their activities in the commercial realm. Such activity was reinforced by social con-ditioning, which perpetuated cultural values. In time, the Ladino speakers produced disproportionately high numbers of entrepre-neurs.

In 1878, when Bulgaria regained independence, the Sephardic Jews received identical rights as other Bulgarians. Economic segre-gation continued, and the former specialized in commercial activi-ties. They worked as self-employed merchants and independent arti-sans or craftspeople (e.g., jewelers, shoemakers, tailors, etc.). As such, they were appreciated entrepreneurs, performing an important economic task. When Bulgaria sided with the Nazis during World War II, the Bulgarian people prevented the deportation of these Jews. In 1941, the Nazi-dominated government forced the Jews to give up their shops. Often, stores were sold (on paper only) to Bulgarian friends who served as *prête-noms,* sharing the profits. Increasingly as of 1941, Jews in Bulgaria concentrated on home-based industries such as sewing. This continued until liberation by the Soviets on Sep-tember 9, 1944.

Communism arrived with the nationalization of banks, factories, rental property, and other businesses on December 23, 1947. There were 50,000 Jews in Bulgaria at the time; 45,000 of these moved to Israel shortly thereafter. Among those who remained in Bulgaria, en-trepreneurship was a common occupation, even under communist rule. Some were suppliers of mechanical components. Others were owner-managers of restaurants.

Situated along the overland route linking Europe to Asia, Plovdiv was once a principal trading center. Consequently, Jews maintained a continuous presence there. In fact, Roman ruins indicate the exis-tence of Jews in Plovdiv over 1,700 years ago. With the return of capi-talism to Bulgaria, in 1990 the Ladino-speaking community of Plovdiv (consisting of 700 Sephardis) incorporated a unique com-pany, Maccabi Ltd. This is a community enterprise that perpetuates entrepreneurial spirit. Its first president, Josef Mitrani, was born in Is-rael to a Bulgarian family who returned to Bulgaria in 1938. Under his leadership, the firm reports considerable dealings with former Bulgarian Jews who now live in Israel (interviews conducted with representatives of Maccabi Ltd., Plovdiv).

Maccabi Ltd. is involved in a variety of activities. It operates a fashion boutique and a restaurant in Plovdiv, exports labor to Israel for construction, serves as a commission agent for import/export activities, and even introduced language courses. Not surprisingly, one can now buy South African juice in Plovdiv, with the label in Hebrew.

Symbolic of its being a hub of mercantilism, the name of the town Pazardzik is derived from the word bazaar. Located at the foothills of mountains, the region is ideal for growing potatoes, as well as for raising animals for milk, cheese, and meat. The dependence on imported wheat made this area ideal for the Ladino-speaking minority, who served as tradesmen. Whereas these people were the backbone of the local economy, the community of Pazardzik was concentrated in the geographic center of town, near the principal market. They lived and worked in the central business district where they established their institutions near the main market (interviews conducted with elders of Pazardzik). Here, too, is a node of commerce sustained by Sephardic Jews who shuttle between Bulgaria and Israel.

Among many examples is a store, built in 1922, which belonged to a member of the Ladino-speaking community who moved to Israel in 1948. The building was nationalized and transformed into a fish store. When the property was returned to him with the privatization act of 1990, he reconverted it back into a cosmetics store. Although he prefers to live in Israel, he shuttles to Bulgaria when necessary. While he is away, another Ladino-speaking entrepreneur, Asher Danon, who still lives in Pazardzik, administers the enterprise. (Asher Danon, officially a chemical engineer during the communist years, was a small-scale entrepreneur throughout the communist era.)

The State of Entrepreneurship and the Small-Business Sector

Since the 1990s, small and medium enterprises have played an important role in the national economy, formerly dominated by the large-scale state-owned enterprises. However, Bulgarian entrepreneurship still suffers from the limited availability of venture capital, a relatively poor banking infrastructure, and difficulty in obtaining loans. Usually, substantial collateral is necessary, often greater than the value of the loan; this may involve jewelry as well as hard currency. At times the cost of debt has been high. Bulgarian banks have charged a spread of up to 18 percent between their cost of capital and their lending rate, and interest rates have exceeded 60 percent before receding to the 10 percent range. Most new ventures depend on private savings from an informal network. With annual salaries of state employees being so low, few Bulgarians manage to accumulate much capital legally. Some talk of winning a lottery (see Photo 4.11).

According to the Agency for Small and Medium-Sized Enterprises in Sofia, 99 percent of all firms in Bulgaria are small and medium enterprises. Agency sources suggest that 92 percent are microenterprises (see Photo 4.12), many with very little capital. Some depend on public transport (see Photo 4.13). The rail system serves major towns (see Photo 4.14), but it bypasses most mountain villages. In some cases, people travel by donkey or mule-drawn cart (see Photo 4.15).

Bulgaria also has its share of entrepreneurs who operate in the covert sector. Cockburn wrote,

> Any bar owner or group of bar owners in Greece can send someone up to southern Bulgaria to buy women for cash. The cost of a girl in that area is $1,000, or, if you negotiate, you might be able to get two for $1,000. Best to try on a Monday for cheap prices, because most trafficking happens at the weekends, Mondays are slow, so you can get the leftovers. (2003, p. 10)

Toward the Future

Under communist rule, the state intervened to encourage urbanization and industrialization, creating jobs in state-run factories. Although production was inefficient and quality was poor, centralized planning ensured a captive market. With the collapse of the Soviet bloc, Bulgaria lost its principal trading partner. Urban entrepreneurship has since been decreed to be the cure-all. Yet a variety of obstacles plague the sector, while bakeries, dairies, grocery stores, and woodwork plants in rural areas have been ignored. Farmers have been given land, but they lack equipment (see Photo 4.16). Government policy should address this in the immediate future in order to avoid uncontrolled urbanization.

PHOTO 4.11. "May I have a winning ticket, please?"

PHOTO 4.12. Microenterprise with low fixed costs.

PHOTO 4.13. Electric-powered trolley bus.

PHOTO 4.14. Train station at Varna.

PHOTO 4.15. Reliable transport.

PHOTO 4.16. Limited equipment.

Full membership in the European Union is expected in 2007. Meanwhile, an increase in transparency in decision making, coupled with a reduction in administrative requirements, will likely contribute to the success of entrepreneurship in Bulgaria.

THE CZECH REPUBLIC

In accordance with a 1992 law passed in the Czech and Slovak Federal Republic (formerly Czechoslovakia) on January 1, 1993, the Czech Republic became an independent country, with Czech as the official language (see Photo 4.17)[4]. Covering 30,497 square miles, the Czech Republic borders Austria, Germany, Poland, and Slovakia.

The Czechs were among the first in Eastern Europe to witness mass privatization. When its Velvet Divorce resulted in the dissolution of Czech and Slovak Federal Republic, the Czech Republic rushed into a market economy. The Czech Republic soon became the first former member of the Warsaw Pact to be invited to join NATO and the European Union.

Historical Overview

The capital of today's Czech Republic, Prague, was already flourishing as the imperial capital of Bohemia's first Holy Roman emperor during the late fourteenth century. In 1648, following thirty years of war, the Austrians took over Bohemia and Moravia. The Czechs lost more than half of their population and their vibrant Protestant culture. Under Austro-Hungarian rule, the Czechs were influenced by the

PHOTO 4.17. Advertisement in the Czech language.

Austrians and by the Germans. This is still reflected in the architecture (see Photo 4.18).

After World War I, the Czechs and the Slovaks found themselves united in an independent Czechoslovakia. The new country was enlarged in 1919, with the annexation of Ruthenia (which is now a part of today's Ukraine). The constitution was ratified on February 29, 1920, and Constitution Day was henceforth celebrated every four years (Patric, 1938a).

During the interwar period, the Czechoslovak Škoda works provided munition to China, Romania, and Yugoslavia (Patric, 1938a). President Eduard Benes told Patric during an interview, "Jews, free as in England or the United States, are no problem here" (1938a, p. 225).

In March 1939, the Nazis arrived in Prague. In the words of Ronayne, "without resistance the balance of Czechoslovakia was incorporated into the *Reich*" (2002, p. 25). Prague was finally liberated by the Soviets on May 9, 1945.

PHOTO 4.18. Typical building in Bohemia.

In 1948, the communists took over the country[5] and all means of production in Czechoslovakia were nationalized. As the state took over all industrial activities, large firms became monopolistic organizations pushing entrepreneurship out of the economy. Authorities issued commands that reflected centralized planning, which was directed at satisfying production goals with no concern for market needs. State enterprises became the dominant employers (see Photo 4.19).

The role of business was primarily to fulfill the central plan. Production seldom met demand, quality deteriorated, and work ethics and spirit dwindled. In 1959, small shops and family businesses were taken over by the state (see Photo 4.20). In 1968, Soviet tanks crushed Prague's attempt to revolt and reform the economy. This delayed transition in Czechoslovakia.

Following similar reforms in Yugoslavia (in 1967), Hungary (in 1972), Romania (in 1972), and Poland (in 1976), in 1987 Czechoslovakia changed its foreign direct-investment regulations, making it possible for foreign investors to own up to 45 percent of a firm. Finally, communism was ousted in 1989.

In April 1990, Czechoslovakia became the Czech and Slovak Federal Republic. In June 1992, the Czech Civil Democratic Party (with an economic policy of rapid reform) won the Czech elections. The Movement for Democratic Slovakia (with a platform reflecting Slo-

PHOTO 4.19. Paid by the state.

PHOTO 4.20. Formerly in private hands.

vak cultural values) won the support of the Slovaks. Differences being irreconcilable, a political agreement reached on June 20, 1992,
recognized disagreements. A decision was made to divide the federation into two countries by December 31 of that year. On January 1,
1993, two new republics emerged from the Velvet Divorce: the Czech
Republic and Slovakia. Self-determination is a new concept for the
Czechs. Their internal affairs had been dominated by foreign powers,
including the Romans, the Austro-Hungarians, the Nazis, and the
Soviets.

Whereas Czechoslovakia's GDP had contracted nearly 20 percent
between 1990 and 1992, the Czech Republic's GDP grew in 1993 and
1994. Income tax rates were reduced in 1994, but some people had
little income to speak of. The reforms brought about by transition did
not have the same effect on everybody. Restitutions benefited the former owners of confiscated property. However, price liberalization
was a shock to many people, as wages were kept artificially low in accordance with a March 1991 agreement between the state, employers, and unions. In addition, more than half a million people were
unemployed.

In September 1994, the Czech Republic repaid its IMF loans five
years ahead of schedule. In 1995, GDP growth exceeded 5 percent,
and until 1997, the Czechs continued to hear good news about their

economy and its successful transformation toward a free-enterprise system. Western Bohemia prospered, as its proximity to Germany accelerated the development of tourism (see Photo 4.21) as well as industry. Old buildings were restored to their former splendor (see Photo 4.22).

The state welcomed foreign investment. Coca-Cola, Pepsi, Kodak, Minolta, Marlboro, and Head & Shoulders became household terms, along with Budweiser (see Photo 4.23). Falafel and McDonald's replaced sausages, dry bread, and *knedlikee*. Audis, BMWs, Fords, Peugeots, Renaults, and Toyotas replaced Ladas and Skodas. A problem, however, was that the effective marketing that created an increased demand for Western goods also contributed to the Czech Republic's growing trade deficit.

On April 16, 1997, the Czech government announced the Redirection of Economic Policy and Other Transformation Measures. This included the introduction of non-interest-bearing import deposits, equal to as much as 60 percent of the value of the imports. The purpose was to discourage imports of consumer goods and food products. In effect, the import deposit also froze the inception of new importers and threatened to wipe out existing small-scale importers. It was also speculated that importers would be forced to raise prices. Another disappointment for Czech entrepreneurs came when the Czech government approved the raising of the VAT on energy con-

PHOTO 4.21. Grand Hotel Europa in Prague.

PHOTO 4.22. Plzeň.

PHOTO 4.23. Prague.

sumption, from 5 percent in 1997 to 22 percent in 1998. During the first quarter of 1998, GDP began to decline. By the second quarter, several big banks were in major trouble.

In May 1998, several thousand Czechs demonstrated against the growing influence of multinational corporations. The protest reflected the feeling of many Czechs who were concerned that in the rush into a market economy, their society had lost sight of humanist values. In fact, the introduction of capitalism did widen the gap between rich and poor. Education and health care budgets were slashed, and Prague witnessed a new phenomenon—homeless people.

In preparation for the general elections of June 20, 1998, Milos Zeman attacked tax-evading entrepreneurs and corrupt beneficiaries of privatization. The Czech people, feeling the jolt of rapid reform, expressed their discontent with this approach to transition. With a platform of increasing welfare, minimum wage, and import tariffs, while slowing down the privatization of banks, the Social Democrats, led by Zeman, won seventy-four seats in Parliament—more than any other party. Interestingly, the Czechs elected more Communists than was the case in the 1996 election.

Promoting Entrepreneurship

Czechoslovakia began its privatization program in April 1990, preparing to dismantle state monopolies and to encourage entrepreneurship. In November, the government passed the Small Restitution Reform, allowing entrepreneurs (or their descendants) to claim businesses, that had been nationalized in 1959. Also in November 1990, the Small Privatization Measure was introduced, setting the framework for privatizing state-created firms. Entrepreneurs were invited to prepare privatization proposals, each suggesting a purchase price. Entrepreneurs were given the right to hire employees as well as to own means of production. In January 1991, traditional subsidies were eliminated and prices were liberalized, leading to an average price jump of 54 percent. A five-pronged reform policy was adopted:

1. The government agreed to return property to those who owned it on February 25, 1948 (see Photo 4.24).
2. The government identified 70,000 small enterprises (including retail stores and eating/drinking establishments[6]) to be privat-

ized and began putting these up for sale by auction. Foreigners were banned from participating in these auctions, except when a minimum price threshold could not be reached among local bidders. It was originally expected that this process of privatization of small businesses by auction would be completed in 1993, and the process took only slightly longer than had been planned.

3. The government passed a joint-venture law, leading to the establishment of 3,000 internationally held microenterprises and another 1,000 larger deals.

4. The government actively encouraged foreign direct investment, and in most industries, 100 percent foreign ownership was permitted.

5. The government privatized 3,000 firms by means of a voucher scheme, allowing each adult citizen to receive equity as early as 1992. This not only allowed individuals to participate in the privatization process, but also served as a learning tool for ordinary citizens. Although the daily press did not guarantee symmetric information, it increased general knowledge of market economics. Bids occurred in sequential rounds, causing those with privileged information to reveal it, thus resulting in the spread of price information and price equilibrium.

Another round of privatization took place in late 1993, and a venture capital pool, the Regionalni Podnikatesky Fond (Regional De-

PHOTO 4.24. Back in private hands.

velopment Fund), was launched in Ostrava in 1994. At the end of 1994, it was announced that privatization in the Czech Republic was almost complete. In 1995, the Fond Rizikoveho Kapitalu (Venture Capital Fund) was launched with money from the European Union. Since January 2003, Act N° 47 has been in effect, supporting entrepreneurship development.

Today, the Czech government provides a variety of state funds to facilitate the start-up and strengthening of small and medium enterprises with up to 500 employees. The Ministry of Agriculture has an Agricultural and Forestry Fund that provides loan guarantees and interest-rate subsidies. The Ministry of Economy has a budget to promote technical and technological development and to provide consulting services. The Ministry of Industry and Trade also provides consulting services through its Energy Agency. Finally, the Ministry of Labor and Social Affairs has funds to assist with skill development and job creation (see Photo 4.25). Czech Trade is more specific, providing leads to export opportunities.

Entrepreneurs in the Czech Republic can also benefit from nongovernmental support. The European Union's PHARE Program Management Unit for small and medium enterprises is the Small Business Development Agency, which provides services for entrepreneurs, financial schemes, and support to institutions. The Association of Czech Entrepreneurs and the Association of Small and Me-

PHOTO 4.25. Skill development.

dium Enterprises are also active in the promotion of entrepreneurship in the Czech Republic.

Foreign Entrepreneurs

The Czech Republic was quick to reduce import tariffs and to welcome foreign investment. In 1994, Vladimir Dlouhy (the Czech Minister of Industry and Trade) created CzechInvest, an agency to attract direct investment from abroad. Moody's Investors Service upgraded the republic's rating from Baa3 to Baa2, and in 1995, the Czech Republic became the first in the region to be awarded an A-stable investment rating by Standard & Poor's, a U.S.-based credit rating agency. This attracted some entrepreneurs from the West. However, the Czech Republic implemented a standard corporate income rate of 35 percent and provided incentives only for enterprises with $10 million or more. This made the Czech Republic more attractive to large multinationals than to entrepreneurs.

Numerous German firms shifted production from Germany to Bohemia. About 50 members of the Regensburg Chamber of Commerce, in Bavaria, moved some of their operations to the Czech Republic. Yet, when ranked according to volume of foreign direct investment in the region, the Czech Republic came only in fourth place with $5.5 billion, only 12 percent of the region's foreign investment (World Bank, 1997).

When compared to established foreign enterprises, Czech entrepreneurs lacked competitive advantage. Local entrepreneurs had relatively less access to capital, technology, effective management, and marketing skills. Lacking economies of scale, Czech entrepreneurs became vulnerable to foreign competitors.

The State of Entrepreneurship and the Small-Business Sector

During the period from 1991 to 1997, two thirds of all capital invested was destined for small and medium enterprises. In 1998, 69 percent was invested in large enterprises and only 31 percent in smaller firms. Although small and medium enterprises absorbed a large number of employees released from the restructuring and closure of large enterprises, the unemployment rate in 1999 was double that in 1996. Many firms have been struggling, and the Czech cabinet has discussed renationalization as a measure to correct the republic's rapid privatization of the past.

Toward the Future

The Czech Republic rushed into a into a market economy with a policy of rapid privatization. Incentives were provided to firms with more than $10 million. This gave the economy a jump-start, and on the surface, all looked well. In November 1995, the Czech Republic was the first postcommunist nation to be accepted in the Organization for Economic Cooperation and Development (OECD). However, the pace of reform led to unemployment and inequalities. The Czech koruna—the first convertible currency in Eastern Europe—appeared to be healthy, but experts warned that it was overvalued. Rapid reform led to inevitable political and economic problems. A lesson to be learned is that privatization can be fast, but the implementation of market mechanisms takes longer.

A recent wave of high-tech investment into the Czech Republic has made this country a leading technology workshop, as the production of electronics and optical appliances became the fastest-growing processing industry in the republic (Petrus, 2003). This will provide skilled jobs and new opportunities for entrepreneurship in the very near future. In the slightly longer term, this sector may surpass the automotive industry in terms of sales (see Photo 4.26). For entrepreneurs, this will mean opportunities to subcontract to larger firms.

THE GERMAN DEMOCRATIC REPUBLIC
(EAST GERMANY)

On July 1, 1990, a treaty on economic, monetary, and social union came into effect, introducing to the German Democratic Republic (East Germany) a social market economy.[7] The document regulating this reform is 243 pages long. On October 3, 1990, in accordance with Article 23 of the constitution of the Federal Republic of Germany (West Germany), the territory that had comprised East Germany became five *Länder* of the federal republic. At the time, East Germany had 16.6 million people living in an area of 41,772 square miles, while West Germany was home to 62 million people in an area

PHOTO 4.26. The Czechs have been producers of automobiles for a long time.

of 95,974 square miles. Unified, Germany would have 23 percent of the population of the European Economic Community, the predecessor to the European Union. An autonomous government agency, Treuhandanstalt was created to handle sales of state-owned property. Having succeeded in its mission, it was closed in 1995.

Historical Overview

At the end of World War II (see Photo 4.27), Germany was partitioned into two countries, formally known as the Federal Republic of Germany and the German Democratic Republic. Severely damaged by the war (see Photo 4.28), Berlin was further divided into sectors (see Photo 4.29).

Under Soviet guidance, East Germany worked toward becoming a showpiece of communism (see Photo 4.30). East German farmers were banished from their counties as estates were subdivided. The restructuring of land tenure eliminated the family farm, formerly a significant element of the small-business sector. Entrepreneurs in other industries were required to sell their firms to the state, and some former owner-managers became employees of the nationalized firm that they had owned. The military became a national priority (see Photo 4.31).

PHOTO 4.27. War memorial in Berlin.

PHOTO 4.28. War damage in Berlin.

PHOTO 4.29. End of the British sector.

PHOTO 4.30. Showpiece of East Berlin.

PHOTO 4.31. Military parade in East Berlin.

In 1961, the erection of the Berlin Wall shattered dreams of reunification (see Photo 4.32). For decades, family members would be separated from one another (see Photo 4.33).

The East German government formally eliminated independent small business in 1972, when all small and medium-sized firms were nationalized. The number of enterprises in East Germany with 100 or fewer employees was thus reduced from almost 10,000 to fewer than 1,000. Of 855,000 farms that were operating in 1952, only 3,850 remained in 1989.

Marshall described democracy in East Germany:

> In the Communist era, compulsory "voting" consisted only of folding a pre-marked ballot and putting it in the box—an exercise derisively called "going folding." Those who had not "voted" by midday were quickly visited by authorities. The only thing worse than voting late, East Germans recall, was asking to use a voting booth. This was a clear act of defiance, since it signaled an intention to alter the ballot. (1990, p. B1)

On November 9, 1989, East Berliners breached the Berlin Wall. By March 1990, East Germany was losing 2,000 emigrants a day (Marshall, 1990). On Sunday, March 18, 1990, the East Germans went to

PHOTO 4.32. Brandenburg Gate behind the Berlin Wall.

PHOTO 4.33. East German train turning at the Berlin Wall.

vote for real. Now, reunification became imminent. On June 13, 1990, at Bernauerstrasse, 300 East German border guards began the official destruction of the Berlin Wall.

On July 1, 1990, East Germany shifted from using East German Ostmarks to using West German marks, and East German products lost their traditional markets across Eastern Europe because Eastern European consumers could not afford to pay in hard currency. As the economy of East Germany (1989 per capita GDP = $4,500) was grafted to the dynamic and successful one of the federal republic (1989 per capita GDP = $19,300), thousands of East German enterprises could not survive. Unemployment in East Germany skyrocketed. Range (1996) reported that 36 percent of East Berlin jobs disappeared between 1990 and 1995.

For entrepreneurs, however, there were countless opportunities. Small enterprises could provide employment with relatively low inputs; they could also curb existing monopolies. Although the psychological environment was not highly conducive to becoming an entrepreneur (Lechner and Pfeiffer, 1993), people looked up to tradesmen who had been self-employed before 1990. Utsch et al. (1999) reported that there was little knowledge about entrepreneurship. Furthermore, a new venture involved burdensome paperwork requirements. Nevertheless, 150,000 new ventures were registered during the summer of 1990.

Entrepreneurs were about to be Barthian social agents of change (1963, 1966, 1967a,b, 1981), as well as pathfinders for economic growth, and this included West German entrepreneurs who were quick to begin their search for opportunities. Given their experience with a market-oriented economy, coupled with the availability of venture capital in the West, they had a competitive edge over their less-experienced counterparts. Foreign entrepreneurs also identified possibilities in former East Germany, but unfamiliarity with the German language, culture, and market needs increased risk and decreased the expected value of various transactions.

In the course of replacing the centrally planned economy in East Germany, 8,000 government-owned firms, formerly the backbone of East German business, were available to be privatized as of 1990. Yet disputed property claims, poor infrastructure, and low labor productivity deterred Western enterprises from acquiring many of the state-run, money-losing giants of East Germany. Entrepreneurs turned down factories that they could have obtained for gratis. Sources at the Berlin Economic Development Corporation indicated to me that 70 percent of existing East German firms were expected to collapse.

As defunct industry needed to be replaced, the role of entrepreneurs increased, creating new ventures and jobs for former state workers. Reiseburo, the former East German government-owned travel agency, was ordered in 1990 to reduce the number of its outlets by a third. By August 1990, 2,500 entrepreneurs had applied to set up travel agencies.

By October 1990, 1,800,000 civil servants of the former communist regime were jobless, and another 1,500,000 East Germans were working only part-time. This represented a large pool of labor from which entrepreneurs could recruit. Self-employment and entrepreneurship were the optimal choice for many.

The East Germans lived through four decades of shortages of consumer goods. Finally, the opportunity arose to supply the high demand. There was also a tremendous demand for support services such as Western accounting, previously nonexistent in East Germany (Cheney, 1990). Furthermore, there was high demand for technical, management, and marketing skills. East German farmers, for example, were unsure how to sell their livestock on an open market; the result was imported meat on store shelves and a surplus of local cattle in the fields.

Annex IX of the GEMU (German Economic and Monetary Union) Treaty indicated that to facilitate new venture creation, the government officially committed itself to provide "adequate property for private enterprise." Moreover, investors in the East received a 12 percent grant from the federal government. With the world's largest trade surplus in 1989, the federal government poured a great deal of money into its new states, particularly into a much-needed infrastructure, which would in turn enhance the business environment (see Photo 4.34). Meanwhile, for entrepreneurs in construction or providing infrastructure, tremendous opportunities were available.

Banks, too, were active in encouraging entrepreneurial activity. Although East German banks were reluctant to give loans, as of May 1990, West German banks gave thousands of East German entrepreneurs advice on how to start a new venture. Given that post–1972 nationalizations were declared reversible, banks also offered consulta-

PHOTO 4.34. Freeway passes through former border that separated one Germany from the other.

tions to entrepreneurs on how to buy back a family business from the state.

Enhancing balance sheets was the fact that although savings had been converted from East German Ostmarks to West German marks at par, the conversion rate for debits was two to one, thereby effectively reducing debts by 50 percent. (The unofficial exchange rate had been ten Ostmarks to one West German mark.)

West German entrepreneurs contributed to joint ventures with East Germans by providing market skills almost nonexistent in former East Germany. On the other hand, given that in 1988 28 percent of East German exports went to Eastern Europe and 37 percent to the Union of Soviet Socialist Republics, East German networks introduced new export opportunities for entrepreneurs from the West.

Indeed, German unification resulted in unprecedented opportunities for entrepreneurship. In addition, important advantages that entrepreneurs in former East Germany enjoyed, included

1. availability of hard currency as of July 1, 1990;
2. considerable federal funds from Bonn;
3. easy access to sophisticated technology;
4. access to markets of the European Economic Community; and

5. contact with West German entrepreneurs and their networks, which contributed to a rekindling of an entrepreneurial spirit.

Nonetheless, despite the numerous opportunities inherent in reunification, transition was not entirely smooth. Several obstacles were encountered:

1. Legal uncertainty increased levels of risk. Although many nationalizations were reversible and the former entrepreneur may apply to buy back a small business from the state, reaching an agreement as to price was not straightforward. After forty years of conditioning under communist rule, bureaucratic mentality was still strong and a tradition of communist bookkeeping added to the confusion as to the worth of assets. Furthermore, there was a debate as to *which* entrepreneur had the right to buy back a given firm. East German proprietors who had fled to the West now wanted their property back, while interim occupants had claims as well. Some complex East German rules continued to exist, while red tape, low productivity, and a poor infrastructure deterred venture capital.

2. The technological environment in East Germany needed substantial upgrading. Obstacles in the technological environment discouraged entrepreneurs from manufacturing in the east, where the lack of technology and infrastructure could hinder productivity. An obstacle to manufacturing, in particular, was an energy shortage. Before reunification, 73 percent of East Germany's electricity and heat came from coal (Thompson, 1991), rich in toxic sulfur and far from Western European environmental standards (see Photo 4.35). For technical reasons, the quantity of electricity imported from the West could not be immediately increased.

3. The regulatory environment needed streamlining, as some East German regulations survived after unification. Remnants of East German regulations include the stipulation that employees were allowed one paid day off each month up to the end of 1991 for housekeeping. In some cases, West German regulations were added to East German rules. When a firm was purchased, its new owner could not easily reduce the number of employees during the first year. This may have swayed some entrepreneurs

away from certain acquisitions in former East Germany. A more controversial regulation adopted in the East was that West Germany's inflexible shopping hours began to apply to stores, which formerly stayed open late. Shops were required to close at 6:30 p.m. except on Thursday, and then only with trade union permission could they remain open later.

4. There were infrastructural difficulties. In particular, the shift toward trucking caused considerable problems. Before 1990, all shipments of freight traveling in excess of 50 kilometers (approximately 30 miles) were required to be railed. After reunification, enterprises leaned toward trucking, but East German roads had not been designed for heavy truck traffic.

5. There was an adjustment period with regard to pricing. In the past, subsidies made necessities affordable to all. Agricultural producers in East Germany used to depend heavily on subsidized pricing. It used to be that food subsidies allowed East German farmers to fatten pigs on subsidized potatoes and bread. Reunification meant an end to subsidized food, animal feed, fertilizer, and fuel.

6. A competitive disadvantage in East Germany was the lack of marketing expertise, packaging, and presentation skills. These were less necessary when demand exceeded supply and no effort was needed to sell. With reunification, East German entrepreneurs needed to seek marketing expertise from the West, from either partners or consultants.

7. There were concerns about the level of initiative exhibited by people in the East. Frese et al. (1996) showed that there was lower initiative at work in the East; Speier and Frese (1997) elaborated on this.

Toward the Future

Ironic it is indeed that in 1989, *The Economist* reported, "East Germany says it needs no *perestroika* at all" (Anonymous, 1989b, p. 6). Fay and Frese (2000) examined changes that have occurred and trends taking place. A united Germany translated massive shortages in the East into opportunities for entrepreneurs, the pathfinders for economic development.

PHOTO 4.35. Coal.

THE REPUBLIC OF HUNGARY

Hungary covers an area of 35,911 square miles, bordering Austria, Croatia, Romania, Serbia and Montenegro, Slovakia, Slovenia, and the Ukraine.[8] Hungary was among the first countries in Eastern Europe to take bold initiatives toward a market-led economy, with emphasis on small and medium enterprises; the Hungarian economy soon became the soundest of the former Soviet bloc. In contrast to other Eastern European countries that opted early during their transitional period to distribute free assets to the public by means of a voucher scheme, Hungary was reluctant to do so on the basis that several state-owned enterprises had negative net worth. Hungary, today, is among the most stable emerging economies.

Historical Overview

While the word "Hungarian" is derived from *Onogur,* meaning "ten tribes," the Hungarians call themselves *Magyar,* Ugric in origin. Unlike their Slav neighbors, the Hungarians are descendents of nomadic horsemen who arrived in the late ninth century. Of Finno-Ugric stock, the Hungarians are related to the Finns and the Estonians.

Christianity was introduced to the Hungarians under St. Stephen, who centralized political power over 1,000 years ago. In 1526, Louis II, the last king of an independent Hungary, died after falling off his horse while escaping the advancing Ottomans who were being led by Sultan Suleiman the Magnificent. The Ottomans were driven out of Hungary in 1683, and the Hapsburgs took over most of the Hungarian lands. In response to a revolt in 1848, the *Ausgleich* (compromise) of 1867 established the Austro-Hungarian dual monarchy, in which Hungary was an equal to Austria. In 1872, the Industrial Law prescribed the liquidation of guilds, which had formerly hindered industrial development in Hungary.

On July 28, 1914, the Austro-Hungarian government sided with Germany and declared war on Serbia. During the course of World War I, the former Austro-Hungarian monarchy ceased to exist and was replaced in Hungary by a national Hungarian government (see Photo 4.36).

On June 4, 1920, the Treaty of Peace between the Allied and Associated Powers and Hungary (also known as the Treaty of Trianon) greatly reduced the area of Hungary. A western strip of Hungary was ceded to Austria; Slovakia went to Czechoslovakia; Transylvania went to Romania; and southern Hungary was absorbed by the Kingdom of Serbs, Croats, and Slovenes.[9]

In November 1940, Hungary joined the Axis, as the alliance of Germany and Italy was called. In June 1941, Hungary declared war on the Soviets. The Nazis occupied Hungary from March 1944 until the Soviets arrived in late 1944. During the few months of Nazi occupation, the courtyard behind Budapest's Central Synagogue (see Photo 4.37) served as the departure point for Nazi transports to concentration camps, where 700,000 Hungarian Jews perished.

In 1948, a Soviet-style constitution made Hungary a one-party state. Hungarian firms with more than 100 employees were national-

PHOTO 4.36. Neogothic spires of Parliament building on Pest side of the nation's capital.

PHOTO 4.37. The largest synagogue outside the United States.

ized. In October 1956, Soviet tanks crushed a bloody revolution. As a follow-up to Moscow's original five-year plan to industrialize Hungary, a less ambitious three-year plan was drafted for 1958 to 1960, followed by a five-year plan for 1960 to 1965.

Reform was initiated in 1968, when the New Economic Mechanism decentralized planning from the state to the enterprise level. McDowell (1971) noted that the government no longer fixed all prices, and unlike citizens of some other communist countries, Hungarians could own land privately. Licensed artisans could form new ventures, but private ownership and partnerships were limited to small firms (Lyles, Baird, and Orris, 1995). In 1981, the number of employees an entrepreneur could hire was raised from six to nine. In 1983, the number was raised to twelve. As indicated by Hisrich and Fulop (1995), from 1982 to 1985 the number of private firms in Hungary doubled almost every year, and the number of shopkeepers almost tripled between 1982 and 1987.

In 1984, the Hungarian National Association of Entrepreneurs (VOSZ) was established within the Hungarian Chamber of Commerce. This was the first independent economic-interest federation in Hungary. Noar (1985) reviewed the small-business reforms that were taking place in Hungary at the time.

In 1987, private enterprises owned 2 percent of gross fixed assets in Hungary (Crook, 1990). Major liberalization began in 1988, when Hungary introduced its Companies Act. That year, private enterprise provided 7 percent of the jobs in Hungary and accounted for 11 percent of retail trade turnover (Crook, 1990). In 1988, entrepreneurs were permitted to have as many as thirty employees; this was raised to 500 the following year.

A stock exchange opened in January 1989. A new constitution[10] was approved on October 18, 1989, and the People's Republic of Hungary was abolished on October 23, 1989.

Hungary's secondary economy of small private firms and cooperatives grew remarkably fast, providing part-time employment for many state employees. State-owned enterprises and cooperatives accounted for 85 percent of the Hungarian economy in 1990, and it was estimated that the secondary economy provided at least some income to two-thirds of Hungary's families (Crook, 1990).

As of 1991, foreign trade was liberalized, requiring no specific license. Yet in 1991 Hungary still had 2,000 state enterprises with a book value of $25 billion. This accounted for 90 percent of productive assets in the country.

By the end of 1991, state-owned firms in Hungary were required to become profit oriented. Privatization took place quickly, and multinational enterprises rushed into Hungary. By 1994, it was estimated that Hungarian entrepreneurs already accounted for a quarter of the nation's GDP (Fulop, 1994).

To assist with the development of small and medium-sized enterprises, December 1999 legislation assigned responsibilities to the Enterprise Development Council. In 2000, the Széchenyi Plan was launched, with an Enterprise Development Plan oriented toward

1. facilitating the establishment of innovative small and medium-sized enterprises;
2. promoting the expansion of existing small businesses;
3. promoting the internationalization of existing small and medium-sized enterprises; and
4. assisting with the establishment of links to the information economy.

In October 2002, Hungary launched a medium-term investment promotion program called SMART Hungary. Also, an Action Program was designed to prepare small and medium-sized enterprises for integration with the European Union.

In June 2003, the National Bank of Hungary devalued the forint and subsequently raised its key, two-week deposit rate by 1 percent, to 7.5 percent. This was interpreted as a move toward instability (Feher, 2003).

Promoting Entrepreneurship

A state initiative launched in 1990, the Hungarian Foundation for Enterprise Promotion, fosters the establishment of small and medium-sized enterprises and helps existing ones stay profitable. The mission of the foundation is to provide long-term training for prospective and active entrepreneurs, thus promoting the professional and market-related development of small and medium-sized enterprises.

In 1991, the Hungarian Foundation for Enterprise Promotion began setting up rural enterprise development centers, and a national network was soon assisting entrepreneurs in all counties. In 2005 there were about 100 contact points for entrepreneurs. To account for regional differences and local needs, the network is decentralized, allowing a different enterprise development program to be created in each region. The foundation's microcredit scheme has met with considerable success.

Since 1992, the National Union of Handicraftsmen (IPOSZ) has owned and operated the For Market Entrepreneurial Trading House Corporation, with the mission to assist handicraftspeople and their small enterprises in production, marketing, and export. The union's network of expertise in ceramics, glasswork, metallurgy, precision engineering, and woodwork allows small batches of products to be custom-made, with a short turnaround period.

In 1993, the nonprofit Hungarian Investment and Trade Development Agency was established by the Ministry of Industry, Trade, and Tourism to promote investment and trade development. Supervised by the Ministry of Economy and Transport and by the Ministry of Foreign Affairs, this agency provides advisory services, identifies opportunities for entrepreneurship, and conducts matchmaking between firms in Hungary and others abroad. The Ministry of Foreign Affairs maintains the agency's Foreign Trade Network Services.

A Law on Small and Medium Enterprises has been in effect since 1999. The National Development Plan calls for an entrepreneurship development program, and this includes an Incubator Program. The Incubator Program supports centers that offer infrastructure and low-cost professional services to assist small and medium-sized enterprises.

The chambers of commerce in Hungary are also promoting entrepreneurship. According to Hungarian law, the role of chambers of commerce includes vocational training and business development.

None of the entrepreneurs I interviewed complained about a serious difficulty in obtaining finance. For those just starting out, German Start Credit is available. According to some respondents, microcredit is plentiful for those in business. According to others, it is less plentiful than was the case in the recent past. Nevertheless, financing is available for Hungarians wishing to buy state property. In addition, the Hungarian women's World Bank microcredit scheme provides finance to women who operate small firms.

Foreign Entrepreneurs

In 1972, foreigners were allowed to hold 49 percent of an enterprise in Hungary. The law was changed to allow majority ownership in 1985. In 1989, foreign entrepreneurs were permitted to exercise 100 percent ownership, eliminating the need to form a partnership with a Hungarian entity. Yet when it came to privatization, the government decided that local entrepreneurs would be preferred over foreign investors in the case of similar bids.

Since 1994, non-Hungarians have been able to create Hungarian offshore limited-liability companies, provided that the majority of directors and employees are Hungarian and that the principal bank account of the firm is in Hungary. Although offshore limited-liability companies have become popular investment instruments, they cannot trade within Hungary or become involved in the finance sector. Most foreign investors operate through limited-liability companies (Kft) incorporated in Hungary. The Kft resembles the German GmbH.

The forint has been freely convertible since the 1995 Act on Foreign Exchange. Controls are limited to portfolio investment and real estate purchases. Since May 9, 2001, the value of the forint has been free to float against the euro within a 15 percent band.

The State of Entrepreneurship and the Small-Business Sector

The constitution in Hungary provides Hungarian citizens with several basic rights, one of which is the right to launch a business. The government defines sole proprietorship as "a business launched by a sole proprietor (entrepreneur)." The official definition elaborates,

> A sole proprietor is an individual who performs business activities in Hungary in his own name, at his own risks, on a regular basis, for profits, holding an entrepreneurial card, along with a private person whose activities are categorized by the law as business activities.

Thus, the entrepreneur is (by definition) equated with a sole proprietor, and an entrepreneurial card is mandatory. An individual may receive only one entrepreneurial card, and the holder is allowed to engage only in entrepreneurial activities that are specified on the entrepreneurial card issued to that particular individual.

In 2003, over 400,000 sole proprietorships were operating in Hungary, representing the same number of entrepreneurs and entrepreneurial cards. The authorities, for a variety of reasons, may revoke an entrepreneurial card. A sole proprietor has the option to hire employees. Even when employees have been hired, the proprietor is required, according to Hungarian law, to personally participate in the business.

When discussing entrepreneurial cards with respondents, it was suggested to me that countless individuals are dealing in activities beyond those specified in their respective entrepreneurial cards. It was also explained that some individuals who have had their entrepreneurial cards revoked are still engaged in business activities, due to economic necessity.

Toward the Future

As early as the 1960s, Hungarians working on state farms and co-operatives were allowed to use their household plots for private gain. Further steps toward private ownership were taken during the 1970s, when tenants were permitted to purchase the apartments (see Photo 4.38) in which they resided. After privatization, residents took better care of their homes (see Photo 4.39). Today, entrepreneurship is not only allowed, but also encouraged. Small firms have grown in performance as well as in number. Hungary's private sector, which accounted for 20 percent of GDP in 1990, now produces more than 80 percent of GDP; this is among the highest ratios on Europe.

Yet entrepreneurship is not without its current problems in Hungary. Zoltan Vereczkey of the Chamber of Commerce and Industry of Pest County described to me three types of entrepreneurial firms in Hungary: (1) artisanal enterprises; (2) small-scale independent subcontractors selling to large firms; and (3) high-tech innovators. He expressed concerns to me, citing that most of these private sector entrepreneurs in Hungary operate their firms only on a part-time basis, to earn sideline income.

Janos Fonagy, former undersecretary of state at the Ministry of Economic Affairs, told me that only a third of registered enterprises are really working. He also expressed concern that small and medium

PHOTO 4.38. Housing was poorly maintained under central planning.

PHOTO 4.39. Privately owned and well-kept housing.

sectors consist of a very high number of microenterprises, and their economic situation was fragile as a result of very low capitalization. Policy should therefore focus on enhancing competitiveness and self-financing capabilities, moderating the shortage of capital prevailing as a general characteristic.

Nevertheless, entrepreneurship is generally developing at a fine pace in Hungary. The government has created an enterprise-friendly business environment, and the excellent infrastructure may be regarded as a facilitator (see Photo 4.40).

Among the 600,000 Hungarians in Romania and Slovakia, many are keen to develop business networks with entrepreneurs in Hungary. In 2003, Hungary proposed to issue documents to these people, indicating Hungarian ethnicity. These networks may become significant in the future.

THE REPUBLIC OF POLAND

The Polish Republic covers an area of 120,725 square miles, bordering the Baltic Sea, Belarus, the Czech Republic, Germany, Lithuania, Russia, Slovakia, and the Ukraine.[11] Poland was the first country in Eastern Europe to form a noncommunist, multiparty parliament,

PHOTO 4.40. Hungary has one of the most reliable postal systems in Eastern Europe.

and the first to pioneer a shock-therapy approach to transition. At first, this tripled poverty, but it soon paid off, and Poland became one of Eastern Europe's most successful reformers, also known as the "Eagle Economy." During the 1990s, Poland avoided the recessions and currency crises that afflicted the Czech Republic, Hungary, and others. However, support for mass privatization was limited in Poland, and the nation's National Investment Funds Program became operational only in 1995. According to records at the World Bank, 95 percent of adult Poles participated in privatization by 1996. Unlike the situation in some other Eastern European countries, Polish interviewees did not mention social networks in their discussions of postcommunist entrepreneurship in Poland. This supports research by Johnson, McMillan, and Woodruff (2002), who found that the use of social networks for business in Poland is infrequent.

Historical Overview

Poland emerged as a political entity in 966, when the dukes of Polanie united several tribes. During the fourteenth century, Casimir the Great encouraged trade and made Poland a significant power in Europe. He bequeathed the crown to Louis of Anjou, King of Hungary.

Under the Krëva Act of 1385, Louis' daughter, the Polish Crown Princess Jadwiga, married the Grand Duke of Lithuania, Jogaila. The Jogaila dynasty then ruled over Poland and Lithuania for almost 200 years. In 1569, Poland was united with the Grand Duchy of Lithuania, forming the Commonwealth of Poland and Lithuania, an empire that spread from the Baltic Sea to the Black Sea.

As a result of their links with Jewish entrepreneurs in other countries, Polish Jews developed a sophisticated trade network, acting as intermediaries with Hungary and beyond. During the sixteenth and seventeenth centuries, Jewish entrepreneurs in Gdansk developed trade networks with England and the Netherlands. Meanwhile, other Jews developed trade links with the Hungarians and the Turks via Kraków and Lviv. These people exported Polish cattle and agricultural produce, as well as ready-made clothing. Their trade networks, at the time, were notable. During the mid-sixteenth century, Jewish entrepreneurs from Brest Litovsk, Grodno, Sledzew, and Tykocin established a company to trade with Gdansk. In 1616, merchants from Kraków, Lublin, Lviv, and Poznan established a similar company.

Between 1772 and 1795, Austria, Prussia, and Russia carved up Poland, each taking a piece. Poland as a country no longer existed, until the nineteenth century, when Napoleon conquered Austria and Poland and reestablished a Polish state. Following the collapse of Napoleon's campaign in Russia, the Duchy of Warsaw fell under Russian rule in 1813. As a result of the Congress of Vienna, the Russian-ruled Kingdom of Poland was established in 1815.

Following World War I, the Treaty of Versailles recognized an independent Poland; the new country became a parliamentary republic. By the terms of the Treaty of Versailles, the former capital of East Prussia, namely Danzig (as Gdansk was known in German), became a Free State, administered by the League of Nations. A customs union between Danzig and Poland lasted until September 1, 1939.

Hosmer (1939) gave an account of Poland shortly before occupation by the Nazis, on September 1, 1939; this included discussions of Poland's Jews and Ukrainians. Then, World War II transformed Poland. Kuhn and Kuhn wrote that with the war, "Poland lost the farming skill of the Ukrainians, the technical and managerial talents of the Germans, the commercial enterprise of the Jews" (1958, p. 390). Denuelle (1973) elaborated on the Holocaust against the Jews.

After World War II, the Allied Powers established modern Poland and its present borders. The country shifted over 100 miles to the west, roughly outlining the Polish country that existed 1,000 years ago. "No fewer than 8,000,000 Germans fled or were expelled from what became western Poland, and more than 5,000,000 Poles, most of them from territory seized by Russia, moved in to take their places" (Kuhn and Kuhn, 1958, p. 386).

Under Soviet guidance, Poland became a satellite state and the industrial revolution transformed the granary. As a gift to the Poles, Josef Stalin sent 5,000 Russians to Warsaw to erect the thirty-storey Palace of Culture and Science (see Photo 4.41). Completed in 1955, the building contains more than 2,000 rooms.

After their revolution of October 1956, the Poles regained some liberties. The state reformed its compulsory delivery program and farmers were allowed to sell milk and more grain at market prices (see Photo 4.42).

PHOTO 4.41. The Palace of Culture and Science.

PHOTO 4.42. Motivated by market prices.

The government relaxed its efforts to force small-scale farmers into collectives, but it did little to assist them. Four-fifths of the land continued to be owned by private farmers (see Photo 4.43), although their tiny farms lacked economies of scale and so mechanization was seldom a viable option (see Photo 4.44).

Until 1970, food prices were very heavily subsidized. Luxuries, however, were expensive. The price of refrigerators, for example, was beyond the means of some farmers (see Photo 4.45).

On December 12, 1970, the government announced significant increases in food prices, along with lower prices for refrigerators (meat jumped 17 percent). This led to riots along with strikes in Gdansk, Gdynia, and Szczecin (known as the German port of Stettin until 1945). During the 1970s, the Polish economy went from crisis to crisis, as the government enforced communist ideology, steered by the Central Committee of the Communist Party, officially known as the Polish United Workers' Party.

In August 1980, as another strike at the Lenin Shipyard in Gdansk was about to end, former shipyard electrician Lech Wałęsa made additional demands. These were met, and the government agreed to the formation of an independent self-governing trade union, Solidarity. The union was registered officially on October 24, 1980.

In December 1981, General Wojciech Jaruzelski declared martial law and Lech Wałęsa was arrested. The Solidarity movement was

PHOTO 4.43. Traditional small-scale farmers.

PHOTO 4.44. Lacking economies of scale.

PHOTO 4.45. Christmas dinner preserved in a cold bedroom.

forced underground. Wałęsa was awarded the Nobel Peace Prize in October 1983.

By the late 1980s, Solidarity counted 10 million members. In May 1988, workers went on strike demanding the legalization of Solidarity and the end of food price increases. In April 1989, Wałęsa halted the strike and obtained semidemocratic reforms, in addition to re-legalization of Solidarity. It should be noted that owners of property could not be members of Solidarity. Instead, Polish artisans could join a separate trade union, namely the Solidarity of Artisans.

Elections took place on June 4, 1989, and Solidarity won all of the seats it was allowed to contest in the lower house, in addition to 99 out of 100 seats in the Senate. However, the Communist Party and its allies retained a majority of the seats in the lower house, through a reserved list. The private sector, at the time, accounted for about 5 percent of economic activity. In July, Communist Party leader Wojciech Jaruzelski (who had smashed Solidarity in 1981, and interned Wałęsa) became Poland's president.

Nonetheless, the Communist Party was losing power. Johnson wrote, "Beset by strikes, debt ridden, repudiated by an overwhelming majority of voters in elections in June, the regime was drained of the ability to govern. . . . Suddenly last week, the inconceivable happened" (1989, p. 16). In August 1989, Jaruzelski asked Tadeusz Mazowiecki, a Solidarity lawyer, to become the first noncommunist prime minister in the Soviet bloc since 1948. This opened a new chapter in history. Meanwhile, the *Moscow News* reported about Poland, "There can be no government of national accord without communists" (Masterov, 1989, p. 1).

In October, Radyshevsky reported, "Yesterday's underground are today's ministers . . . the monthly tuition at private schools is equal to the average Polish wage" (1989, p. 6). He elaborated that "crowds of black marketers . . . fearlessly change currency outside state banks. . . . A kilogram of sausage costs 20,000 złoty . . . whereas the average wage of a physician, for example, is 70,000" (Radyshevsky, 1989, p. 6).

On January 1, 1990, Poland embarked on its big-bang shock therapy model of transition, as many price and monetary restrictions were abandoned. As prices rose by 80 percent that month, Crook described the reforms as "frighteningly bold" (1990, p. Survey 4). The Balcero-wicz Plan was aimed at stabilizing the economy while creating a free market. Reform liberalized prices, enacted comprehensive privatization measures, and created the Ministry for Ownership Changes, charged with overseeing the process of privatization. The Ministry for Ownership Changes was given a very specific mandate:

1. to work out and implement guidelines on state policy regarding privatization;
2. to work with the Ministry for International Economic Cooperation, establishing guidelines on state policy concerning cooperation with foreigners;
3. to analyze the progress of privatization;
4. to contribute to the fostering of start-ups and the development of privately owned firms; and
5. to launch training courses.[12]

The privatization of firms was usually straightforward, but the privatization of immoveable property gave rise to many issues, as there were often difficulties proving title to land and buildings. This varied from place to place, but tracing ownership was a particular problem in areas where there had been large numbers of Jewish landlords, simply because so many people were victims (see Photo 4.46).

Privatization of enterprises was structured according to the size of firms. Although 8,000 large enterprises were set aside for privatiza-

PHOTO 4.46. Krakow was home to 60,000 Jews.

tion on a case-by-case basis, approximately 60,000 small firms were privatized primarily by means of auctions. The State Enterprise Privatization Act was passed on July 13, 1990. This introduced two paths to ownership transfers: (1) privatization by the transfer of equity, and (2) privatization via the liquidation of assets, as per Article 37 of the act. Firms did not necessarily do well after privatization. Outside the co-operative sector, there was a significant shortage of management skills.

Among several steps taken in 1990, bankruptcy laws were amended and the Polish currency, known as the złoty, was made convertible. Lech Wałęsa became president of his country in December that year. Inflation in Poland was 684 percent in 1990, falling to 80 percent in 1991. Industrial production fell 28.8 percent in 1990, and another 5.7 percent in 1991.

Trading on the Warsaw Stock Exchange began on April 16, 1991. In July, the Warsaw Pact was dissolved. On December 16, 1991, Poland signed the European Treaty of Association, which came into effect in February 1994. Dandridge and Dziedziczak (1992) emphasized the success of economic reform in Poland. By 1993, Poland's private sector was contributing half of the nation's GNP (Michaels, 1993).

The new złoty (worth 10,000 old ones) was introduced on January 1, 1995. Poland joined the World Trade Organization (WTO) on July 1, 1995, and NATO on March 12, 1999. On November 19, 1999, Parliament passed the new Law on Economic Activity. It had been hoped that entrepreneurs would create jobs as fast as job-protection clauses in privatization contracts expired, but this did not happen. Unemployment edged up from 10 percent in 1998 to 16 percent in 2001. The Privatization Agency was dissolved in April 2001.

In December 2002, at the Copenhagen Summit, Poland completed talks for accession to the European Union. In last-minute negotiations, Poland obtained a set of financial arrangements to help cover the costs of accession. The new deal appealed considerably more to farmers in Poland than did the former proposal.

Given extremely weak price pressures in late 2002, the *Economist Intelligence Unit* revised downward its forecast of inflation for the year 2003. It was projected that inflation at the end of 2003 would be near the lower 2 percent limit of the central bank's target range. In 2003, according to Goodale, "The infrastructure indispensable to join a knowledge-based economy remains beyond the reach of the 38 per cent of Poles living in rural areas" (Anonymous, 2003, p. 77).

The Polish Craft and Small Business Association

Even under communist rule, craftspeople and peasants could own land in Poland as well as the equipment required to practice their trades. As explained by Radyshevsky (1989), they could also employ workers. Across Poland, 300,000 enterprises have evolved from crafts, and another 300,000 are members of craft self-government organizations.

The Polish Craft and Small Business Association was established before World War II and has been active ever since. The association includes 484 guilds as well as twenty-six regional chambers of crafts and small and medium enterprises. Its mandate is fivefold:

1. to represent the craft and small- and medium-enterprise community, in contacts with governmental bodies, state administration, and economic and social organizations;
2. to inspire and work out legal solutions pertaining to crafts and small and medium enterprises, especially those connected with improving the competitiveness of the sector;
3. to provide comprehensive assistance in fulfilling statutory duties to associated organizations;
4. to provide specialized consulting services in organization, economics, and finance; and
5. to coordinate vocational training.

The Polish Craft and Small Business Association has participated actively in the work of the following: the Economic Council of the Ministry of Economy; the European Association of Crafts and Small and Medium Enterprises; the International Association of Crafts and Small and Medium Enterprises; the National Council for European Integration; the Parliamentary Committee for Small and Medium Enterprises; the Polish Foundation for Promotion and Development of Small and Medium Enterprises; the Polish Standardization Committee; and the World Association for Small and Medium Enterprises (WASME), with an advisory role to the UN.

Promoting Entrepreneurship

Although it can be argued that the macroeconomic environment (factors such as inflation, etc.) did not favor small firms (Piaseski and Fogel, 1995), Hull (1999) noted that the success of SMEs (small- and medium-sized enterprises) in Poland was due mainly to microeconomic conditions rather than to active promotion of the sector. It may be stated, nevertheless, that the goal of the state, concerning entrepreneurs and their firms, is to create conditions conducive to the development of this sector and to the optimum utilization of its potential. Until 2000, the body responsible for the promotion of Polish entrepreneurs and their small and medium enterprises was the Polish Foundation for Promotion and Development of Small and Medium Enterprises. Legislation on November 9, 2000, replaced this foundation, creating as its successor the Polish Agency for Enterprise Development. Projects initiated by the Polish Foundation for Promotion and Development of Small and Medium Enterprises were simply taken over by the new agency.

The Polish Agency for Enterprise Development was launched on January 1, 2001, as the successor to the Polish Foundation for Promotion and Development of Small and Medium Enterprises. The mission of this agency, which is financed by the state budget, is to participate in the implementation of economic-development programs with an emphasis on supporting small and medium enterprises. The agency provides advisory services to entrepreneurs, as well as grants for managerial training. The agency collects information of possible usefulness to entrepreneurs, administers databases, and conducts analyses. It also prepares and publishes documentation in accordance with its mandate to disseminate knowledge and to facilitate access to information. In addition, the agency encourages participation at trade fairs and exhibitions in Poland and abroad, and it financially supports the attendance of Polish entrepreneurs at these events. The agency is managed by its president, under the supervision of a board that consists of nine members. As well as assisting entrepreneurs, the Polish Agency for Enterprise Development provides assistance to governmental bodies with regard to the needs of small and medium enterprises. It also provides assistance to loan and credit-guarantee funds, through financial support as well as advisory services.

In February 2002, the Council of Ministers approved the Entrepreneurship-Development-Employment Program. This was praised for shifting expenditures away from transfers and toward growth-enhancing policies that promote the growth of entrepreneurial firms, thereby reducing the high level of unemployment. To further encourage new-venture creation, in July 2002, Poland introduced a tax credit for small-scale entrepreneurs just starting out. The Government Program on Capital for Entrepreneurs was introduced in September 2002.

A paradox is that while entrepreneurship is being promoted in Poland, entrepreneurs I interviewed stated that a bureaucratic regulatory regime has been an obstacle to entrepreneurial activity. Since January 2001, all business activities must be registered in the National Juridical Register, except natural persons who have registered with the Business Activity Register before January 2004. Other registration requirements include registration with the statistical office and the tax office. Another complaint cited by entrepreneurs in Poland was their disadvantageous position in obtaining loans.

Foreign Entrepreneurs

In 1976 foreign ownership of firms in Poland was permitted, up to a maximum of 49 percent. New regulation in 1986 permitted majority ownership by foreign parties, but some Polish control was required. The limit was raised to 100 percent in 1989.

Meanwhile, in December 1988, new legislation created the Foreign Investment Agency, responsible for the issuance of permits. This facilitated foreign investment, from the perspective of foreign entrepreneurs, as obtaining approval became much easier than had been the case when dealing with workers councils. As discussed by Stoever (1995), most applicants were small-scale entrepreneurs.

In September 1992, foreign entrepreneurs were permitted to participate in fast-track privatization of firms that could reduce unemployment, provided that payment would be made in cash.

The new Law on Economic Activity, passed on November 19, 1999, introduced the principle of equal treatment for all firms, regardless of their country of origin. This seems to have had a positive impact, as foreigners invested a record $13 billion in Poland during

2000. More important, foreigners have been bringing expertise, helping to improve productivity.

Since 2001, foreign entrepreneurs can benefit from a hotline provided by the Polish Agency for Enterprise Development and offering useful information. This includes details about starting a business in Poland, financing and assistance programs, taxation and customs requirements, and possibilities for entering the financial market. Foreign entrepreneurs may also link up with Polish business partners through this agency. Poland's attempts to promote foreign investment have been very successful.

The State of Entrepreneurship and the Small-Business Sector

The Polish Foundation for Promotion and Development of Small and Medium Enterprises has defined small and medium enterprises according to net sales as well as the number of employees. Small firms are those with up to fifty employees and net sales of up to 7 million euro; medium companies may have up to 250 employees and sales of up to 40 million euro. Of Poland's 2 million registered enterprises, over 99 percent are small and medium enterprises, and 92 percent employ fewer than six people (unpublished documents at the Polish Foundation for Promotion and Development of SMEs, Warsaw).

Zapalska (1997b) identified five categories of entrepreneurs in Poland. These are corporate spin-offs; former bureaucrats; experienced managers; traditional traders; and former part-time entrepreneurs. Zapalska (1997a) compared Polish entrepreneurs by gender. She reported that about 99 percent of male respondents stated that they had begun entrepreneurial activities for the purpose of short-term economic gain. In contrast, 89 percent of women respondents considered long-term capital accumulation to be very important. The study noted that female entrepreneurs in Poland borrowed extensively from the technological and organizational innovations of the West and innovated themselves as well.

Although urban small and medium enterprises have been prospering, the largest 20 percent of farms in Poland (mostly in the north and west of the country) produce 80 percent of the country's agricultural output. In contrast, life is often modest for the people living on Poland's 2 million family farms (see Photo 4.47).

The traditional Polish farmer has a smallholding on which his family grows fruit, vegetables (e.g., cabbage and leeks), and cereals, and raises poultry (see Photo 4.48). He typically has a horse, a cow or two, along with some pigs. Because of this lack of specialization, agriculture in Poland is often quite labor-intensive (see Photo 4.49).

In eastern Poland, subsistence farms prevail; three hectares is a typical size. Cows sleep indoors during winter nights, but during the daytime, they graze in fields usually some distance away. Often, an elderly woman walks the cow to pasture (see Photo 4.50). Wealthier families may escort their cows by bicycle. Twice a day, a family member milks the cow(s) by hand, often in the field, returning home with milk for the family. The surplus milk is poured into metal containers (milk cans), which are later picked up by a local dairy, in some cases by horse-drawn cart (see Photo 4.51). By lunchtime, the milk cans are emptied and returned to the farms (see Photo 4.52).

Some families sell surplus produce by the roadside. This includes apples, cabbage, carrots, cucumbers, leeks, pears, plums, potatoes, and tomatoes, as well as sunflower seeds (see Photo 4.53). Others sell berries or mushrooms picked in the wild.

To supplement their income, members of some farming families sojourn abroad; they work in strawberry fields in Finland and in vineyards of Germany. Others work on tobacco plantations in France, where they perfect the skills to plant and harvest their own tobacco crop upon their return to Poland (see Photo 4.54).

Toward the Future

The state supports entrepreneurs and their activities. Sixty Enterprise Support Centers have been established, along with over forty business incubators, over thirty Guarantee and Loan Funds, thirty Business Support Centers, and ten Technology Transfer Centers. The private sector already dominates construction and the retail sector[13] across Poland, even in rural areas (see Photo 4.55).

According to unpublished documents at the Ministry of Industry and Trade in Warsaw, small and medium enterprises account for more than half of the nation's GDP. This includes microscale producers (see Photo 4.56).

PHOTO 4.47. Three generations on the farm.

PHOTO 4.48. Typical farm.

PHOTO 4.49. Labor-intensive agriculture.

PHOTO 4.50. Morning walk.

PHOTO 4.51. Milk carts.

PHOTO 4.52. Suctioning milk from metal containers.

PHOTO 4.53. Fresh produce for sale.

PHOTO 4.54. Drying tobacco.

PHOTO 4.55. Selection of drinks at rural retail store.

PHOTO 4.56. A calf being taken to the market.

Wasilczuk (2000) found small business owners to be well-educated. Nevertheless, he identified shortsightedness and passiveness, and concluded that Polish owner-managers blame the transformation and the market for their firms' problems.

The entrepreneurs I interviewed expressed optimism concerning the impact of joining the European Union. They are keen to have a wider range of suppliers, and possibly an increase in discipline and efficiency among the workforce.

Yet the picture is not all rosy. Farmers expressed their concern to me that if Poland upgrades its farm technology to Western standards, half a million jobs would become obsolete, consequently displacing a considerable number of people. Entrepreneurs expressed concern to me that integration into the European Union will allow European multinationals to dominate the distribution channels in Poland. To compete with more established firms in the European Union, Polish entrepreneurs may need to refine their management style, such as to be more responsive to consumer needs and more accountable.

An element that should become more widespread is corporate well-being through personal effort. Under central planning, it was understandable that state employees did not feel responsible for their firms. Service quality was poor, but consumers had no choice. Now consumers have a choice, but some firms still provide poor service, with no regard for accountability. In 2002, I noted that the restaurant at Hotel Gosciniec Praski in Warsaw closed from noon until 2:00 p.m., during which time employees ate lunch. Elsewhere, lunch is available, but the main course comes at the same time as the appetizer, and coffee arrives in the middle of the meal. Of course, Poland has better restaurants, but these are often unaffordable for the average Pole. Hotels are also perceived as expensive or overpriced, relative to wages, and parking may cost 50 percent of the price of a room. Car theft is especially high in eastern Poland, where vehicles disappear into Lithuania and the Ukraine. Another issue to be addressed is quality control. There is a broad range of quality in Poland, ranging from poor to excellent, but finding hairs and foreign particles in bread is not an unlikely occurrence. How can the consumer perceive good value when sold toilet paper with almost the same softness as cardboard, but more brittle?

It may not be easy to change such a mind-set. As discussed by Kosmala-MacLullich, Sikorska, and Gierusz (2003), there is no exact Polish equivalent for the Western notion of accountability, so the English word is loosely translated into Polish as *odpowiedzialność,* but this means "official responsibility" rather than "accountability."

THE REPUBLIC OF ROMANIA

Romania covers an area of 91,699 square miles, bordering the Black Sea, Bulgaria, Hungary, Moldova, Serbia and Montenegro, and the Ukraine.[14] Not surprisingly, the Romanians call themselves Latins in a sea of Slavs. Romania was the first Eastern European country to mount a successful revolt against communism, as a 1989 demonstration in Timisoara ignited the revolution that ended communist dictatorship in Romania. Yet a model of gradual transition led to slow reform for this country, which entered the path to a market economy with great structural distortions in terms of concentration on heavy industry. Although entrepreneurs in Romania complain of overregulation, bureaucracy, nontariff barriers, and high taxation, the United States Trade Representative estimates that half of Romania's GDP emanates from the informal sector (see Photo 4.57).

PHOTO 4.57. Informal transaction.

Historical Overview

Unlike their Slav and Magyar neighbors, the Romanians claim to be direct descendents of the Romans who settled in the area, after A.D. 106. In time, the region became home to two Christian principalities, namely Moldavia (a Polish satellite) and Wallachia (controlled by the Hungarians, along with Transylvania). The region fell to the Ottomans in 1526.

In 1859, with the help of the French, Alexandru Ioan Cuza was placed on the thrones of Moldavia and Wallachia, and these provinces were united as the autonomous state of Romania within the Ottoman Empire. Independence was declared in 1877, and the Ottoman Empire gave official recognition to the new nation at the 1878 Congress of Berlin. In 1881, Carol of Hohenzolern, a German officer, was proclaimed king of Romania.

On August 27, 1916, Romania joined the Allies and invaded Transylvania, but in December, Bucharest fell to the Central Powers. In 1918, Romania was awarded Transylvania from the Austro-Hungarian Empire, and Bessarabia from Russia. Different architectural styles are still prominent in regions of Romania. Transylvania has remnants of Austro-Hungarian influence (see Photo 4.58), contrasting with the predominant style of Bucharest (see Photo 4.59).

PHOTO 4.58. Grand Hotel in Oradea.

PHOTO 4.59. The Academy of Economic Studies in Bucharest.

Interwar Romania included Bessarabia, Moldavia, Transylvania, and Wallachia. Its economy prospered as the nation became a major exporter of agricultural products and fuel. Romanian currency was strong and widely accepted. In 1938, Romania was the second biggest supplier of oil in Europe, and seventh in the world.

Writing just prior to World War II, Hosmer noted the multiculturalism in Romania: "there remain five distinct peoples: Romanians, Hungarians, Saxons, Jews, and Gypsies" (1938, p. 570). She elaborated regarding the subject of occupational clustering, "The *Caldarari* make the huge copper kettles which they peddle from village to village. . . . The *Ferarii* put the hoops on cart wheels and shoe the horses" (p. 579). Hosmer (1940) focused on ethnic Russians who were fishermen in Romania.

In 1940, the Soviets occupied Bessarabia and northern Bukovina, and these regions were incorporated into the Union of Soviet Socialist Republics. In August 1940, Romania was forced to cede the northwestern part of Transylvania to Hungary. In September, Bulgaria took over southern Dobrudja. King Carol II abdicated in favor of his son Michael, but Marshall Ion Antonescu imposed a pro-Nazi dictatorship. With the hope of taking back Bessarabia, in 1941 Romania joined the Nazis and attacked the Soviets. In August 1944, King Michael organized a coup and Romania changed sides.

Following the abdication of King Michael, a republic was proclaimed on December 30, 1947. Most agriculture and industry were nationalized, except in parts of Banat, Bukovina, and Transylvania, where private enterprise was heavily regulated, resulting in distortions in the use of land. Soviet troops remained in Romania until reparation payments were completed in 1958. Michael and his family lived in exile (see Photo 4.60).

The country followed Soviet directives until 1962 and then experimented with its own model of central planning. In 1965, Nicolae Ceauşescu took over the country's leadership and changed its horizon (see Photo 4.61).

Ellis wrote of Romania during the 1970s, "State direction of the economy is nearly total: Only small pockets of mountain land and artisans' shops remain in private hands" (1975, p. 698). Describing store windows, he noted, "most windows were as bare as the trees of winter" (p. 692). During the 1980s, outdoor markets provided a relatively good range of fresh produce (see Photo 4.62).

PHOTO 4.60. King Michael, Queen Ana, and Princess Margareta.

PHOTO 4.61. Ceauşescu's Palace of the People, now known as the Palace of Parliament.

PHOTO 4.62. Market in Cluj.

Romanians spoke of the state firms that employed them, "They pretend that they are paying us, and we pretend to work." By August 1989, according to *The Economist,* Romanians had "the tightest food rationing in Eastern Europe, sometimes only a few hours' electricity a day, the continent's highest infant mortality rate" (Anonymous, 1989, p. 15).

Romania's economy changed hands only after a bloody revolution. Ceauşescu was executed on December 25, 1989, and elections took place in May 1990. Many of those elected, however, were former communists. Land was distributed to peasants, but not more than ten hectares per person; a problem arose, as this eliminated economies of scale (see Photo 4.63).

In November 1990, state subsidies were reduced, prompting price increases. That same month, the Romanian currency, known as the leu (the plural of which is lei), was devalued from 20 lei per dollar to 35 lei per dollar.

PHOTO 4.63. No economy of scale.

On January 30, 1991, Tax on Profit Law N° 12 introduced a corporate income tax. Later that year, state-owned banks and enterprises were decentralized, some converted to autonomous state-managed monopolies, and others to commercial companies subject to state-appointed directors as per Privatization Law N° 58 of August 14, 1991.

In 1991, a macroeconomic stabilization plan was introduced, supported by the IMF, and this was coupled with a program of structural reforms. In November 1991, the leu again devalued, this time from 60 lei to the dollar to 180 lei. A new constitution was voted by Parliament on November 21, 1991, and validated by a referendum on December 8, 1991.

The IMF supported a second program of reform in May 1992, including a stand-by arrangement involving 314 million Special Drawing Rights and a Contingency and Compensatory Financing Facility of 76.8 million Special Drawing Rights. In June, the World Bank approved a $400 million structural adjustment loan.

Also in June 1992, the Agricultural Bank (Banca Agricolă S.A., Strada Smirdan N° 3, Bucharest) and the Romanian Bank for Development (Banca Română pentru Dezvoltare S.A., Strada Doamnei N° 4, Bucharest) came to an agreement with the International Bank for Reconstruction and Development in Washington, DC, regarding a

Private Farmer and Enterprise Support Project. The objective of this project, according to Schedule 2 of the unpublished Loan Agreement Between Romania and the International Bank for Reconstruction and Development, was "to promote the economic and social development of rural areas through increased private sector agricultural and business activities" (Loan Number 3486 RO, dated June 15, 1992, p. 13). The same schedule elaborates, "The Project consists of the operation of a credit facility for the financing of specific development projects by private farmers and private sector businesses to increase on-farm production and to establish and expand the operations of agro-processing marketing and service enterprises." The International Bank for Reconstruction and Development made available an amount in various currencies, equivalent to $100 million on the condition that the Romanian banks ensure the objectives of the project, specifically to support small-scale self-employed people, such as private farmers (see Photo 4.64).

By December 1992, privatization vouchers had been distributed to the Romanian people. Although private-sector activity grew rapidly in the fields of agriculture, construction, services, and trade, this could not offset the decline in industrial activity, and GDP fell considerably. Consumers felt an additional pinch when a VAT of 18 percent was introduced on July 1, 1993. The exchange rate was liberalized in October 1993. Much entrepreneurial activity during the

PHOTO 4.64. Private farmers on the way to Drajna.

PHOTO 4.65. Headed toward the black market.

mid-1990s took place in the parallel economy (see Photo 4.65). During the international embargo on Serbia, Romanian entrepreneurs profiteered by selling oil to Serbs.

In December 1996, a reformist coalition was elected, with promises to speed privatization, to cut taxes, to encourage foreign investment, and to curb inflation. In February 1997, the administration of President Emil Constantinescu launched an economic-reform program, and this improved prospects for the national economy. The pace of privatization was accelerated, land transactions were permitted, tariffs were reduced, and quotas were eliminated. However, as prices were liberalized, inflation for 1997 exceeded 150 percent and the economy shrank by 6.6 percent. For entrepreneurs, a major change took place in December 1998, when the National Agency for Small and Medium Enterprises of Romania was established.

Promoting Entrepreneurship

Directly coordinated by the prime minister, the National Agency for Small and Medium Enterprises took over the responsibility of small- and medium-enterprise development, from the Council of Reform. The mandate given to this national agency was

1. to elaborate and propose programs to stimulate new venture start-ups and the development of small and medium enterprises;
2. to endorse programs for small- and medium-enterprise development;
3. to design studies to analyze the legal, institutional, and economic framework for small and medium enterprises;
4. to cooperate with government departments and with other administrative bodies, and coordinate the development and implementation of small- and medium-enterprise development programs;
5. to design small- and medium-enterprise development programs, in cooperation with chambers of industry and commerce, and with other organizations whose aim is to support the development of small and medium enterprises;
6. to gather information about the small- and medium-enterprise sector, and to provide it to interested parties;
7. to make recommendations regarding the state financing of programs to stimulate new-venture creation and to develop existing small and medium enterprises;
8. to prepare the annual report regarding the efficiency of the policies and the small- and medium-enterprise development programs;
9. to propose by October 1 of each year governmental programs for the year to come;
10. to cooperate with international institutions, ensuring the coordination of the technical and financial assistance offered to Romania for stimulating the small- and medium-enterprise sector; and
11. to represent the Government of Romania in international organizations, in order to elaborate small- and medium-enterprise policies and programs.

In its first few years of existence, the National Agency for Small and Medium Enterprises focused much of its efforts on improving the legal environment for entrepreneurship. In 1998, it was decided to finance marketing activities of small and medium enterprises in order to increase exports (Government Decision 789). In 1999, guaranteed funds were established in accordance with the regional development law (Ordinance 23/1999). The agency coordinates and gives financial support to the Permanent Secretariat of the Balkan Center for Cooperation among small and medium enterprises. This provides a link with Albania, Armenia, Azerbaijan, Bulgaria, Greece, Moldova, Romania, Russia, Turkey, and the Ukraine.

Thanks to a program initiated by the Romanian Development Agency, small-scale entrepreneurs can receive credits amounting to 50 percent of the interest of the National Bank of Romania (Banca Naţională a României), provided that their activities are in construction, industry, research, services, or tourism. This has made possible the creation of thousands of jobs. With the participation of the Bank for Small Industry and Free Enterprise (Banca pentru Mică Industrie şi Liberă Iniţiativă, MINDBANK) and the commercial bank Ion Tiriac (Banca Comercială Ion Tiriac), employers may receive a credit of up to 50 million lei. The reimbursement period is three years.

Foreign Entrepreneurs and the Romanian Development Agency

Since Decree Law N° 96 was passed in March 1990, wholly owned foreign investments have been permitted in Romania. Foreign investment is governed by Company Law N° 31 of 1990, and by Foreign Investment Law N° 35 of 1991. Subsidiaries are governed by Law N° 105 of 1992.

Although the National Agency for Small and Medium Enterprises caters to local entrepreneurs, the Romanian Development Agency serves as a first stop for foreign parties considering investment in Romania. The mandate of this development agency is to attract international investment. Its services include the provision of economic data and details of investment opportunities to interested parties. This agency identifies local partners, provides advisory services to potential investors, and supports foreign entrepreneurs operating in Romania (see Photo 4.66). All foreign enterprises are required to register with the Romanian Development Agency.

PHOTO 4.66. The Valencia, a joint venture between Romanian and Spanish partners.

The State of Entrepreneurship and the Small-Business Sector

Decree Law N° 54 authorized the establishment of small businesses in February 1990. Small and medium enterprises are defined by the National Agency for Small and Medium Enterprises of Romania as firms with fewer than 250 employees. In 2003, such enterprises represented over 99 percent of total active firms in this country; over 97 percent of these are privately held (unpublished documents at the National Agency for Small and Medium Enterprises of Romania, Bucharest).

There are definite advantages to operating a small or medium enterprise in Romania. Since January 1, 1995, Romania has distinguished between "small taxpayers" and "big taxpayers." A Romanian legal person with no more than 299 employees and whose annual turnover does not exceed 10 billion lei can be treated as a small tax-payer. Upon reaching 300 employees a firm is considered "big" and is no longer eligible to be treated as a small taxpayer.

Most members of the Chamber of Commerce and Industry of Romania are small and medium enterprises, and the chamber has long lobbied for the state to serve small- and medium-enterprise interests. Since 2000, the chamber has organized conferences, seminars, and workshops, providing information on how to launch a new venture, how to develop a business, and how to internationalize it.

In January 2001, the government of Romania established a Ministry for Small and Medium Enterprises and Cooperatives, with policies and strategies designed upon consultations with the Chamber of Commerce and Industry of Romania. The ministry's key function is to elaborate a national strategy for small and medium firms. Twice each year, the ministry presents the government an action on removing regulatory hurdles.

The Basic Law on Small and Medium Enterprises (Law N° 133), passed in February 2001, calls for the creation of a favorable environment for the establishment and development of small and medium enterprises, and regulates the fostering of small and medium enterprises, including family associations.

- Article 2 defines the entrepreneur as "an authorized natural or legal person which, individually or in association with other authorized natural or legal persons, organizes a company, that will be further called enterprise in order to develop commercial facts and deeds, according to the provision of Article 3."
- Article 3 then defines an enterprise as "any kind of an economic activity organization, with autonomous patrimony and authorized by the actual laws to make deeds and actions of commerce in order to obtain a profit from producing goods or services, and from selling them on the market, in competitive conditions."
- Article 4 defines microenterprises as having nine or fewer employees, small enterprises as having between ten and forty-nine employees, and medium firms as having between fifty and 249 employees.

Law N° 133 facilitates the establishment of small and medium enterprises and guarantees their access to public services and to assets belonging to commercial companies with state-share capital. Authorities are thus obliged to offer support to small and medium enterprises to facilitate their access to communications, energy, transportation, and utilities. This law also grants small and medium enterprises priority in leasing and preemptive rights to purchase assets offered for sale in their vicinity. In addition, this law allows small and medium enterprises to benefit from information services, assistance, consultancy, research, and technological innovation in finance, banking, management, and marketing, in order to develop business activities. Small and medium enterprises are also entitled to professional management training. This law provides financial, fiscal, and banking incentives. Only firms with an annual turnover not exceeding 8 million euro are entitled to benefit from the provisions of this law.

Numerous financial support programs exist for small and medium enterprises in Romania. The Micro-Credit Program gives loans of up to 5,000 euro for a period of up to three years. Larger loans are provided by the European Union and by the governments of Germany and the United States.

Toward the Future

Transition in Romania was designed as a two-phase process, starting with decentralization and followed by sufficient investment and restructuring to allow for privatization with minimal job losses (see Photo 4.67). Central to the Romanian model of transition has been a commitment to gradualism. This was based on the belief that a phased approach to price liberalization was needed to protect consumers and that jobs could be best protected by means of gradual reform. Efforts were thus focused on controlling inflation and limiting the displacement of labor and related social costs. As a result, while other transitional economies faced the shock of significant unemployment during the early phases of transition, change in Romania came more gradually. Likewise, price controls were justified by the desire to minimize social costs. It was decided that a slow decrease in state intervention would be the best way to assure the supply of raw materials to industry and essential goods to the people.

Agriculture was privatized, re-creating a class of smallholding farmers and shepherds (see Photo 4.68). The small-enterprise sector was largely privatized, as the state sold or leased firms in the retail

PHOTO 4.67. Plenty of jobs in snow removal.

PHOTO 4.68. Shepherd and his flock.

and service sectors. Prices were allowed to rise gradually. Foreign trade was liberalized, and Law N° 84 established free-trade zones. A voucher system was introduced by Law N° 58 of 1991, and pursuant to the Law for Acceleration of Privatization (Law N° 55), a mass privatization program was launched in June 1995. An Office for Consumers Protection has been set up. All this suggests a large step toward a Western-style market economy. However, it should be noted that although the legal framework for a market economy was rapidly established, its implementation moved ahead slowly.

Manrai, Lascu, and Manrai (1999) noted that although Romanian consumers found an increase in the availability of products after the fall of communism, they reported that the affordability decreased (see Photo 4.69). As suggested by Marinov et al. (2001), this represents an opportunity for entrepreneurs who will provide consumer goods at affordable prices in the future.

A challenge for the state will be to develop an environment conducive to the sustainable growth of entrepreneurship in Romania. This includes the reduction of corruption. In regions of Romania that were formerly under Ottoman rule (Moldavia and Wallachia), the "baksheesh" culture has survived; a move away from bribes will certainly help entrepreneurship in the future.

Also of importance to the future of Romania are the management of cultural diversity and the fostering of harmony among ethnic

PHOTO 4.69. Unhappy consumer.

groups within this country. Romanians in Romania have established networks with Romanians outside the country; Hungarian-speaking Romanians appear keen to do business with firms in Hungary. Such networking may develop into significant trade in the future.

THE SLOVAK REPUBLIC (SLOVAKIA)

In accordance with a law passed in the Czech and Slovak Federal Republic in November 1992, Slovakia became an independent country on January 1, 1993.[15] The Slovak Republic covers an area of 18,921 square miles, bordering Austria, the Czech Republic, Hungary, Poland, and the Ukraine. Although Slovakia shared much of the twentieth century with the Czech Republic, the two nations have gone distinctly different ways since the breakup of the Czech and Slovak Federal Republic. In contrast to the Czech Republic, Slovakia adopted a policy of slow and gradual reform, with special assistance provided to microenterprise. The capital of Slovakia is Bratislava (see Photo 4.70), a city that before 1918 was known as Pozsony in Hungarian and Presporok in Slovak.

PHOTO 4.70. Bratislava.

Historical Overview

The Slavs settled the area that is now Slovakia during the fifth century. This land became part of the Moravian Empire and remained so until the Magyar invasion of the tenth century. An agricultural land, Slovakia was divided between the Kingdom of Hungary and the Ottoman Empire. Castles were many (see Photo 4.71). In 1848, the Slovaks attempted to revolt against the Magyars. The Hungarian response was to ban the Slovak language in churches and schools.

In 1918, Slovakia was detached from Hungary and attached to Bohemia and Moravia, creating Czechoslovakia. Thus, the Slovaks found themselves united with the Czechs in an independent and multicultural Czechoslovakia. However, there was concern about regional differences. Just prior to World War II, Patric wrote that some people "fear that this Republic will fall apart. Your peoples are so diverse . . ." (1938a, p. 225).

In March 1939, the independence of the Slovak state was announced. A Nazi puppet state, under the leadership of Reverend Josef Tiso, the Slovak state persecuted Czechs, gypsies, and Jews (see Photo 4.72). It even paid Germany for each Jew deported to a death camp. Reverend Tiso later stood trial for war crimes in Czechoslovakia, and he was hung in 1947. Today he is revered in Slovakia, and some followers wish to make him a saint.

PHOTO 4.71. Among the many castles.

PHOTO 4.72. Synagogue of Lucenec after the Jewish community was exterminated.

Liberated by the Soviets in 1948, Slovakia experienced forceful nationalization, urbanization, and industrialization. The Slovak economy became dependent on that of the Soviets, with a focus on military supplies. Many Slovak towns became dominated by one industry. As was the case in western Czechoslovakia, small shops and family businesses in Slovakia were taken over by the state in 1959. Writing about Slovaks under central planning, Thompson mentioned that in 1972, oil appeared in Bratislava's water supply and "for months half the city had no central water" (1991, p. 58).

The collapse of the Soviet bloc greatly harmed Slovakia, as the Slovak economy had been highly dependent on it for exports. Private enterprise could not absorb the thousands of unemployed workers formerly employed by the public sector. Despite $1.5 billion in annual subsidies from Prague, Slovakia's cumulative GDP fell 18 percent in 1991 and 1992.

Although the Czechs were willing to rush toward a market economy, the Slovaks felt they had less to gain from radical reform. While the Czechs rushed to a modern stock exchange, the Slovaks walked to wooden churches. When President Václav Havel tried to promote national unity, nationalists in Bratislava threw eggs at him. Partition was inevitable; the Czechs and the Slovaks finally took different paths.

A monetary union between the republics lasted only one month. Then, each republic decided to issue its own currency. This led to a flight of capital out of Slovakia, depleting foreign-exchange reserves. Slovaks subsequently converted Slovak krona, expecting a major devaluation. In July 1993, the International Monetary Fund Systemic Transformation Facility led to a devaluation of 10 percent in Slovakia.

In contrast to the Czech Republic, Slovakia began its postcommunist life with negative growth. In 1993, Slovakia had a trade deficit of $800 million, and the nation embarked on a strategy of slow reform. During their first year as separate countries, per capita GDP in Slovakia was $1,161 compared to $3,070 in the Czech Republic. On the other hand, unemployment was 35 percent in the Czech Republic and 13.8 percent in Slovakia, while the inflation rate reached 18.2 percent in the Czech Republic and 14.2 percent in Slovakia.

By 1994, Slovakia accumulated a trade surplus of almost $200 million. Elections in the autumn of 1994 resulted in a return to power of former Prime Minister Vladimir Meciar, a populist who was less than popular among Western investors. He objected to coupon privatization but allowed the Slovak National Agency for Foreign Investment and Development to prepare for privatization by sales. During 1994, Slovakia's GDP grew by 4 percent and the new stock exchange in Bratislava doubled in value. In 1997, Slovakia's GDP grew by 6.5 percent. In January 2002, Slovakia reduced income tax rates for legal persons, and in 2003 the state considered a flat rate of 19 percent to replace the progressive tax system (Condon, 2003).

Promoting Entrepreneurship

Czechs and Slovaks described to me Czechoslovakia's Large-Scale Privatization Law of 1991 quite differently. While Czechs recall the public auctions, the public tenders, and the vouchers, Slovaks dwell on the economic disparity and unemployment, consequences of fast privatization. Not surprisingly, Slovakia adopted a much more cautious pace of privatization than Czechoslovakia had done before the split.

Slovakia was, nevertheless, very active in promoting small business, especially microenterprises. Slovakia adopted the Program of Complex Support to Small and Medium Enterprises in 1993. This established the legislative, financial, and institutional framework for government support to local entrepreneurship. Further legislation introduced a credit support scheme for entrepreneurs, loan guarantees, and the Seed Capital Program. In addition, the state contributed to the establishment of a nongovernmental body, the National Agency for the Development of Small and Medium Enterprises. The Ministry of Economy promotes small and medium enterprises via a network of twelve regional advisory and information centers and five business innovation centers that provide advisory services to entrepreneurs. Some services are subsidized, and others are not.

In 1997, some of the regional advisory and information centers launched a special program for microenterprises. Its purpose is to provide start-up support to very small-scale self-employment (see Photo 4.73). Microenterprises may obtain loans at an interest rate of 1.5 percent above the national bank's discount rate.

In addition, new income-tax legislation was enacted to reduce the financial burden on local entrepreneurs and possibly encourage new-venture creation. Since January 1, 2000, some entrepreneurs pay a lump income tax, unrelated to income; this eliminates the need for bookkeeping.

On September 27, 2000, Slovakia approved several guarantee and credit programs to assist small and medium enterprises:

PHOTO 4.73. Small-scale self-employment.

1. The Program to Support Small and Medium Enterprises through the Provision of Bank Guarantees and Financial Credits
2. The Program to Support Small and Medium Enterprises through the Provision of Guarantees for Foreign Loans
3. The Program to Support Small and Medium Enterprises through the Provision of Bank Guarantees for Pre-Mortgage Loans
4. The Program to Support Flat Construction through the Provision of Bank Guarantees for Loans
5. The Support Credit Program
6. The Region Credit Program

Simultaneously, the state approved the following programs to promote small and medium enterprises up to the year 2005:

1. The Support Loan Program
2. The Micro-loan Program
3. The Slovak Republic's participation in the Third Multi-annual Program for Small and Medium Enterprises
4. The Technology Transfer Program
5. The Advice Program for Small and Medium Entrepreneurs
6. The Program for the Implementation of Quality Management Systems
7. The Program to Support International Cooperation
8. The Education and Training Program for Small and Medium Enterprises
9. The Monitoring and Research in the Field of Small and Medium Enterprises Program
10. The Education, Training and Advice Program for Selected Groups of Potential and Start-up Entrepreneurs

Foreign Entrepreneurs

In July 1998, per capita FDI in Slovakia was only $320. This was seven times less than in Hungary, and almost four times less than in Slovenia. To undertake a review of the situation, the Foreign Investment Advisory Service visited Slovakia in June 1999. (The Foreign Investment Advisory Service is a joint facility of the International Finance Corporation and the World Bank.) It was concluded that Slovakia had an unfair and ineffective incentive framework. In May 2000, the Slovak government created the Slovak Investment and

Trade Development Agency to attract foreign investment as well as promote exports. The agency operates as a one-stop shop, providing a variety of services to potential investors. Considerable investment comes from neighboring Austria (see Photo 4.74).

Slovakian law favors large foreign investors over smaller ones. A foreign investor benefits from an income-tax reduction only when contributing at least 60 percent of an investment that is at least 2 million euro.

The State of Entrepreneurship and the Small-Business Sector

Ivy (1996) found an inverse relationship between regional un-employment in Slovakia and the proportion of the private-sector enterprises that are new ventures as opposed to privatized firms. Many of the 134 towns in Slovakia have limited-liability corporations. These firms, operating in a wide range of sectors, are subsidized in the case of losses.

With annual wages in Slovakia being well below those in the Czech Republic, Hungary, and even Poland, Slovak entrepreneurs benefit from a significant competitive advantage. According to the Ministry of Economy, small and medium enterprises[16] in Slovakia provide 56 percent of the nation's jobs and contribute 58 percent of

PHOTO 4.74. Austrian firm in Banká Bystrica.

the GDP. The averages for the European Union are 66 percent and 60 percent, respectively.

Toward the Future

Linehan quoted a Slovak interviewee: "Czechs are very clever, more rational . . . we drink more wine and liquor than they do. Czechs may have more automobiles, but we have more fun out of life" (1968, p. 170). It appears that there shall always be differences between the Czechs and the Slovaks. Czech Prime Minister Václav Klaus opted for rapid free-market reforms, and Prime Minster Vladimir Meciar of Slovakia found a slow, gradual approach more compatible with Slovak values. Although the Czech Republic exports machinery and service, Slovakia's exports tend to be raw materials, including sugar that is sold to the Czech Republic.

Slovakia has attracted only a small fraction of the amounts invested in the Czech Republic, Hungary, or Poland. Although this may

PHOTO 4.75. Gypsies.

be interpreted as wariness on the part of investors, it has helped local industry develop, protected from overwhelming foreign competition—a rare opportunity for local entrepreneurs.

A unique issue that Slovaks will be facing in the future is that they are bound to become a minority in their own country. Slovakia has one of the highest ratios of gypsies (see Photo 4.75) to *gadje* (non-gypsies) anywhere, and at "current rates of population growth, Gypsies will outnumber Slovaks by about 2060" (Godwin, 2001, p. 84). A problem, according to Anderson, is that "unemployment and discrimination are way of life" (2002, p. 6).

Chapter 5

The Commonwealth of Independent States (CIS)

The Commonwealth of Independent States (CIS) was created on December 8, 1991. That year, eleven former members of the Union of Soviet Socialist Republics joined the organization: Armenia, Azerbaijan, Belarus, Kazakhstan, the Kyrgyz Republic, Moldova, the Russian Federation, Tajikistan, Turkmenistan, the Ukraine, and Uzbekistan. In December 1993, Georgia joined as well, such that, with the exception of the Baltic republics, all of the other former Soviet socialist republics have become members.[1]

THE UNION OF SOVIET SOCIALIST REPUBLICS AND PERESTROIKA

The Union of Soviet Socialist Republics (Soviet Union) was created in December 1922 as the centrally planned successor to the Russian Empire. Covering most of the land that once comprised the Russian Empire, this country was the world's largest, covering 8,649,821 square miles. This is equal to a sixth of the earth's land surface.

In 1922, the original Soviet Union consisted of four republics. At its peak, the Soviet Union consisted of fifteen republics: Armenia, Azerbaijan, Byelorussia (later known as Belarus), Estonia, Georgia, Kazakhstan, Kirghizia (later known as the Kyrgyz Republic), Latvia, Lithuania, Moldavia (later known as Moldova), Russia, Tajikistan, Turkmenistan, the Ukraine, and Uzbekistan. The Soviet Union bordered twelve countries: Afghanistan, China, Czechoslovakia, the Democratic People's Republic of Korea (North Korea), Finland, Hungary, Iran, Mongolia, Norway, Poland, Romania, and Turkey.

Under the leadership of Lenin (see Photo 5.1), private ownership was permitted, and many believed that the union had a bright future. Shaw praised the new union: "At present there is not a hungry child in the fully sovietized regions of Russia, nor a ragged one, nor one who is not getting all the education it is capable of" (1928, p. 460).

In 1929, Joseph Stalin began the collectivization of farms, wiping out the social class of *kulaks* (landed farmers); 10 million people died in the process. Soon, only small agricultural holdings remained in private hands. In 1930, Stalin proclaimed that unemployment no longer existed. Although 350,000 jobless people were registered, employment offices were closed and benefits were cancelled (Gurevich, 1989b).

In 1941, the Soviet Union was home to thousands of Germans, descendants of people whom Catherine the Great had invited to live in the Russian Empire during the eighteenth century. When the Nazis invaded the Soviet Union in 1941,[2] Soviet Germans (citizens of the Soviet Union) were deported from Europe to Kazakhstan, where they eventually numbered a million people. In an act of "social engineering," demographics were changed.

By the 1950s, Soviet agriculture was tightly organized into 70,000 *kolkhozes* (collective farms) and 6,000 *sovkhozes* (state farms with wageworkers). As discussed by Nixon (1959), collective farmers were permitted to till up to one-and-a-quarter acres for their own use, selling surplus in markets (see Photo 5.2).

PHOTO 5.1. Lenin, formerly known as Vladimir Ilyich Ulyanov.

PHOTO 5.2. Selling surplus.

Stalin died in 1953, but there was still little hope of developing wide-scale entrepreneurship in the Soviet Union. Nikita Sergeyevich Khrushchev took control as chief of the Soviet Communist Party, but he failed to break from the system that Stalin had created (Taubman, 2003). In 1961, Khrushchev claimed that communism would bury capitalism.

The Soviet economy was managed by a hierarchy of committees, headed by Gosplan, the State Planning Mission. Gosplan, in turn, took its instructions from the Communist Party. Production goals were centrally planned, ignoring market forces, and prices were independent of supply and demand; this, in turn, led to shortages. Berliner (1957) reported evasion, falsification, misrepresentation of costs, and exaggeration of resource requirements in Soviet firms.

Yet the Soviet Union stunned the world with its Sputnik technology. As well, the country produced large turboprops (see Photo 5.3) and jets (see Photo 5.4) for the communist world.

In 1965, attempts were made to introduce price and profit incentives, but this failed. In 1966, Hammond reported his experience with

PHOTO 5.3. Four-engine Ilyushin Il-18 turboprop produced for Romanian flag carrier Tarom.

PHOTO 5.4. Yakolev Yak-40 trijet used by Vietnam Airlines.

a vendor of ice cream who told him: "I don't like America. . . . There the capitalists are the bosses. Here I'm my own boss. . . . My mother and father were serfs, but now everybody is free" (1966, p. 348). In fact, prices continued to be determined by a State Pricing Board (Rosefielde, 1986).

In 1985, Mikhail Gorbachev came into power and announced that the Soviet Union was entering a new period of its history. He responded to a deepening economic crisis by introducing *perestroika,* which means "rebuilding" or "changing." He admitted that in the previous twenty years industrial production had declined while corruption increased. Thanks to *perestroika,* over sixty cooperative and commercial banks sprung up across the Soviet Union. As well, *glasnost* (openness) was about to change the mind-set. (The root of the word *glasnost* is *golos* [voice], which is also the root of the word for *golosovat* [voting].)

Reforms also affected farms. During the mid-1980s, there were 26,200 collective *kolkhozes* and 22,500 *sovkhozes* in the Soviet Union. Reforms allowed farmers of these entities to freely use the surplus produce that exceeded planned quotas; the surplus could be sold to the state at fixed prices, or to the public at market prices that reflected supply and demand.

Indigenous reindeer herders were often simultaneously employees of a *sovkhoze* and members of a clan cooperative. However, each reindeer was identified as having one personal owner (Jernsletten and Klokov, 2002).

Nevertheless, entrepreneurship had yet to become a socially desirable activity. Reporting from Moscow State University, Kiselev wrote that until 1987, the word entrepreneurship "was associated mainly with criminal activities" (1990, p. 76). In 1987, the Enterprise Law was drafted; the nation was on its way to reform.

In 1987, Gorbachev proposed the formation of cooperatives to supplement and compete with state-run enterprises. Kuteinikov wrote, "Officially the word 'competition' (in its positive sense) first appeared in the USSR in 1988 in the draft Law on Cooperatives" (1989, p. 14). This law was among several that laid the basis for the economic activity of small state enterprises.

Cooperatives were soon springing up, catering to consumer wants. In November 1987, entrepreneur Leonid Onushko left his job at the USSR State Bank, with permission to establish Kontinent, an interregional cooperative bank (Illesh, 1988). During the first half of 1989, the number of cooperatives in the Soviet Union jumped from 78,000 to 133,000 (Crook, 1990). Kuteinikov (1989) reported that most people blamed cooperatives for higher prices, rather than recognizing their positive influence. In the spring of 1989, a crusade against cooperatives was initiated.

In 1989, the "On Measures Concerning the Creation and Development of Small Enterprises" act legitimized new-venture creation. With this act, it became possible for people in the Soviet Union to become entrepreneurs outside the centralized economic system. In March 1989, the Central Committee allowed families to have fifty-year leases on land and to keep their earnings. That year, 5 percent of agricultural land was privately controlled, and this provided almost one-third of the nation's food.

During the summer of 1989, the Supreme Soviet adopted a resolution to allow a switch to cost accounting. Reporting on this issue, Gurevich wrote, "It really is an important event. According to many deputies, nothing of greater importance was discussed by the new Supreme Soviet" (1989a, p. 1). Thus, by 1989 much of the economy had experienced some degree of liberalization. However, prices of labor and raw materials were still kept artificially low (Greenwald, 1989). This resulted in shortages and long lines (see Photo 5.5). Keller

PHOTO 5.5. Waiting.

(1988) explained that the only source of some goods and services was often *na levo,* literally "on the left," but figuratively "under the table."

Another problem was the inconvertibility of the ruble (see Photo 5.6). Castro wrote, "While Moscow says the ruble is worth about $1.60, the currency fetches as little as 10¢ on the black market" (1989, p. 55). In October 1989, Abalkin noted, "Our economic situation continues to grow worse every month" (1989, p. 9). Stankevich suggested, "Emergency efforts are needed to stop the collapse of the national economy" (1989, p. 9).

When Moscow raised the price of diesel fuel, electricity, and transport in January 1990, official trade unions threatened to strike; price hikes were then cancelled. By April 1990, the ruble had several exchange rates. Gardner (1990) explained that there were two official rates of exchange, according to which $1 was worth six rubles, or exactly one tenth of that; on the black market, however, $1 could fetch 20 rubles. The summer of 1990 brought the Soviet Union its largest bumper crop, but management problems caused it to rot, as the system failed to get enough people to harvest (Parker, 1990). By winter, 90 percent of basic industrial goods were in short supply (Kvint, 1991). "Nearly half of perishable crops were wasted due to shortages of packaging materials, storage facilities, outdated processing technology and poor transportation" (Herbig and McCarty, 1995, p. 50). Although corruption, fraud, and politics were blamed for the short-

PHOTO 5.6. One ruble.

ages, Kvint (1991) argued that the real cause was the lack of structural incentives to be efficient.

Despite the existence of some problems, with the monumental changes brought about by *perestroika,* several elements of the former centralized economic system were altered forever. Some of the most important changes included

1. the reduction or elimination of subsidies to unprofitable state enterprises;
2. the introduction of competition within the system, often from outside the country;
3. the breakdown of *Gosnab* (the centralized or "state" supply system) to all enterprises;
4. the elimination of *Gosplan* (the centralized or "state" planning of the economy); and
5. the introduction of market forces.

These changes, and others, have had a profound impact on the Russian people, their economy, their standard of living, and their outlook on life. Yet these reforms were insufficient, as constituent republics of the Soviet Union wanted more autonomy. In March 1990, Estonia and Lithuania pushed for independence from the Soviet Union. Lithuania declared its independence in March 1990. Latvia declared its independence in May 1990. Uzbekistan declared its laws sovereign in June 1990. Byelorussia and Moldavia declared sovereignty in July 1990, followed by Turkmenistan in August. In August 1990, Tajikistan declared its laws supreme over Moscow's. Kazakhstan declared sovereignty in October 1990. Georgia declared independence in March 1991. In August 1991, Soviet warships blockaded the harbor at Tallinn, the Estonian capital (see Photo 5.7).

When Soviet President Mikhail Gorbachev implicitly accepted that decentralization was inevitable in August 1991, a coup by hard-liners temporarily ousted him but ultimately failed. Brzezinski correctly predicted, "The failure of the coup will now make any restoration of central power even less likely. On the contrary, it will accelerate the decentralization and eventually even the partial dissolution of the Soviet Union" (1991, p. B3).

Simultaneously, the economic situation worsened. In July 1991, unemployment insurance was introduced, but the government was

PHOTO 5.7. The vessel Tallinn at Tallinn harbor.

short of cash (Popov, 1991). In October, Oliver (1991) reported that bribes and the mafia were ruling Moscow. By December 1991, barter was used to keep assembly lines working (Kohan and Chelny, 1991). Kohan wrote, "Shoppers have few alternatives short of breeding hens on their apartment roofs or rabbits on their balconies" (1991, p. 17). Once subsistence needs were met, surplus meat, if any, could be sold (see Photo 5.8).

The Soviet Union was soon to be declared defunct, and the hammer and sickle would become a symbol of a bygone era (see Photo 5.9). Soviet citizenship would soon be something out of the past (see Photo 5.10). In the words of Stead et al., "The Soviet empire is dead. A stabler arrangement may be its legacy" (1991, p. 42).

THE REPUBLIC OF BELARUS (WHITE RUSSIA)

Formerly known as Byelorussia, the Republic of Belarus covers 80,134 square miles, bordering Latvia, Lithuania, Poland, Russia, and the Ukraine.[3] When the Byelorussian Soviet Socialist Republic was part of the Soviet Union, the Byelorussian economy was among the most developed in the Soviet Union. More recently, economic development has been hindered by the lack of self-sufficiency in raw

PHOTO 5.8. Two chickens for sale.

PHOTO 5.9. Hammer-and-sickle symbol.

PHOTO 5.10. Soviet passport.

materials. Compared to other economies of Eastern Europe, that of Belarus has been lagging in reform, and its small-business sector has been relatively insignificant; there is, however, a large parallel market.

Historical Overview

The people of Belarus arrived from Central Europe between the sixth and eighth centuries. When the Polish Commonwealth was partitioned during the late eighteenth century the northwestern corner of the land that is now Belarus was taken by Prussia. The remainder of today's Belarus was absorbed into the Russian Empire, where it became known as the "North-West Region" of Russia.

Although Lenin's Bolsheviks seized power in November 1917, in December that year in Minsk, the First All-Byelorussian Congress proclaimed a republican government for Byelorussia. On March 25, 1918, the Executive Committee of the First All-Byelorussian Congress declared the creation of an independent democratic republic, the Byelorussian People's Republic. On January 1, 1919, this became the Byelorussian Soviet Socialist Republic.

The Russo-Polish War began in 1919 and lasted until 1921. On March 18, 1921, Byelorussia was partitioned. The west, including the Bialystok region, was taken by Poland, while the east remained in the Byelorussian Soviet Socialist Republic. Among the people who emigrated from Minsk, some went to Toronto, Canada. In 1930, they built a community center in the Kensington Market area of Toronto (see Photo 5.11).

On September 17, 1939, the Red Army captured western Byelorussia from Poland and reunited it with the Byelorussian Soviet Socialist Republic. On October 10, Moscow realigned the map such that Vilnius would henceforth be in Lithuania, rather than in Byelorussia.

PHOTO 5.11. Meeting place of immigrants from Minsk, 10 St. Andrew Street, Toronto.

The Nazis invaded Byelorussia on June 21, 1941, and occupied it until July 28, 1944.

Although the Byelorussian Soviet Socialist Republic covered less than 1 percent of the area of the Soviet Union, the republic produced more than 4 percent of the union's GNP. Byelorussia was known as the assembly line of the military industrial complex in the Soviet Union (see Photo 5.12).

On July 27, 1990, Byelorussia adopted the Declaration on the State Sovereignty of the Byelorussian Soviet Socialist Republic, and the Republic of Belarus declared its independence on August 25, 1991. On December 8, 1991, Belarus, Russia, and the Ukraine created the Commonwealth of Independent States.

Subsidies were removed in January 1992. However, a reform program in January 1993 allowed most retail prices to be state controlled. An agreement in September 1993 called for the retention of the ruble, and a monetary union with Russia was signed in 1994. A Constitution of the Republic of Belarus was adopted on March 15,

PHOTO 5.12. Industrial production.

1994. In April 1994, a scheme scheduled privatization of about half of the state enterprises.

A treaty of friendship with Russia was signed on February 21, 1995. On June 7, 1995, a new flag, reminiscent of that of the Soviet era, was introduced, replacing the horizontal stripes introduced four years earlier. In 1996, President Aliaksandr Lukasenka adopted a new constitution.

Promoting Entrepreneurship

Since 1991, individuals in Belarus may own land and pass it to their heirs, but not sell it. Fertile soil produces tasty potatoes (see Photo 5.13). Belarus also produces much milk (see Photo 5.14).

With funding from the United States, the Small-Scale Privatization Project was launched in 1993. This project introduced a mechanism for auction-based privatization, along with amendments to the Privatization Law and the State Privatization Program. This resulted in the privatization of over 1,000 enterprises.

To encourage export-oriented production, a law on free economic zones (N° 213-3) was introduced on December 7, 1998. On January 31, 2002, a presidential decree (N° 66) created a free economic zone in Mogilev. Providing favorable conditions for national economic-base adjustment, the objective of the zone is to attract investments for

PHOTO 5.13. Potatoes in abundance.

PHOTO 5.14. Fresh milk.

export development. With an area of 242 hectares, the Free Economic Zone Mogilev provides production and storage facilities. Foreign goods are brought here, exempt from customs duties and taxes. Resident entrepreneurs pay only 50 percent of the profit tax payable elsewhere in the republic.

On another note, the government has requested support from the UNDP. Fighting growing poverty through small- and medium-scale enterprises is an important area of UNDP support, and women have been targeted for entrepreneurship training. Much energy has been focused on microscale financing tools for entrepreneurs and the establishment of incubators for entrepreneurship. A problem that remains, nevertheless, is complex business registration procedures. As a result, many entrepreneurs would rather operate in the parallel economy than in the formal economy.

Foreign Entrepreneurs

Belarusian law dictates that foreigners are not allowed to own land in Belarus. Furthermore, legislation limits foreign investment in banking, insurance, and the stock exchange to 49 percent of outstanding shares. O'Driscoll, Holmes, and Kirkpatrick reported, "Both a lack of structural reform and a climate hostile to business have inhibited foreign investment. . . . Political instability, anti-Western sentiment, an inefficient bureaucracy, corruption, and the lack of privatization all serve to hinder foreign investment" (2001, pp. 91-92). Nevertheless, individuals from Russia have been coming to look for opportunities (see Photo 5.15).

The State of Small Business and Entrepreneurship

Article 1 of the Law on Entrepreneurship in the Republic of Belarus defines entrepreneurship as "independent initiatory activities of citizens, aimed at gaining profits or individual incomes and carried out on one's behalf, at one's risk and with one's own property or on behalf and with responsibility of a legal person." Article 2 elaborates, "Managerial workers and experts of state organizations, whose functions include the solution of issues connected with exercising of entrepreneurial activities or supervision of such activities, shall not be allowed to engage in entrepreneurial activities." Other articles discuss the forms an enterprise may take (Article 3), legislation (Article 4), registration requirements (Article 5), rights (Article 6), responsibilities (Article 7), liabilities (Article 8), the responsibility of the state (Article 9), taxes (Article 10), guarantees (Article 11), and termination (Article 12). Article 11 specifies that "to increase efficiency and provide for a large-scale spreading of entrepreneurial activities, the

PHOTO 5.15. Wearing a shirt from the Soviet era.

state shall set up information, consulting, research and other centers, as well as innovation and insurance funds."

Between 1996 and 1997, small firms in Belarus increased their output by 64.7 percent, and the declared profitability of these firms increased by 13.2 percent. One in eight small firms declared a loss. By 1997, there were 21,300 privately owned small firms in Belarus, and these employed 232,000 people. In addition, 130,000 registered entrepreneurs were doing business independently. This came to a total of 151,300 private players in the economy. Yet numbers slumped suddenly, and in 1998 only 76,000 players were accounted for. House of Representatives Speaker Anatoly Molofeev rightly argued that entrepreneurship and the small-business sector should be regarded as structural elements of a market economy, and he expressed concern over the slow rate of development of this sector (see Photo 5.16). Molofeev judged that state control followed a strategic interventionist policy (Peterson, 1988), favoring protection of self-employed locals, many of whom have microscale operations (see Photo 5.17).

Small businesses provide 5 percent of the jobs in Belarus and produce 9 percent of GDP. Half of the small firms are involved in trade and public food catering. Approximately 15 percent are manufacturers, and about 11 percent are in construction. To help small firms survive, the Post-Privatization Project of the International Finance Corporation established business centers in Belarus. Although these have

PHOTO 5.16. Slow development.

PHOTO 5.17. Limited-scale self-employment.

helped some entrepreneurs obtain financing, many more complain about the lack of access to capital. Banks in Belarus find large-scale borrowers more profitable than smaller-scale entrepreneurs. As a result, small and medium enterprises are often refused loans. Novikova, Petrovskaia, and Daniltchenko (1999) identified the following obstacles to small-business development in Belarus:

1. Lack of government stimulation
2. Lack of financing
3. Lack of subsidies
4. Lack of loans
5. Lack of credits

Toward the Future

The Belarus Small and Medium Enterprises Development Project is funded by USAID to promote small and medium enterprises; however, financial and administrative hurdles are limiting the growth and impact of the sector.

Administrative barriers, including paperwork requirements, are crippling the formal sector of entrepreneurship in Belarus. Yet entrepreneurs are thriving in the parallel economy. If and when Belarus reforms its economic policy, better enforcing property rights and improving the system of taxation, the country may become more attractive for formal entrepreneurship.

THE REPUBLIC OF MOLDOVA

The Republic of Moldova (formerly the Moldavian Soviet Socialist Republic) covers 13,067 square miles, bounded by Romania and the Ukraine.[4] After independence from the Soviet Union, the government introduced a new national currency, the Moldovan leu—worth 1,000 Soviet rubles. A new constitution ushered in private enterprise. Nevertheless, several factors prevented the smooth development of entrepreneurship in Moldova: continued economic dependence on Russia, a small domestic market, a lack of international competitiveness, and the inability to reintegrate with Romania.

Historical Overview

The Kingdom of Moldavia was founded in 1359. Peasants worked the land and nonconformity was met with punishment. In the absence of Weberian values (1904-1905; 1924) present in Western Europe, and in contrast to Islam which permitted the development of a capitalist, mercantile culture in the Ottoman Empire, Orthodoxy in this kingdom emphasized the respect of authority, along with the importance of guilt. A good Moldavian was expected to obey the religion and work the land. A nonmercantile culture did nothing to encourage the development of entrepreneurship. In 1812, when the kingdom lost Bessarabia to Russia, the tsar's feudal system continued to meet nonconformity with punishment.

The fusion of Wallachia with that which remained of the Moldavian kingdom resulted in the birth of Romania in 1859. Bessarabia remained a territory of the Russian Empire.

In the midst of the Bolshevik Revolution, Bessarabia declared itself an independent democratic republic. Complete independence from Russia was declared in 1918, and its people voted to unite with Romania. Writing in 1940, Hosmer explained: "After the World War it [Bessarabia] again became part of Romania. The Soviet Union now looks longingly at this rich granary, which they still consider occupied territory" (1940, p. 411). In June 1940, the Soviets occupied

Bessarabia, and on August 2, 1940, they fused it with the formerly Ukrainian Trans-Dnestr region, creating the Moldavian Soviet Socialist Republic, the capital of which was Kishinëv (in Russian), also known as Chişinău (in Romanian).

The Soviets compiled lists of entrepreneurs and other "especially dangerous elements" of the bourgeoisie. The communists wanted to cleanse Moldavia of any remaining entrepreneurial spirit, and they would do so by what they termed "social engineering." In June 1941, over 5,000 Romanian-speaking families from the danger lists were deported to Siberia. In addition, 53,000 Romanian youths were taken away to forced labor in Russia. Communist specialists in industry and economy were brought from the Soviet Union to participate in the engineering of a new communist Moldavia. When Nazi Romania gained control of Bessarabia in 1941, the very large Jewish community was deported. People moved into homes that belonged to deportees (see Photo 5.18).

In 1944, the Soviet Union regained possession of Bessarabia and promptly implemented communist dictatorship across the territory that would become Soviet Moldavia. Land and business enterprises

PHOTO 5.18. A cottage in Marculesti, a shtetl near Floresti.

were nationalized, and for decades, peasants were not even permitted to own livestock. As was the case in the past, initiative would be perceived as a sign of nonconformity, and it was safer to wait for instructions than to attempt to innovate. The lack of trust in private property was reinforced and, unlike cultures that believed in investment or at least in deferment of gratification, uncertainty about the future inspired Moldavians of Bessarabia to concentrate on surviving the present rather than investing in the future.

Following World War II, the Soviets imposed the industrial production of components, a strategy to make Moldavia dependent on Moscow. Parts of products were produced in Soviet Moldavia, but the completion of many goods relied on other components that came from Russia. Moldavia also had to rely on the Soviet Union for energy as well as machinery and spare parts. At various times, Moldavian assembly lines contributed to the production of agricultural machines, cement, confectionary, electronic equipment, fur products, furniture, linen, refrigerators, scientific equipment, shoes, televisions, tractors, and washing machines (see Photo 5.19).

The Soviets not only spread their economic ideology but also engineered cultural manipulation that had an economic impact half a century later. Given that Moldavia was culturally the eastern limit of Latinity, the Soviets tried to assimilate the Moldavians into Slavic culture. Many speakers of Romanian were shifted to the Ukraine,

PHOTO 5.19. Industry for the Soviets.

where in the absence of Romanian schools, they became a dwindling minority; others were sent to Siberia. Meanwhile, thousands of Russians were brought to Soviet Moldavia, in order to dilute the native Moldavian population and reinforce Russian as the official language. Another factor in the assimilation of native Moldavians was Moscow's decision to include the Trans-Dnestr region in the Moldavian Soviet Socialist Republic. This region was the formerly Ukrainian land which was populated largely by Russians. Thus, social engineering by the Soviets restructured society, and military presence discouraged the development of any nonconformity.

In time, links between Romanian-ruled Moldavia and Soviet Moldavia disintegrated. Families were cut off from one another, and traditional economic links disappeared. More changes took place when Moscow introduced *perestroika* across the Soviet Union. Volin (1989) reported that *perestroika* drastically reduced the number of jobs in Moldavia.

On August 27, 1991, the former Moldavian Soviet Socialist Republic raised its own flag (see Photo 5.20) and declared itself an independent nation—the Republic of Moldova. Even after the break up of the Soviet Union, when travel restrictions were reduced between Romania and the newly born Republic of Moldova, the Bucharest-Chișinău route continued to be one of low-density traffic, not even linked by daily air service. To encourage greater links between Ro-

PHOTO 5.20. Flag of Moldova.

mania and Moldova, airfares between Bucharest and Chişinău were made 58 percent lower for residents of these countries than for foreigners. Yet the airport at Chişinău served so few flights that the airfield and terminal area served as a refuge for stray dogs. During one visit to Moldova, I was personally greeted at the airplane ramp by six hounds. Outside the terminal, a man was sweeping the sidewalk with a broom constructed from small branches.

In September 1991, the Trans-Dnestr region declared itself the independent Pridnestrovskaya Moldavskaya Republica (Transdniestrian Moldovan Republic). This resulted in civil war.

Moldova is heavily dependent on a natural gas pipeline, which crosses the Trans-Dnestr region. During the armed conflict over the future of the Trans-Dnestr region in March 1992, the supply of energy was disrupted, affecting the whole Republic of Moldova. Only in July did the flow resume, but Moldova was charged more than the world price of gas. In some areas, where kitchens used to depend on gas, flow was cut off. Nadia, an interviewee in one town, told me that "only government people and the mafia could get gas here."

Political instability in 1999 led to the suspension of IMF and World Bank funding. Attempts to privatize the national tobacco and wine industries were abandoned in April 2000.

Promoting Entrepreneurship

Privatization in Moldova began in 1993, considerably later than in Romania, but the pace of privatization was much faster in Moldova. Each citizen received coupons with which to buy available shares of state firms. Between April 1993 and November 1995, 1,132 large firms and 613 shops were privatized by means of voucher auctions. A rudimentary stock exchange began operations in June 1995. Coupons remained valid until November 1995 but could not be sold and had no cash value. By 1996, two-thirds of the Moldovan companies had been privatized, mostly via coupons, and the government was seeking foreign investors for the others, as the more successful enterprises were available for sale in exchange for hard currency only. Meanwhile, a few entrepreneurs set up shop (see Photo 5.21).

In 1997, businesspeople met in Chişinău to discuss a variety of issues related to small business, including bureaucracy, management, marketing, and taxation. This resulted in the establishment of the

PHOTO 5.21. "Individual Entrepreneur."

Small Business Association of Moldova, with branches across the country.

In January 2002, BIZPRO Moldova (a project of economic growth through small and medium enterprise development), launched the Entrepreneurs Hotline Program, funded by USAID. This involved the establishment of hotlines in cooperation with business associations in Balti, Cahul, and Chişinău. From January 15 until July 1, hotline operators assisted 2,600 entrepreneurs, half of whom were sole proprietors, while four-fifths of the others represented microenterprises. Almost a quarter of the calls pertained to tax regulations. One-fifth of the calls referred to business registration and the launch of new ventures.

Several organizations promote entrepreneurship in Moldova. In the north of the country, the Association of Small Business Entrepreneurs of Balti encourages small firms in the region. Others function at the national level. The Microfinancing Alliance of Moldova contributes to private institutions of long-term microfinancing and prepares educational materials of use to entrepreneurs. The National Association of the Small Private Enterprises of Moldova promotes the economic, production-related, and commercial interests of small businesses.

Foreign Entrepreneurs

Few foreign entrepreneurs have been successful in Moldova. Some of their deals have not been in the national interest. For instance, during the mid-1990s, it was not possible for an individual in Romania to buy more than $500 of hard currency at an official exchange rate. In contrast, it was possible for a Romanian in Moldova to convert unlimited amounts of nonconvertible Romanian lei into dollars. This left the Moldovan state banks with a surplus of unconvertible Romanian lei.

Constructive entrepreneurship, on the other hand, has shown limited appeal. In 1999, political instability prompted potential investors to pull back from privatization deals (O'Driscoll, Holmes, and Kirkpatrick, 2001). Although foreign entrepreneurs are welcome in Moldova, they may not purchase agricultural land.

The State of Small Business and Entrepreneurship

During the early 1990s, peasants were granted land but no machinery and no financing to buy the necessities for a first harvest. Many opted to remain in cooperatives, but the cooperatives stopped paying their farmers (see Photo 5.22). Therefore, in 1995 there was a great increase in applications for land grants. To the dismay of applicants,

PHOTO 5.22. No longer paid.

however, in February 1995 the state stopped giving farmland to peasants, on the pretext that peasants should no longer have exclusivity on land. As cooperatives were not paying farmers, many peasants found themselves with no cash and no clothes in which to send their children to school.

Poverty among small-scale farmers is ironic given the fertility of the soil and its high productivity (see Photo 5.23). Vineyards and apple orchards have been central to the Bessarabian economy, along with the production of cereals.

Just outside the municipal boundary of the capital city are slopes with seemingly endless rows of grapevines leading up to the horizon (see Photo 5.24). Fine red, white, and sparkling wines are produced, with an untapped potential to penetrate export markets. Poor packaging, however, with inadequate distribution channels and the lack of advertising budget hinder the ability to properly market excellent wines. The leaves of grapevines are also important in the Moldovan diet; a regional specialty consists of vine leaves stuffed with meat and rice.

PHOTO 5.23. Sitting by the oil lamp.

PHOTO 5.24. Vineyards.

Moldova also has very productive orchards, which for years provided tons of apples and pears to the Soviet Union. Once the 1990s crisis began in Russia, demand for Moldovan fruit plummeted, and apples were left to rot on the trees. Other produce from the fertile land of Moldova includes apricots, beans, black currants, cabbage, dill, garlic, onions, potatoes, peaches, peppers, pumpkins, quince, raspberries, strawberries, sunflowers, tomatoes, and walnuts. Beets are grown for the production of sugar. Also plentiful are cucumbers, which many families pickle for their own consumption. It is also common to make homemade hard liquor, as well as jam, from locally grown plums. Growing and preparing food for subsistence results in an almost cashless society among some rural people (see Photo 5.25).

Numerous Moldovans derive their livelihood from work as shepherds with flocks of sheep. Goats are usually kept in smaller numbers. In towns such as Orhei, it is normal to see a goat in a person's garden. In villages such as Ratus, geese roam the main streets. Along the sides of major roads, including the highway between Telenesti and Balti, it is common to see calves grazing, unattended; horse-drawn wagons weave between them. Moldova has excellent dairy cattle, the milk from which is well marketed. Exquisite cream and kefir are industrially produced and sold in glass bottles (see Photo 5.26). A local specialty is chocolate-flavored butter. Cashcaval is produced as well as cream cheese.

PHOTO 5.25. Cashless subsistence.

PHOTO 5.26. Fresh and creamy.

Small numbers of formal-sector entrepreneurs operate in all the major centers. Their businesses, however, are not always popular, as their prices are often high. In Balti, for instance, there is a small, privately owned grocery called Pet Shop (nothing to do with pets); on any given day, business is slower than one might expect, considering that there are few food stores in Balti, which is a major metropolitan area of Moldova. Not surprisingly, formal entrepreneurship, as it is known in the West, is the not very common in this country; individuals often lack the enterprise culture, education, experience, finance, and incentive to become entrepreneurs in the formal sector. Yet informal microenterprises are very common (see Photo 5.27).

Sidewalks in the major centers are crowded with informal vendors lined up side by side trying to sell whatever they can (for example, a used wedding dress or other garments, see Photo 5.28). Beside a woman hunched over, sweeping the street with a broom, stands a vendor, the latter holding two salamis she wishes to sell. Her competition is another woman one meter away, standing with an inventory of three salamis. Both try to sell, but relatively few people have cash.

While some vendors stand still on busy sidewalks, others are ambulant, peddling their goods on buses (see Photo 5.29). Others sell goods from tables (see Photo 5.30). It is common to come across a sidewalk on which several tables have been set up, each attended by a self-employed vendor selling nothing but sunflower seeds, packaged

PHOTO 5.27. Microenterprise.

PHOTO 5.28. Wedding dress for sale.

PHOTO 5.29. On the bus.

PHOTO 5.30. Impromptu retailers.

in recycled sheets of paper. Usually, none has an inventory exceeding a few pounds; turnover is limited. Other vendors set up a table and pace around it. Along highways peasants sell, or attempt to sell, apples and potatoes (see Photo 5.31).

Indeed, informal microenterprise is very widespread in Moldova. Those operating at the microenterprise level may attempt to do all necessary calculations in their heads (see Photo 5.32). The more established and structured vendors use an abacus (see Photo 5.33). Bananas are costly in Moldova, so sidewalk banana vendors have a prestigious social status, and at times an abacus as well.

Subsistence self-employment, involving *no* exchange of money, is also very common in Moldova. The price of food being high relative to average income, it is the norm to supplement one's official income with subsistence self-employment in the internal sector. People grow vegetables. Jam is made in many homes. Chickens are raised for their eggs and goats for their milk from which cheese is produced. Any surplus is bartered in the informal subeconomy. One seventy-nine-

PHOTO 5.31. Roadside vendors.

PHOTO 5.32. Mental calculations.

PHOTO 5.33. Using an abacus.

year-old woman interviewed for this book explained that her monthly pension was hardly enough to live on. The price of eggs being 8 percent of her monthly income, it was normal for her to raise chickens for their eggs (see Photo 5.34). She also grew vegetables in her garden and chopped her own wood. Neighbors could share her produce as long as they brought her homemade wine and cheese.

Formal entrepreneurship, informal microenterprise, and internal-subsistence self-employment are all subject to a variety of constraints and challenges in Moldova. Among these are infrastructural problems, as shortages of power occur and difficulties with banking, power, telecommunications, and transportation are encountered (see Photo 5.35). The covert sector, meanwhile, operates relatively smoothly. Cockburn (2003) wrote about a Moldovan woman who was sold ten times, at an average price of $1,500.

Toward the Future

The lack of affinity between the people of Moldova and Romania has economic implications. A minority of Moldovans advocate the reunification of Bessarabia with Romania. One argument is that the economy of the former German Democratic Republic received a jump-start when it was reunified with the Federal Republic of Germany; similarly (but to a lesser degree), Moldova would have eco-

PHOTO 5.34. Supplementing her meager income.

PHOTO 5.35. Trolley bus being towed to the garage.

nomic gains if merged into Romania. Although such an option is possible, the heterogeneity (resulting from social engineering in Soviet Moldavia) makes this an unpopular option. In 1994, the majority of Moldovans rejected reunification with Romania. Although Moldovan was written in Cyrillic script until 1989, it now uses the Latin alphabet, as does Romanian.

A problem facing Moldova is that half of the GDP takes place in the parallel economy. Another issue involves difficulties in telecommunications. Telephones are valuable for vandals in Moldova because their parts can be removed and sold (see Photo 5.36).

During the mid-1990s, sturdier telephones were installed. As an alternative to tokens, these use Moldtelecom phone cards. Another problem, however, is that the supply of Moldtelecom cards is limited, and their distribution channels not as good as they might be. Many individuals have no phones at home, and so lines at public phones may be long.

Offices often have a telephone, but these are often out of order, and when they are not, employees enjoy taking their time to answer. Frequently, office phones are left off the hook (see Photo 5.37). Long-distance calls may be requested via an operator who calls back later with a connection—often a wrong number.

PHOTO 5.36. Vandalized for parts.

PHOTO 5.37. Out to lunch.

Other issues to be solved in the future are described by O'Driscoll, Holmes, and Kirkpatrick (2001). These include abuse of office by poorly paid civil servants, smuggling, and tax evasion.

THE RUSSIAN FEDERATION

Formerly known as the Russian Soviet Federative Socialist Republic, Russia covers an area of 6,592,735 square miles, neighboring Azerbaijan, Belarus, China, Estonia, Finland, Georgia, Kazakhstan, North Korea, Latvia, Mongolia, Norway, and the Ukraine;[5] Russia's Kaliningrad (formerly known as Königsberg) Oblast borders Lithuania and Poland. In August 1991, Russia declared that it was seceding from the Soviet Union. In October, Moscow City Council held its first auction, to sell off fifteen stores. Drastic economic reforms were instituted the following year, and inflation reached an annual rate of 1,000 percent. As the economy changed hands, the income differential between rich and poor widened. Gone are the shortages of commodities that formerly led to long queues, but new problems have arisen. To defend their interests, entrepreneurs in this country have created a trade union.

Historical Overview

Believed to be the founders of the first Russian state, the Rus were Viking traders who established their rule in Novgorod in 862 (Edwards, 1991). According to some authors, the Mongols conquered the Russians in 1237. After Russia's Ivan the Terrible captured Kazan in 1552, the Volga became an important trade route to the Orient.

Peter the Great's goal to create a class of Russian industrialists became a pork barrel for influential generals and bureaucrats. With few exceptions, his program did little to develop entrepreneurs, and it did not develop the foundation for an entrepreneurial tradition. Herbig and McCarty explained, "Historically, the Russians have been anti-capitalist. During Czarist Russia, the land owning nobles and state officials who governed the empire for the most part looked down on capitalists and decried the profit motive . . . capitalism was denounced as materialist, selfish . . ." (1995, p. 53). Nevertheless, many people in Russia were engaged throughout history in some form of commercial activity. Even after the abolishment of serfdom, during the mid-nineteenth century, Russian slaves were sold in Far East markets (Stamp, 1936). However, Russian entrepreneurs were generally oppressed, heavily taxed, treated as powerless individuals, and regarded as being at the bottom echelon of society. Lieven (1990) explained that the Russian Orthodox Church depicted capitalism as the antithesis of popular Russian values.

Under tsarist rule, Russian entrepreneurs were oppressed by the government. The tsarist government saddled successful entrepreneurs with burdensome obligations, demanded special contributions from entrepreneurs during times of emergency or war, competed with private entrepreneurs previously granted rights and privileges anytime it was expedient, demanded punctual and exact fulfillment of obligations, and confiscated property when these obligations were not met. It is no wonder that entrepreneurs in tsarist Russia were cautious, conservative, and wary of any new venture that would expose them to even more risks and hazards.

Although a 1905 revolution was unsuccessful, the rule of the Romanov dynasty (1613-1917) ended with the revolution of February 1917. In March, Tsar Nicholas II abdicated. The following month, Vladimir Ilyich Ulyanov (Lenin) arrived in Petrograd, as St. Petersburg had been renamed in 1914 (see Photo 5.38). There, he

PHOTO 5.38. Baroque-style Winter Palace, residence of the tsars, in St. Petersburg.

called for socialist revolution. Inspired by the works of Karl Marx (Marx and Engels, 1848), Lenin's slogan was "Peace, Bread, and Land."[6]

In May 1917, Levc Davidovich Bronstein (also known as Leon Trotsky), the son of a Jewish farmer, arrived in Petrograd. He united with Lenin, and their Bolsheviks (from the Russian word for "majority"), later known as the Communists, led the October Revolution. On October 25 of the Julian calendar used in Russia at the time, corresponding to November 7 of the Gregorian calendar, the Bolsheviks took control of Russia. A new currency was issued (see Photo 5.39).

On February 1, 1918, the Julian calendar was phased out in favor of the Gregorian calendar (the Julian calendar had been thirteen days behind the Gregorian calendar). In March 1918, Russia gave up its Finnish province, its Polish lands, the Ukraine, Estonia, Latvia, and Lithuania. Civil war broke out during the summer of 1918. The Communists, too afraid to stay in Petrograd (see Photo 5.40), made Moscow the new capital of Russia. By 1920, the Communists had won the war. In 1921, Lenin's New Economic Policy legalized private ownership, but after Lenin died, his successor Joseph Stalin opted to nationalize the entire country.

The Union of Soviet Socialist Republics, commonly known as the Soviet Union, was born in 1922; Moscow was its capital (see Photo 5.41). In 1924, the name of Petrograd was changed to Leningrad; the name reverted to St. Petersburg in September 1991.

PHOTO 5.39. 1,000 rubles.

PHOTO 5.40. St. Petersburg was known as Petrograd from 1914 to 1924 and as Leningrad between 1924 and 1991.

PHOTO 5.41. Moscow, the new capital city.

Several years before becoming president of the United States, Richard Nixon gave an account of his visit to Russia (Nixon, 1959). Myalo discussed the corruption and lack of work ethic during the 1970s: "in the 70s the whirlpool of corruption and careless work, work which had become sort of not obligatory for all—failed to engulf all people" (1988, p. 11).

Under central planning, state firms offered lifelong employment (see Photo 5.42). An important national priority was the military (see Photo 5.43). For consumers, choice was limited (see Photo 5.44). Shortages and lines became the norm (see Photo 5.45).

As was the case elsewhere across the Soviet Union, *perestroika* and *glasnost* during the 1980s brought a variety of changes to Russia. Khamidulin reported, "Perestroika offers more opportunities for people everywhere . . ." (1988, p. 5). *Perestroika* even provided opportunities in the covert sector. In 1988, several publications introduced the word "mafia" into Russian, to describe the organized crime networks involved in embezzlement, extortion, bribery, black-market profiteering, and drug trafficking (Keller, 1988). It was still not permitted to import rubles into the Soviet Union, yet the import was tolerated (Mitchell, 1989).

Urbanization was contributing to a growth in Moscow's population (see Photo 5.46); in 1989, there were more people than jobs in this city. Ivanov (1989) reported that effective July 15, 1989, industrial enterprises were required to pay 31,000 rubles for each non-Muscovite hired (see Photo 5.47). This amount was payable to the Fund of Additional Financial Resources of the Moscow City Soviet Executive Committee.

On November 28, 1989, entrepreneurs in Russia formed a trade union, with the aim of protecting private property at large, as well as professional interests of entrepreneurs and their employees. In 1991, this became the Russian Union of Medium and Small Business Workers.

In 1990, Russia legalized private farming. By the end of the year, the 2 percent of total Soviet farmland that was in private hands produced 60 percent of Russia's potatoes and almost 30 percent of its eggs, meat, milk, and vegetables. As fixed prices failed to reflect demand, shortages were common, especially in urban stores.

Massive price increases on January 2, 1992, reduced shortages and queues. A presidential decree permitted unrestricted trading on pub-

PHOTO 5.42. Providing jobs.

PHOTO 5.43. Military personnel had special privileges.

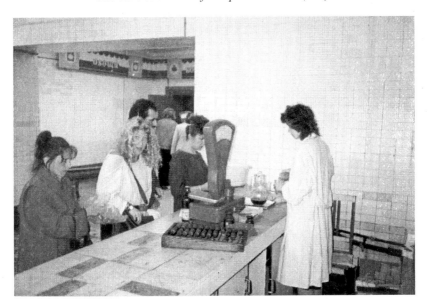

PHOTO 5.44. Store in Leningrad.

PHOTO 5.45. Waiting to enter a shop.

PHOTO 5.46. Crowded mall in Moscow.

PHOTO 5.47. Non-Muscovites.

lic streets (see Photo 5.48). Nevertheless, some items (for which prices were set below production costs) remained scarce (McKinsey, 1992).

Regarding the issue of market pricing in Russia, Reichlin reported on an unexpected situation, explaining that it

> hasn't yet reached Vasileostrovsky Farmers' Market in St. Petersburg, where prices . . . aren't set by supply and demand. Instead, pricing is dictated by hard-nosed traders from Azerbaijan. . . . For years, traders . . . had little competition because state-owned food stores were mostly empty. But on Jan. 2, Boris Yeltsin freed most prices. State stores started to fill up as prices rose. Traders in other countries might be tempted to cut their prices to make them competitive with the state ones. Not the Azeris . . . They are organized like U.S. mobsters. . . . To keep out competitors, such as Uzbeks,[7] the Azeri enforcers first offer to buy their inventory before they start unloading it. . . . Should competitors refuse to sell, they are warned by the Azeris to sell at going prices or else. Punishment, sometimes death, can come swiftly to the stubborn. (1992, p. 51)

PHOTO 5.48. Public trading.

By 1992, the Russian Union of Medium and Small Business Workers had conducted negotiations on issues of entrepreneurs' interests in legislative bodies and other organs of power, leading to the signing of the Decree About Organizational Measures on Development of Small and Medium Business in the Russian Federation.[8] The union interacted with deputies, participated in the lawmaking initiative, and through mass media swayed public opinion in favor of entrepreneurs. By 1993, the union had reached an agreement with the State Committee of the Russian Federation, taking into account the interests of Russian entrepreneurs and a developing banking infrastructure (Johnson, Kroll, and Horton, 1993). Yet not everything was rosy for entrepreneurs. Bohlen (1994) described how criminals were suppressing entrepreneurship; she reported that ninety-four entrepreneurs were murdered in Russia during 1993. Boylan (1996) reported that during the mid-1990s over 70 percent of enterprises were paying extortion money, and 80 percent of American firms in Russia were paying bribes.

In contrast to the situation in Poland, where state enterprises were restructured while still in state hands, business establishments in Russia saw little restructuring. This was true even among privatized firms, as subsidies continued to distort the Russian economy (Belyanova and Rozinsky, 1995). Boycko and Shleifer (1994) explained that most enterprises were being managed by preprivatization teams who lacked the interest to initiate significant changes. Aoki (1995) confirmed that privatized firms were doing as little restructuring as was the case among state-owned enterprises. Vamosi summarized the situation: "In other words, the same administrative technology, the same physical frames and the same 'old' culture prevail!" (2003, p. 195).

In 1995, the federal government introduced a new law on small enterprises. According to this law, a firm with over 100 employees could no longer qualify as a small enterprise.

Writing about Moscow during the mid-1990s, Remnick noted, "The rule of the dollar has brought the city riches and hunger, freedom and anxiety, commerce and crime" (1997, p. 79). Alon and McKee (1999) reported that banks, business, and government have been coerced to cooperate with the mafia. Resistance has resulted in death (Ahmed, Robinson, and Dana, 2001).

A major devaluation increased the price of imports while reducing the disposable income of Russians; this led Russia into a recession in August 1998. Notwithstanding, a weak ruble boosted domestic production, and it was suggested that the ruble crash brought a wave of investment (Cottrell, 2002). Russia's economy grew by 5 percent in 1999, and by 8 percent in 2000. However, not everybody benefited. Johnson et al. (2000) found that Russians faced worse bureaucratic corruption, more mafia extortion, higher taxes, and a less-effective court system at the turn of the millennium than was the case under communist rule.

In 2001, an inflation rate of 18.6 percent pushed up the real exchange rate of the ruble (Cottrell, 2002). One in seven Russians was living below the official poverty line of $31 monthly per person.

Alon and Banai (2001) concluded that the Russian market is hostile, with many threats to established firms as well as new entrants. They cited corruption and "a high level of crime, ranging from petty thievery to street gangs and organized criminal networks" (2001, p. 135).[9]

Promoting Entrepreneurship

Herbig and McCarty (1995) noted that Russian culture does not have underlying innovative tendencies or an entrepreneurial history. They discussed how religion and the lack of individualism were traditionally coupled with inherent biases against risk taking. Along similar lines, Lewis suggested,

> If a religion lays stress upon material values, upon thrift and productive investment, upon honesty in commercial relations, upon experimentation and risk-bearing and upon equality of opportunity, it will be helpful to growth, whereas in so far as it is hostile to these things, it tends to inhibit growth. (1955, p. 105)

With financing from the Russian Federal Science and Technology budget, in 1994 Russia established the Fund for Assistance to Small Innovative Enterprises. Yet the lack of managerial competence appears to have limited growth of such enterprises. Zhuplev et al. (1998) found that although network skills were important for Russian entrepreneurs, people gave little value to people skills. The study concluded that Russia was making far less progress in developing entrepreneurship than was Kazakhstan.[10]

The Citizens Democracy Corps is an economic development organization committed to nurturing small and medium enterprises. This organization provides access to a network of support organizations and has successfully mobilized significant resources for small and medium entrepreneurs (Dilts, 2000). Incubators were also set up to assist entrepreneurs.[11] More recently, the reduction of bureaucracy, coupled with cuts in tax rates, "made it a bit easier to start a business" (Anonymous, 2003, p. 66).

Foreign Entrepreneurs

After fourteen years of planning, on January 1, 1990, McDonald's opened its first restaurant in Russia (Dana, 1997b). This was a joint venture between McDonald's Canada and Mosobschepit. The joint venture had considerable success, and several outlets were opened. American entrepreneurs Ben Cohen and Jerry Greenfield launched Ben & Jerry's in Russia, but problems led to its closure (Dana and Dana, 1999).

In July 1999, a new law on foreign investment was introduced that granted national treatment to foreign entrepreneurs in most sectors (see Photo 5.49). Although foreign entrepreneurs can establish their own ventures, registration is complicated. Other obstacles include corruption, crime, and legal uncertainty.

The problem that was most frequently brought up by the foreign entrepreneurs I interviewed was the cost of *krysha*—mafia protection. Some entrepreneurs have been forced to pay 20 percent of profits to one of several extortion groups.

The State of Entrepreneurship and the Small-Business Sector

Radaev (1993) reported that the typical small-scale businessperson in Russia is educated, often with an engineering or technical background. Yet Hisrich and Gratchev (1995) found that despite their technical education, these individuals are often lacking business skills. Glinkina (1999) focused on entrepreneurship in Russia's parallel economy.

PHOTO 5.49. Foreign entrepreneurs in Moscow.

An empirical study by Robinson et al. (2001) identified mind-set as a source of problems challenging the small-business sector. Their study found the following:

1. Russian respondents tended to ignore the concept of price elasticity.
2. Some people believed that if one succeeded, it must be by doing something wrong, illegal, or unethical and ultimately bad for society. It was perceived that a successful entrepreneur took unfair advantage of workers, customers, and/or suppliers;
3. Respondents did not demonstrate the ability to think innovatively.
4. A common perception was that rules were made to be broken.

It should be mentioned that setting up a new venture in Russia can be time-consuming and costly. Djankov et al. (2002) showed that it takes two months to set up a firm and that official fees are the equivalent of 38 percent of per capita GDP.

Once an enterprise is established, more challenges lie ahead. In 2003, entrepreneurs I interviewed discussed the following as problems facing them and their small firms in Russia:

1. Capital for small firms is scarce.
2. Frustration over perceiving themselves to be at a disadvantage, when compared with larger firms, with respect to access to and adoption of technology.
3. Discontent that they perceive themselves to be at a disadvantage, when compared with larger firms, with respect to receiving fair treatment in government matters.
4. Feeling like victims of unfairly implemented regulations, more often than was the case among larger companies that could exercise more *blat* (influence).
5. Belief that they were asking for a disproportionate amount of bribes, when compared to larger companies.
6. Security problems.

Toward the Future

"Gorbachev observed that to achieve *glasnost* and *perestroika,* Russian culture would have to change" (Behrman and Rondinelli, 1999, p. 10). Almost two decades since the launch of *perestroika,* structural changes to the Russian economy are relatively easy to orchestrate when compared to changes in culture and human nature (i.e., the attitudes that comprise paradigms regarding salient aspects of life). The processes involved in changing one's mind-set differ significantly from the decrees used by the Russian president to initiate and regulate the change to the market economy.

In the case of Russia, the greatest difficulty in converting from a centralized economy to a free-market economy has *not* been the lack of technical knowledge for designing, engineering, and building products. Russia has a highly educated workforce with a much higher proportion of college-educated people per capita than Western countries. Western travelers to the country can easily encounter numerous unemployed or underemployed engineers. A lack of experience with the firm-type economy, as it works in the West, is an important barrier in the development of enterprising culture across Russia. There is admittedly a lag in the retraining of older managers in the practical application of business skills and knowledge in the emerging new market economy.

Kuznetsov, McDonald, and Kuznetsova (2000) explained how, in Russia, the relationship between participants in a transaction is characterized by mistrust, and the business environment is marred by the fact that organized crime controls much of the economy. Hough (2001) argued that economic reform in Russia did not go wrong because of corruption. He suggested that Russia could have fared better had it saved its manufacturing core by investing in it and protecting it from foreign competition. An alternate opinion is that of Herbig and McCarty (1995), who recommended that foreign entrepreneurs be recruited to settle and thrive, to be emulated, over time, by local people.

THE UKRAINE (LITTLE RUSSIA)

The Ukraine covers an area of 231,990 square miles, neighboring Belarus, Hungary, Moldova, Poland, Romania, Russia, and Slovakia, with shores along the Sea of Azov as well as on the Black Sea.[12] Due to scarcity of oil and other cheap sources of energy, the Ukraine has approached privatization with far greater caution than has Russia. State-owned industries in the Ukraine were subsidized, stifling the development of private enterprise. As the monthly inflation rate reached 30 percent, the Ukrainian currency devalued faster than the Russian ruble. Johnson, Kaufmann, and Shleifer (1997) reported that unofficial Ukrainian GDP was 49 percent of official GDP, remarkably high compared to 6 percent in neighboring Slovakia. Johnson et al. (2000) found that 41 percent of sales in the Ukraine are unreported, compared with 29 percent in Russia. Only 1 percent of their sample said that no sales were hidden, compared with 74 percent in Poland. Barriers to entry in the formal corporate sector have contributed to the attractiveness of the parallel market. Formal entrepreneurship is concentrated in Kiev (see Photo 5.50) and in Odessa (see Photo 5.51).

PHOTO 5.50. Kiev.

PHOTO 5.51. Odessa.

Historical Overview

The ancestors of today's Ukrainians arrived from central Europe between the sixth and eighth centuries, displacing indigenous Finnic tribes. The medieval principality of Kiev was founded in the ninth century. By the end of the fourteenth century, the Grand Duchy of Lithuania ruled much of today's Ukraine. Ukrainians were also governed by the Ottoman Empire. With the partition of the Polish-Lithuanian Commonwealth and with acquisitions from the Ottoman Empire, the Russian Empire eventually obtained most of the Ukraine, while the western Ukraine became part of the Austro-Hungarian Empire. Although Ukrainian and Russian are similar languages, the tsars banned the Ukrainian language during the nineteenth century. During the 1880s an unusually large sum of money was allocated for the promotion of non-Ukranian culture. A considerable sum financed the construction of the Opera in Odessa, built between 1884 and 1887 (see Photo 5.52).

PHOTO 5.52. The Opera in Odessa.

After World War I, the Ukraine declared its independence. Although Lenin had promised to recognize a sovereign Ukraine, the Bolsheviks put an end to independence in 1920. Western areas of the Ukraine were divided among Czechoslovakia, Poland, and Romania; the eastern Ukraine became the Ukrainian Soviet Socialist Republic. In the west, the city of Lviv was Austro-Hungarian before 1918, and subsequently situated in Poland until 1939.

In 1939, the Soviet Union annexed Polish sections of the Ukraine. The German invasion of the Soviet Union resulted in Nazi occupation of the entire Ukraine. The region returned to Soviet rule when the Soviets defeated the Nazis there.

Under communist rule, life was grand for just a few (see Photo 5.53). For the masses, there were shortages and long lines for consumer goods (see Photo 5.54).

In August 1991, the Ukraine proclaimed its independence from the Soviet Union. On December 8, 1991, the Ukraine joined Russia and Belarus in the CIS. Although the Ukraine declared itself politically independent, Soviet (and later Russian) rubles remained legal tender in the Ukraine, and the economic environment was affected by Moscow's policies. The Ukraine followed Russia's example and liberalized prices. During the first six months of 1992, the nominal volume of money in circulation decreased by a factor of seven, due to the increase of prices made possible by liberalization. Such a serious disproportion between the value of goods and the availability of money resulted in a nonpayment crisis. This led to the breakdown of relations between enterprises and an unprecedented decrease in production. Conditions gave rise to barter operations.

In October 1992, Russia eliminated state control of oil and natural gas prices. This was particularly harmful for the Ukraine, where the nonpayment crisis worsened. Most of the state banks tried to accumulate resources from enterprises as well as from the National Bank of the Ukraine. The rate of inflation increased rapidly. The Ukrainian government signed a protocol with Russia in October 1992, whereby the Ukraine took responsibility for debts of entrepreneurs, resulting in substantial artificial growth of external debt of the Ukraine.

The nonpayment crisis prompted the Ukrainian government to cancel the circulation of Russian rubles in the Ukraine, effective November 16, 1992. Although the koupon (see Photo 5.55) or karbovanet became the local currency, the ruble remained useful for inter-

PHOTO 5.53. Only the elite had cars.

PHOTO 5.54. Long line to enter a store.

PHOTO 5.55. 100,000-Koupon note.

national transactions. An illegal black market emerged for Russian rubles, while koupons flooded the domestic market. The financial and economic crisis in the Ukraine was growing.

Although the situation improved for industrial enterprises in Russia, the limited market for Ukrainian products aggravated the economic crisis in the Ukraine. The koupon was devalued by a factor of 1.5, in order to decrease the cost of exports, mainly to Russia. Although the intention was to get more rubles into the Ukraine, the opposite happened. Russia banned the import of Ukrainian products, and the Ukraine lacked rubles to buy raw materials from Russia. This was especially harmful due to very tight business integration between Russian and Ukrainian enterprises in the post-Soviet economic space. Large-scale economic stagnation, coupled with hyperinflation, led to stagflation.

An exploratory phase of currency introduction lasted until mid-1993. It was a period of search for a new financial policy for the Ukraine, as the monthly rate of inflation was typically 47 percent during this phase. Although the rate of hyperinflation peaked at 10,255 percent, in 1993, banks were keen to do business. Johnson et al. (1993) observed that banks started lending even before the establishment of a legal framework.

Capital construction investments were 22 percent lower in 1993 than in 1992, and approximately half of that in 1991. Agriculture suffered due to the high difference in prices between agricultural and industrial products. The bulk industrial price index increased by 3,900 times, in comparison to 1991.

Deficit became the normal state of affairs in the Ukraine, and business plans became meaningless due to hyperinflation. Under such conditions, the koupon could not promote the accumulation of reserve, as people spent their local currency to acquire dollars, rubles, or goods. As a result, the koupon tumbled and prices escalated. The money emission in 1993 increased by seventeen times in comparison to 1992, and the value of the koupon decreased by a factor of 36. Taking into consideration the triple devaluation of koupons against the dollar, the purchasing power of the koupons decreased by more than 100-fold.

Economic instability was discouraging. Ahmed et al. (1998) summarized the situation during the 1990s:

1. there appeared to be irresponsibility among the administration, with respect to what was happening in the economy and society as a whole;
2. the system was still centered around state property, and groups of former Communists and *Komsomol* (Young Communist League) leaders used income from state property, for personal gain;
3. former Communist leaders, who had neither the appropriate education nor experience in business, and whose primary goal is personal profit, were in positions that control large banks and commercial firms;
4. there was a lack of qualified managers in industry;
5. there appeared to be political and economic pressure from Russia;
6. an all-penetrating mafia was very powerful;
7. hyperinflation practically eliminated bank savings for a majority of people in the country, and this affected consumption patterns;
8. taxes were increased on several occasions;
9. a high excise tax was introduced;
10. financial policy was naive;
11. state credits were stolen by some bureaucrats;
12. the banks in the Ukraine tried to generate profits by raising interest rates, creating substantial difficulties for entrepreneurs; and
13. due to poor workmanship, Ukrainian products were inferior to world standards, thus inhibiting their exports, and the volume of external trade decreased.

An important positive step in financial policy was the organization of the Ukrainian Stock Fund and in June 1993 the signing of a contract with the French Stock Society to computerize the fund. The French party provided 25 million French francs to buy appropriate software.

In October 1994, President Leonid Kuchma froze salaries and restricted the printing of money. His new policy decreased the state budget deficit, liberalized trade, and accelerated the rate of privatization. Liberalized trade allowed more imports. The port of Odessa was busy (see Photo 5.56). However, perhaps more than ever before, food stores were filled with imported products. Never before were the shelves so poorly supplied with food produced in the Ukraine. Industrial produce dropped to 40 percent of the 1990 level. Yet the top of the administration pyramid seemed prosperous. Although official salaries were low, bureaucrats were not poor. Unofficial payments became required for export licenses, contracts, and permits. For those with good connections, life was easy (see Photo 5.57).

In contrast, consider a university professor's monthly income in 1995: about 18 million koupons or $90 at the time. If he or she lived in a two-room apartment, he or she had to pay 3.5 million koupons in rent. (Energy for cooking, heating, and light was prohibitively expen-

PHOTO 5.56. Odessa, port on the Black Sea.

PHOTO 5.57. More equal than others.

sive.) One million koupons per month was required for public transportation. Little remained for food and clothing. Dividing 12 million by thirty days, the budget to be spent on food was 400,000 koupons per day, corresponding to $2.22. This was the cost of about 800 grams (1.76 pounds) of low-quality sausage, 6.5 kilograms (14.3 pounds) of bread, 5.5 kilograms (12.1 pounds) of potatoes, 7 liters (1.85 gallons) of milk, less than 3 kilograms (6.6 pounds) of sugar, or about one liter of vodka— not very much if we take into account that the professor may have a family to care for. At the end of some months, the government claimed not to have money to pay salaries and professors had to survive without pay. Yet high-ranking officials continued their expensive trips abroad.

Progressive steps were taken in 1995, when new legislation eliminated the double taxing of salaries. However, there were still twenty-nine types of taxes, and this was a burden on owner-managers of small businesses with limited time and resources. The first positive results of financial stabilization were achieved in the middle of 1995. Between April and July 1995, the credit interest rate decreased by 5.8 percent. Although the credit cycle was shifted to the long-term, substantial changes to investments did not happen. By 1996, commercial banks accumulated about $2.3 billion, but only half of the sum belonged to deposits; all other money was related to current accounts.

In September 1996, the hryvnia was introduced to replace the koupon. One hryvnia was given the value of 100,000 koupons; $1 was worth 1.8 hryvnias. In June 1997, a new corporate tax introduced a switch from revenue taxation to profit taxation, and a 30 percent base taxation rate.

Thanks to a strict monetary policy, a positive result has been achieved in the area of financial stabilization. The currency market has been developed, and commercial banks have obtained the right to purchase hard currency and to sell it through their exchange offices. Commercial banks have been allowed to perform hard-currency operations directly with entrepreneurs and consumers.

Although life is not bright for everyone, it appears to be improving for many. Marinov et al. (2001) noted a 1998 study by the Ukrainian Trade Union Federation, revealing that 74 percent of the population lived below the poverty line. More recently, Bird reported, "Some 30 percent of Ukraine's 48 million people live below the poverty line of $63 a month; most survive on an average wage of $70 a month"

(2002, p. 24). For many, life is improving (see Photo 5.58); but this is not the case for everybody. Cockburn noted that owners of brothels can buy young Ukrainians "for around \$4000 each" (2003, p. 5).

Promoting Entrepreneurship

Gilmore described the situation during World War II: "One of the interesting features of reconstruction of the Ukraine is the Government's encouragement of individuals opening small enterprises for private profit" (1944, p. 513). Of course, the promotion of entrepreneurship was short-lived.

Following independence from the Soviet Union, the explosive liberalization of prices, hyperinflation, the delay of mutual payments between firms, and the unwillingness of industrial plants to adapt to new economic conditions resulted in disaster for entrepreneurship. The approach to reforms proposed by the IMF and supported by the

PHOTO 5.58. Enjoying a good meal.

Ukrainian government failed to produce significant effects on Ukrainian entrepreneurship. Sudden freedom resulted in chaos.

In 1992, the Government of the Ukraine invited the International Finance Corporation to launch a small-scale privatization project. Funded by the USAID, this project eventually helped privatize over 50,000 firms across the Ukraine. There were delays, however, as the privatization of small enterprises planned for 1993 did not materialize because of the following factors:

- the absence of appropriate clear methodology, norms, and experience of privatization;
- counteraction of the state structures responsible for the enterprises to be privatized;
- slow development of the local privatizing institutions;
- the absence of laws providing the possibility for privatizing the land where private enterprises were situated;
- the absence of laws providing the legal protection for individual property rights; and
- the policy of stripping government enterprises from their assets and simultaneously sabotaging privatization involving non-corrupt Ukrainian individuals and foreign corporate interests.

The privatization of small enterprises finally began in 1994. With financing from the United Kingdom's Know How Fund, as well as from USAID, the International Finance Corporation managed a business development project, with centers across the Ukraine assisting small firms with training, information, and access to finance.

By 1997, about 40,000 small and medium enterprises were functioning; however, only half exhibited adequate results. A large number of private enterprises showed worse results compared to the state-owned ones. Reasons for their poor state included the lack of appropriate investments; the lack of appropriate internal structuring of economy; low technologies unsuitable for market competition; and stringent resistance from the corrupted local government bureaucrats.

In the countryside, subsistence self-employment became the norm (see Photo 5.59). An average family usually possesses 0.5 to 0.8 hectares of land upon which it is normal to plant cabbage, carrots, cucumbers, onions, potatoes, and tomatoes. Sometimes, corn and wheat are

PHOTO 5.59. Subsistence farming.

also grown. The output is consumed by the family itself, and surplus is used to feed a couple of pigs, a cow, and fifteen to twenty chickens.

Among the most prosperous people in the countryside are those who can steal wheat or sugar from a *kolkhoz* and sell it abroad. These are mainly heads of collective farms and those who are responsible for reserves of beans, cereal, corn, flower, honey, sugar, wheat, etc. They consider themselves clever entrepreneurs because they identify opportunities to profit from theft. The situation in industry is not much different. Writing about the formal sector, Bird reported, "This state does not want small businesses to prosper" (2002, p. 24).

Foreign Entrepreneurs

In spite of a potentially large investment market, rich natural resources, substantial industrial and scientific potential, and qualified and relatively cheap human capital, the Ukraine did not attract many entrepreneurs from abroad. Ahmed et al. (1998) explained:

1. economic turmoil in the Ukraine, an unstable financial system, hyperinflation, a very heavy tax burden, and mafia rule rendered the Ukraine unattractive for foreign entrepreneurs;

2. investors usually received very low returns from investments in the Ukraine;
3. a large volume of Ukrainian capital was transferred abroad secretly, influencing the volume of possible investments into the Ukrainian economy;
4. the transfer of capital out of the Ukraine contributed to an image of a country in which government was unable to provide appropriate conditions for foreign direct investment; and
5. the lack of a substantial financial infrastructure complicated matters.

The State of Entrepreneurship and the Small-Business Sector

Although entrepreneurship has much potential in the Ukraine, entrepreneurs I interviewed expressed concern about the following obstacles:

- the sourcing of raw materials can be problematic;
- bad debts among buyers harms suppliers;
- uncertainties make it difficult to write a business plan;
- consulting services and legal firms are very expensive;
- regulation is perceived to be excessive and haphazardly implemented;
- protection of intellectual rights is poor;
- taxation rates are perceived to be high and formalities complex, given the number of different taxes and changing regulations; and
- the atmosphere of irresponsibility in the Ukraine helps bureaucrats to shift more wealth into their own hands.

Another issue brought up by entrepreneurs during interviews was corruption. One respondent cited the fact that, on a scale of 10, the Ukraine scored 2.1 in the 2002 Transparency International corruption rating. This was lower than Russia, scoring 2.3, and much lower than Finland, scoring 9.9. Bird summarized an interview that she conducted in Kiev: "The only way to defend yourself is to slip a bribe to someone" (2002, p. 24).

Toward the Future

Gilmore wrote about the Ukraine: "It has much of the richest agricultural land in the Soviet Union" (1944, p. 528). As recently as the 1980s, the Ukraine (with 2.7 percent of the land area of the Soviet Union) produced "26 percent of the wheat, 32 percent of the corn, 58 percent of the sugar beets, 22 percent of the cattle, [and] 27 percent of the hogs" (Edwards, 1987, p. 610) for the country. It is ironic, therefore, that the Ukraine is faring poorly now.

A study by Marinov et al. (2001) concluded that the Ukraine is considered a very difficult environment for business. The government would benefit if it were to take measures to change this and to revive entrepreneurship in agriculture (see Photo 5.60) as well as in industry.

Whereas the existing tax system has been encouraging about 50 percent of the economy to take place in the black market, an overhaul of the taxation system might facilitate emergence from the parallel economy. This includes reducing the number of different taxes payable and making compliance more affordable. For instance, there should no longer be retroactive changes to reporting. From the state's perspective, an efficient tax system should be easy to administer.

Government paperwork requirements are numerous, which is costly and time-consuming for entrepreneurs in the formal sector.

PHOTO 5.60. Traditional farm.

Simultaneously, this encourages others to remain in the parallel economy. If reporting requirements were simplified, more entrepreneurs might comply.

Some people perceive the Ukraine to be a temporary place for grabbing fast money before an escape abroad. Efforts to curb in-house, large-scale stealing might yield visible improvements to profitability.

Culture in the Ukraine does not contribute to the social desirability of being an entrepreneur in this country. A public campaign might contribute to improving the general perception of entrepreneurs, making entrepreneurship more socially desirable in the future (see Photo 5.61).

PHOTO 5.61. Toward a bright future.

Chapter 6

The Baltic States

Estonia, Latvia, and Lithuania had been under Russian rule since the eighteenth century. After World War I, however, they enjoyed a brief period of independence with free-market economics. Given their geographic position on the Baltic Sea (see Photo 6.1), these countries are collectively referred to as the Baltic States.

On August 23, 1939, the Molotov-Ribbentrop Pact changed the course of history, as the Nazis and the Soviets agreed to divide Eastern Europe into spheres of influence. In accordance with this agreement, the three Baltic republics were annexed by the Soviet Union in 1940.

In March 1949, the Baltic nations lost 3 percent of their native population, as 60,000 people were deported from Estonia; 50,000 from Latvia; and 40,000 from Lithuania (Misiunas and Taagepera, 1983).

PHOTO 6.1. On the Baltic Sea.

Each was given the status of Soviet republic, but the respective national flags were outlawed until 1988.

During the 1980s, when Moscow introduced *glasnost* (openness) and *perestroika* (restructuring) across the Soviet Union, the Baltic States were the only constituents with a living memory of free-market economics. Although the three share openness toward market economies, cultural differences must not be underestimated. Estonians, most of whom are Lutherans, have a Finno-Ugric tongue, similar to the Finns and the Hungarians. Latvians have an Indo-European language. Many Latvians are Lutherans. Lithuanians are mostly Roman Catholics. Although the Estonians and the Latvians are culturally similar to the Germans, the Lithuanians have cultural ties with Poland (Vesilind, 1990).

Of course, there are also differences within each nation. Vesilind wrote, "wherever you have three Estonians, you find a social club— but wherever you have at least four Estonians you find two clubs" (1980, p. 494). Although most Estonians are Lutherans (see Photo 6.2), a small number belong to the Orthodox Church (see Photo 6.3), and their traditional dress is reflective of historical differences.

Among the Soviet republics, per capita GNP varied considerably. In 1989, per capita GNP was $6,740 in Latvia, $6,240 in Estonia, $5,960 in Belarus, $5,880 in Lithuania, and only $2,340 in Tajikistan; in Poland, the figure was $3,910 (Anonymous, 1991).

Some 60 percent of people in Estonia were ethnic Estonians in 1989, compared to 94 percent in 1945. Of people living in Latvia, about half were ethnic Latvians, compared to 83 percent in 1945. In Lithuania, 80 percent were ethnic Lithuanians, compared to 79 percent in 1945 (Misiunas and Taagepera, 1991). Since the Baltic States gained their independence, the Latin alphabet has become more prominent, and Cyrillic script less so (see Photo 6.4).

In 1997, Estonia was invited to negotiations regarding joining the European Union; Latvia and Lithuania were invited to join in 1999. In 2001, a free-trade zone was formed, encompassing the three Baltic States, the European Union, and other countries in Eastern Europe.

THE REPUBLIC OF ESTONIA

The Republic of Estonia is 17,462 square miles, bordering the Baltic Sea, the Gulf of Finland, the Gulf of Riga, Latvia, and Russia.[2]

PHOTO 6.2. Lutheran Estonian in national costume with traditional headcover.

PHOTO 6.3. Orthodox Estonian in traditional dress with headscarf.

PHOTO 6.4. Bilingual sign.

Since its reindependence in 1991, Estonia has implemented a wide spectrum of reforms, along with tight fiscal policies. Most small and medium firms were privatized by 1994, and most large ones by 1996. By 1997, Estonia already had a functioning market economy, and in November 2001, the Heritage Foundation and *The Wall Street Journal* ranked Estonia fourth in the world in terms of economic freedom. Only Hong Kong, Singapore, and New Zealand scored better, while fourth place was tied with Ireland, Luxembourg, the Netherlands, and the United States. The IMF and the World Bank have noted the remarkable economic progress achieved in Estonia. Multinationals feel comfortable in this country (see Photo 6.5), while locals increase their standard of living as well. The selection of goods is unprecedented (see Photo 6.6).

Historical Overview

According to the most widespread theory, the ancestors of Estonians were people from the region of the Ural Mountains. "Seafarers, hunters, beekeepers, fishermen, farmers, they lived in peace with the spirits of the land, asking permission of the forest to hew its trees, and praying for forgiveness to the spirit of the bear when they slew him" (Vesilind, 1980, p. 494).

PHOTO 6.5. Canon, Johnson, and Whirlpool in Tallinn.

PHOTO 6.6. Free samples of Mars bars.

Estonia was among the last regions in Europe to be Christianized. At the beginning of the thirteenth century, Estonia was invaded by German crusaders, then Swedes and Danes. Later, German knights conquered the country. The Germans were said to have "looked upon the natives more or less as their property. Later, the Swedish kings intervened in favor of the suppressed population" (Ungern-Sternberg, 1939, p. 805).

After the thirteenth-century conquest, commerce became a significant presence for the Estonian urban centers. Tallinn, Tartu, Pärnu, and Narva were members of the Hanseatic League, organized by merchants in northern Europe and the Baltic to protect their trading interests.

The Livonian War lasted from 1558 to 1583. During this time, and in the wars that followed almost continuously until 1620, Sweden took over much of the area that is present-day Estonia. In 1632, *Academia Gustaviana* (named after Gustav, the Swedish king) was opened by the Swedes in Tartu, a town then known as Dorpat.

Peter the Great took Estonia from the Swedes in 1710, and Estonia became one of the Baltic provinces of the Russian Empire. In 1819, peasants were freed from serfdom. On March 26, 1819, Tsar Alexander I passed an act requiring that each head of a freed household choose a surname for himself and his family. The adoption of names began in 1823, and the process lasted until 1834. The year 1860 marked the beginning of a period of national awakening, and circumstances led to the deepening of the conviction to secede from Russia.

In most of rural Estonia, peasants were required to grind grain in their respective manor's mill, but in the western regions, peasants could own a windmill and obtain revenue from it. The owner of a mill typically kept 8.5 percent of the grain milled as payment in lieu of cash. Entrepreneur Jüri Ling still operates a mill on Eemu Farm, near the village of Linnuse, on the island of Muhu. His mill (see Photo 6.7) can grind 50 kilograms (approximately 110 pounds) of flour per hour.

In the nation's largest port, Reval, a construction boom took place during the early twentieth century. Although earlier buildings were traditionally made of wood (see Photo 6.8), turn-of-the century buildings were more elaborate. Photo 6.9 shows a building constructed during the years 1908 and 1909. Photo 6.10 shows another built during 1909 and 1910.

PHOTO 6.7. The Eemu windmill on Muhu.

PHOTO 6.8. Traditional wooden buildings in Tallinn.

PHOTO 6.9. Built 1908-1909.

PHOTO 6.10. Built 1909-1910 on Pikk Street.

In January 1918, the Bolsheviks cancelled the elections to the Estonian Constituent Assembly and established a dictatorship. Representatives of the larger parties in the Land Council formed the Estonian Salvation Committee, and on February 24, 1918, Estonia declared its independence. The Germans immediately occupied Estonia, retreating only on November 11. Invasion by the Bolsheviks prompted the Estonian War of Independence. Infrastructure was destroyed, and the flight of capital was coupled with the severance of ties with traditional markets in Russia (Raun, 1987). A new post office was opened in Reval on November 13, 1918 (see Photo 6.11).

With the Land Act of 1919, estates owned by Baltic Germans were expropriated. The land was then distributed to workers and those who participated in the struggle for independence. The War of Independence ended with the Tartu Peace Treaty, which was signed on February 2, 1920. The treaty specified that Moscow renounced claims to the territory:

> Russia recognizes with no additional conditions the independence and sovereignty of the Estonian state, abandoning voluntarily and forever, all sovereign demands which Russia has had over the people and land of Estonia under the legal state government or international agreements which now in their formal sense are not valid any more in the future. Estonian people and land are not under any obligations to Russia proceeding from their former attachment to Russia.

The Estonian Republic was thus created as a parliamentary democracy, and its capital city, Reval, was renamed Tallinn (see Photo 6.12). The name is derived from Taani Linn (Danish town). The new government nationalized estates in excess of 330 acres and subdivided these. The land was then distributed to farmers. In 1921, Estonia became a member of the League of Nations.

On February 12, 1925, Parliament passed the first Cultural Autonomy of Ethnic Minorities Act. This granted minority groups consisting of at least 3,000 individuals the right to establish cultural self-governments, where they could organize, administer, and monitor public and private educational institutions in their native language, and where they could attend to their other cultural needs and administer institutions and enterprises established for that purpose. This included Germans, Jews, Russians, and Swedes.

PHOTO 6.11. New post office.

PHOTO 6.12. Tallinn market square.

By the mid-1930s, the majority of industrial enterprises in Estonia were small workshops, and Estonian entrepreneurship was becoming increasingly urban (Liuhto, 1996). According to the Estonian Institute, the number of farms in Estonia increased to 139,984 by 1939. This provided permanent employment for 342,050 people, and temporary jobs to another 35,083. In addition, 62,619 wageworkers were employed in Estonia's agricultural sector. The average farm covered 22.7 hectares (about 56 acres), and had 3.3 cows and 2.7 pigs.

In 1939, Estonia was pressured into signing a treaty allowing the Soviets to establish bases in Estonian territories. Following the agreement set out in the "Secret Additional Protocol" of the Soviet-German Molotov-Ribbentrop Pact, Moscow annexed Estonia on August 6, 1941. Then came Nazi occupation, lasting until the return of the Soviets in 1944. Forced collectivization took place between 1947 and 1950. Land once home to feudal manors was divided into 2,213 *kolhoos* (collective farms) and 160 *sovhoos* (state farms). Until 1959, members of a collective were partly paid in-kind, for their work; this included grain and potatoes. In 1959, Estonia became the first Soviet republic to abolish payment in-kind.

In 1967, collective farms were put on a self-management system, and a portion of their profits could be used for bonuses. By the 1970s, agriculture in Estonia was the most efficient in the Soviet Union (see Photo 6.13).

As of 1987, Gorbachev's *perestroika* allowed the creation of new ventures in some industries, including construction. Estonian entrepreneurs demonstrated their initiatives. Given that the USSR's Enterprise Law was not implemented successfully, Estonia drafted its own legislation. On November 16, 1988, the Supreme Soviet of the Estonian Soviet Socialist Republic declared Estonian sovereignty. Estonia was drafting plans for economic autonomy. Vesilind (1989) reported that of all the joint ventures between the Soviet Union and the West, Estonia (with less than 1 percent of the population of the Soviet Union) had over 50 percent of these.

The year 1991 turned out to be one of major changes. The independence of Estonia was restored on August 20 and recognized by the Russian Federation a few days later. Romania soon opened its embassy in Tallinn (see Photo 6.14).

Estonia joined the UN on September 17, 1991. The passing of the Land Reform Act of 1991 led the path for land to be returned to its

PHOTO 6.13. Healthy livestock.

PHOTO 6.14. The Romanian Embassy in Estonia.

previous owners. In 1992, the Agrarian Reform Act reorganized and privatized farmland (see Photo 6.15).

Estonia was the first of the former Soviet republics to issue its own currency, the Eesti kroon (EEK), which was introduced on June 20, 1992. Its value was pegged at the rate of 8 EEK to the German mark. When the euro was introduced, the kroon was pegged at the rate of 15.6466 EEK to the euro.

The process of privatization was streamlined in 1993, with the (now defunct) Estonian Privatization Agency. By 1994, approximately 1,500 small and medium companies had been auctioned, and privatization of the sector was almost complete. Old Soviet industries were abandoned (see Photo 6.16). On January 1, 1995, a free-trade agreement with the European Union came into effect.

On February 15, 1995, the Estonian Commercial Code was adopted, to become effective in September that year. This defines and governs the different types of business entities that can legally operate in Estonia. The types of businesses include

1. the general partnership, known as *täisühing* (TÜ);
2. the limited partnership, known as *usaldusühing* (UÜ);
3. the private limited company, known as *osaühing* (OÜ); and
4. the public limited company, known as *aktsiaselts* (AS).

Estonia joined the WTO on November 13, 1999. By 2001, 75 percent of Estonia's GDP was produced by the private sector (European Bank for Reconstruction and Development). Its task having been successfully accomplished, the Estonian Privatization Agency closed on November 1, 2001.

Promoting Entrepreneurship

As discussed by Blawatt (1995), the Estonian government believes that the entrepreneur and a supportive environment are the keys to a successful economy. A Law on State Aid to Enterprises came into effect in 1994, providing government funds to small and medium enterprises in Estonia. To qualify for financial assistance, a firm could not employ more than 80 employees, and its turnover could not exceed 15 million EEK. This law is no longer in force. Instead, the Law of Competition regulates state aid to enterprises; such aid to small and me-

PHOTO 6.15. Privatized fields.

PHOTO 6.16. No longer in use.

dium enterprises in Estonia is limited to training courses and consulting support.

In 1995, the Nordic Council of Ministers supported an Export Development Program for Estonian companies. This was a joint effort that included the participation of the Helsinki School of Economics, the Trade Council of Iceland, and local talent. After the training sessions, each participant was required to develop an export-marketing plan. The Estonian Chamber of Commerce and Industry decided to become involved in subsequent programs. The largest private organization of business, it promotes export and business contacts between Estonian and foreign enterprises. The Estonian Credit and Export Guarantee Fund, KredEx, provides credits and guarantees for the development of entrepreneurship and the encouragement of exports.

A large variety of export training and consulting options are offered by the Estonian Chamber of Commerce and Industry, by the Estonian Trade Council, by universities, and by training enterprises. Enterprise Estonia is a foundation that provides business training, counseling, and start-up grants to new ventures. It also offers grants to growing small and medium enterprises interested in staff training, and research and development. The Agricultural and Rural Life Credit Fund provides loans to farm-related enterprises. The Estonian Technology Agency (ESTAG) finances technology-related enterprises. The Tartu Biotechnology Park (TBP) promotes biotechnological entrepreneurship.

Since 2000, corporate income tax is no longer payable on reinvested profits. This has created incentives for increasing investment and has made tax paying more transparent and profit declaring more desirable. The retail sector has had notable success (see Photo 6.17).

Foreign Entrepreneurs

Estonia treats entrepreneurs equally, whether they are local or foreign. A governmental body, the Estonian Investment Agency (EIA), promotes foreign direct investment in Estonia. By 2001, accumulated foreign investments in Estonia were 2625 euro per capita, among the highest in Eastern Europe. Entrepreneurs from Finland and Sweden have been especially active in Estonia. Four-fifths of foreign direct investment in Estonia is in Tallinn.

PHOTO 6.17 Rüütli retail area in Pärnu.

Restrictions on foreigners are few. Regulations are transparent, and applied in a fair manner. The country is essentially duty-free, with almost no barriers to trade.

The State of Entrepreneurship and the Small-Business Sector

The privatization of small and medium enterprises was completed very rapidly. The Ministry of Economic Affairs and Communications refers to firms with up to nine employees as microenterprises, those with ten to forty-nine employees are considered small enterprises, and those with fifty to 249 workers are called medium enterprises. According to unpublished sources at the Estonian Chamber of Commerce and Industry, 94 percent of registered firms have less than 100 employees, while the average has about eighteen.

The number of firms grew quickly during the early 1990s. Estimates jumped from three per 1,000 inhabitants in 1990, to seven in 1991, twelve in 1992, and thirteen in 1993. The national average reached twenty-four firms per 1,000 people, but this is not evenly spread. A third of Estonia's population lives in Tallinn where there are forty-five firms per 1,000 inhabitants. Given the vast contrast with eastern and southern regions, the national average is reduced to twenty-four.

In contrast to 1995, when public limited companies represented over 70 percent of firms in Estonia (Elenurm, 2004), private limited companies have recently become the most common form of business entity in this country. In 2002, there were over 20,000 sole proprietorships and 55,000 enterprises in the commercial register.

Liberal foreign trade regulations, coupled with a stable currency, have facilitated the internationalization of Estonian entrepreneurs. In addition, subcontractors have benefited from exemptions of duties. As a result, several sectors have been thriving with international sub-contractual work; these include clothing, machinery, metalwork, and textiles. Elenurm (2004) discussed the results of a survey revealing that Estonian firms were more likely to be involved in foreign subcontracting than were Bulgarian or Polish enterprises. Unlike the situation in advanced industrial economies, subcontracting is less common within Estonia.

Since 1998, the Estonian Export Agency has commissioned surveys on export prospects and constraints. The agency sees Finland, Latvia, and Sweden as important destinations for Estonian goods, and findings support a stage model of internationalization (Elenurm, 2001) resembling that of the Uppsala School (Johanson and Vahlne, 1977; Johanson and Wiedersheim-Paul, 1975).

Estonia also has its share of small-scale farmers, who grow carrots, onions, potatoes, strawberries, and tomatoes on small plots. Pigs and sheep are raised along with dairy cattle and chickens. This is typical on the traditional island of Kihnu, located in the Gulf of Livonia.

Kihnu is home to several small-scale fishing ventures. Teams of fishermen go to sea in wooden boats, much as they did generations ago. Spring fishing season typically begins in May, with the catching of Baltic herring, and lasts through June (see Photo 6.18). The fish are sold to various companies on the mainland, as well as to the local firm Kihnu Kala. Much of the catch thus gets exported to Russia. From mid-July until early September, eel is caught by longlines, along with perch. Eel is a local specialty, as is milk pudding with jam. Starting in October, flounder, pike perch, and perch are caught in nets.

The island of Kihnu is more traditional than is the mainland, and people on this island often retain an element of folklore in their clothing (see Photo 6.19). An abacus is preferred over a cash register. Dur-

PHOTO 6.18. Fishing crew at Kihnu.

PHOTO 6.19. Traditional attire.

ing the ice-free period, from May to December, boats link Kihnu with the mainland. In winter, airplanes use the unpaved landing strip near the village of Sääreküla. A paradox is that islanders, who do not have a toilet with running water, nevertheless use mobile phones and Internet facilities. Agriculture and fishing are no longer as important as they once were. The largest components of Estonia's exports are electronics, machinery, and timber-related products.

Toward the Future

Estonia conducts two-thirds of its international trade with members of the European Union. In 2002, Estonia's applied tariffs averaged 3 percent on fishery products (compared to the European Union average of 12.4 percent); and 14.9 percent on agricultural products (compared to the European Union average of 16.2). Estonia had no tariffs on industrial products (compared to the European Union average of 3.6 percent). Estonia's average tariff on all products was 3.2 percent (compared to the European Union average of 6.3 percent). A requirement for entering the European Union was for Estonia to raise tariffs.

Estonia has a promising future, with an environment of openness, favorable for business, and a tax policy conducive to investment and innovation. The nation has embraced technology, while maintaining family values (see Photo 6.20). Although Estonian small and medium enterprises identified a niche, subcontracting to firms abroad, Estonian innovations and new products are becoming increasingly important. Young Estonians are acquiring an entrepreneurial spirit from an early age (see Photo 6.21).

THE REPUBLIC OF LATVIA

The Republic of Latvia covers 24,595 square miles, bordering Belarus, Estonia, Lithuania, Russia, the Baltic Sea, and the Gulf of Riga.[3] The first Baltic state to become a member of the WTO, Latvia has committed itself to the liberalization of international trade and the elimination of protectionism. In 2002, Latvia was invited to join the European Union as well as NATO. The country was proud to host Eurovision in May 2003.

PHOTO 6.20. Three generations.

Historical Overview

"Latvia's original tribes, the Letts and the Livs, became fused into one through reaction to the crusading efforts of the Brothers of the Sword and the Teutonic Knights" (Chandler, 1938, p. 776). During the Polish-Swedish War that lasted from 1600 to 1629, Sweden won the north of Latvia. The southern provinces were united into a duchy that later won the island of Tobago, subsequently traded for Gambia. The following century brought more fighting, as Russia and Sweden battled for Livonia. The Russians won and came to control all of Latvia, including Livonia. Between 1817 and 1819, serfdom in Latvia was abolished.

On January 24, 1905, 50,000 workers protested during a general strike, and eighty people were killed during clashes with tsarist troops. During World War I, Latvians in the Russian army fought the Germans. The latter occupied half of Latvia by 1915, and Riga on

PHOTO 6.21. Young newsies.

September 3, 1917. With the Brest-Litovsk Treaty of March 1918, the Bolsheviks abandoned all of Latvia. When Germany surrendered on November 11, 1918, Latvia got its opportunity to become its own country, and on November 18, independence was declared (see Photo 6.22).

War against the Russians started in 1919. Chandler wrote, "During the . . . Communist invasion of 1919 . . . we were forced to eat . . . porcupines and armadillos . . . and the elephant at the Riga zoo" (1938, p. 785). The war ended with the Treaty of Riga, at which time Russia vowed to respect Latvia's independence. The international community recognized Latvia on January 26, 1921. The Latvian constitution was adopted on February 15, 1922.

During the period between the World Wars, English was a compulsory language in Latvian schools (see Photo 6.23). About Riga (see Photo 6.24), Chandler explained, "A trilingual city is this beehive of the Daugava" (1938, p. 785). Latvia prospered until Soviet troops invaded on June 17, 1940, and took the republic into the Soviet Union.

In July 1941, the Nazis penetrated Latvia, and during three years of occupation, they killed 90 percent of the country's Jews, many of whom were entrepreneurs. The Red Army returned to Latvia in 1944, reinstating a communist regime and forcing collectivization (see Photo 6.25).

PHOTO 6.22. Independence marked a new era.

PHOTO 6.23. Fluent in English.

PHOTO 6.24. Riga.

PHOTO 6.25. During communist era.

On May 31, 1989, the Latvian Popular Front called for independ-ence from the Soviet Union. That summer Latvians tried to get public support for their cause. If Latvia was to declare independence, which countries would recognize the renegade state? In August 1989, for-mer Prime Minister Joe Clark was asked whether Canada would rec-ognize a Latvian declaration of independence (see Photo 6.26). On December 20, 1989, the Communist Party of Lithuania voted over-whelmingly to break away from the leadership in Moscow (Fein, 1989). This was the first time that a local party organization defied the Kremlin. On May 4, 1990, the Supreme Council of Latvia adopted a declaration to eventually restore independence. On July 16, 1990, the Supreme Council voted to allow private property. On August 21, 1991, the Latvian Parliament voted in favor of independence, recog-nized by Moscow on September 6. On September 17, Latvia joined the UN along with Estonia and Lithuania.

PHOTO 6.26. The Right Honorable Joe Clark with a Latvian flag in Ottawa, August 1989.

The transitional Latvian ruble was introduced on May 7, 1992. This currency was replaced by the lat (LVL), on March 5, 1993. Registration of land began in 1993. The same year, the Agricultural Finance Company established a rural financial system that was later adopted by commercial banks; in its first five years of operations, it approved 2,860 loans, before being taken over by the Mortgage and Land Bank in 1997.

The Agricultural Development Project, financed by the World Bank, was approved in 1994. However, not everything was rosy that year. In 1994, Latvian farmers demanded more price supports, as well as protection from imports. The Farmers' Union, a government coalition partner, accused the Latvian Way faction of violating promises to support agriculture and ignoring demands to impose high customs duties on imported farm products. This prompted a political crisis, leading Prime Minister Valdis Birkavs to announce his resignation.

By 1995, most Latvians had taken out privatization vouchers; 230 state firms were privatized during that year. On February 10, 1999, Latvia became a full member of the WTO. By the end of the year, registration of land in Latvia was completed. On December 10, 1999, Vaira Vike-Freiberga, formerly a psychology professor at the Université de Montréal, became Latvia's first female president. A new law required the use of the Latvian language at most public functions and in business.

In December 2001, the Cabinet of Ministers approved the National Development Plan. A new Commercial Law came into effect on January 1, 2002, simplifying the environment for business in Latvia. In 2002, Estonia implemented new legislation making company income nontaxable until it is distributed, and the response of the Latvian Ministry of Economics was to consider applying local administrative measures to prevent Latvian entrepreneurs from relocating their enterprises. By 2003, over 600,000 properties were registered in the Latvian Landbook, fostering a vibrant market.

Promoting Entrepreneurship

The first National Program for the Development of Small and Medium Enterprises in Latvia was adopted in 1997. Since then, the government has paid special attention to the promotion of small business in rural areas. To this end, the Rural Development Project, approved in 1997, provides a special credit line to subsidize small-scale farmers and entrepreneurs.

Since July 1, 2000, the Innovation Promotion Center has supported Latvian entrepreneurs with technology transfers. Support is also available for members of industrial clusters to participate at international fairs and trade missions. A Latvian National Innovation Program for 2003-2006 was developed in 2002. Its goals include the creation of an innovation-friendly environment; the creation of a sustainable base for the creation and growth of innovative firms; and the promotion of a competitive economic structure.

To encourage the entrepreneurship sector, Latvia has adopted what it terms "a favorable legislative regime" toward entrepreneurs. The corporate income tax rate was temporarily set at 22 percent in 2002, falling to 19 percent in 2003, and 15 percent in 2004. Small and medium enterprises benefit from a 20 percent reduction in income tax payable. To qualify as a small or medium enterprise, the book value of fixed assets must not exceed 70,000 LVL, net turnover must not exceed 200,000 LVL, and the firm must employ an average of 25 persons or less. In the case of supported projects, income tax payable is reduced by 40 percent of the total investment if the total investment exceeds 10 million LVL and is invested within a period of less than three years (*Economic Development of Latvia,* Ministry of Economics, Riga, December 2002).

Latvia has four free zones, designed to develop and promote trade, industry, and transport: the Liepàja[4] Special Economic Zone; the Rezekne Special Economic Zone; the Riga Free Port; and Ventspils Free Port. A variety of industrial, commercial, and service activities are permitted in these zones, and there is no limit on the duration during which goods may be stored here. No VAT is assessed for most goods and services provided in these zones. The Liepàja Special Economic Zone and the Rezekne Special Economic Zone provide additional tax incentives. These include a rebate of 80 to 100 percent of property taxes, and an 80 percent rebate on corporate income tax applicable to income derived within the zone. Although these zones may seem attractive on paper, interviewees told me that the zones are ineffective. A commonly heard complaint is that Latvia lacks good governmental support for small and medium firms (see Photo 6.27).

PHOTO 6.27. What about SMEs?

Although the government appears to have good intentions, non-governmental organizations are also trying to promote entrepreneurship in Latvia. Among these is the Latvian Chamber of Commerce and Industry, a voluntary and politically neutral organization of firms from a variety of sectors across the country. This chamber has over 900 members, of which 85 percent are small and medium enterprises.

The American Chamber of Commerce in Latvia also promotes entrepreneurship there. Among its annual events is the Student Business Plan Competition, designed to foster entrepreneurship. This chamber also lobbies the Latvian government to create a stable business environment. In 2003, the American Chamber of Commerce was working on a bankruptcy law for Latvia.

Foreign Entrepreneurs

The Ministry of Economics consulted extensively with Western economists and lawyers to prepare an appropriate policy for foreign investment (Pavlovskis, 1990). The Law on Foreign Investment, adopted November 5, 1991, and later amended, provides foreign investors with national treatment. An added advantage is that foreign investors are exempt from paying customs duties when importing fixed assets. In addition, the Latvian Development Agency offers foreign partners one-stop-shop services to help with the successful entry of foreign direct investment. Entrepreneurs receive all required services in one place.

The State of Entrepreneurship and the Small-Business Sector

In 2002, there were 42,534 economically active businesses in Latvia, of which 42,252 were small and medium enterprises with a maximum of 250 employees. Four percent of the firms were considered medium firms (defined as having between fifty and 250 employees), 20 percent qualified as small businesses (with ten to fifty employees), and 76 percent were microenterprises (with no more than nine employees). Half of the small and medium enterprises were operating in Riga (see Photo 6.28). Documents at the Latvian Chamber of Commerce and Industry indicate that Latvia had fewer than twenty enter-

PHOTO 6.28. Riga.

prises per 1,000 people. In the European Union, the rate was two to three times that, depending on the region.

At the request of the Ministry of Economics, the Central Statistical Board of Latvia conducted a study of small and medium enterprises in 2002. Respondents cited the following as factors hindering the development of their firms:

1. shortage of resources;
2. late payment or nonpayment by customers;
3. difficulties with access to credit;
4. a growing shortage of skilled employees; and
5. inadequate information about state assistance.

Toward the Future

Latvia has been highly dedicated to fighting corruption, and the government has established an anticorruption bureau (the KNAB) to tackle this issue. Much has been done to improve the environment for entrepreneurship in Latvia. The future looks bright for entrepreneurship in this country, especially with membership in the European Union and NATO.

THE REPUBLIC OF LITHUANIA

With a coastline of about sixty miles along the Baltic Sea, the Republic of Lithuania is 25,170 square miles, neighboring Belarus, Latvia, Poland, and Russia.[5] Lithuania was the first Soviet republic to challenge the monopoly of the Communist Party and the first to declare its independence from the Soviet Union. Since independence, the nation has benefited from its adherence to strict policies imposed by the IMF, constraining the money supply and reducing inflation. Privatization in Lithuania has been among the fastest and most comprehensive of Eastern Europe, thanks to a voucher program. Lithuania enjoys a solid currency, an export boom, zero inflation, shrinking unemployment, and the highest growth rate in Europe. Efforts are being made to further foster entrepreneurship in this country; however, entrepreneurs still perceive many constraints.

Historical Overview

In 1236, Duke Mindaugas united local chieftains to defeat the Livonian knights, thus establishing Lithuania. In 1253, he was crowned king. Under the Krëva Act of 1385, Lithuanian Grand Duke Jogaila married the Polish Crown Princess Jadwiga. By the end of the fourteenth century, the Grand Duchy of Lithuania ruled a vast territory. Among its castles was that at Trakai (see Photo 6.29).

Jews were allowed into the Grand Duchy of Lithuania in 1503. They became very active in establishing international trade links. In 1569, Poland was united with the Grand Duchy of Lithuania, forming the Commonwealth of Poland and Lithuania, an empire that spread from the Baltic Sea to the Black Sea. In 1795, Lithuania was absorbed by Russia. Tsarist rule banned the Latin script. Until 1861, serfs were legally attached to the land and transferred with it in sales and leases. Serfdom was eliminated in 1861, at which time the serfs were granted personal freedom.

In 1905, an autonomous Lithuania was created as a province of the Russian Empire. In 1915, German forces occupied Lithuania, and under German tutelage, which lasted from 1915 to 1918, the Lithuanian Council proclaimed the independence of Lithuania on February 16, 1918. Vilnius became the capital city of the Republic of Lithuania. Soviet troops entered Lithuania in January 1919, followed by Polish

PHOTO 6.29. Castle at Trakai.

forces in April 1919. In October 1919, Poland occupied Vilnius. In 1920, Kaunas became the national capital. In 1922, a major land reform was initiated, and properties belonging to feudal manors were distributed to the peasantry. In 1923, Poland annexed Vilnius. Kaunas served as capital city of Lithuania until 1939.

Since 1871, Memelland (the capital of which was Memel) had been the northern part of the German province of East Prussia. With World War I, Memelland came under the French Sector of Allied occupation. In 1923, Memelland was annexed to Lithuania, and Memel's ethnic Germans were given a degree of autonomy. Memel was annexed to Germany in March 1939. After the war, its name was changed to Klaipėda.

As was the case with Estonia and Latvia, Lithuania's independence came to an end after the 1939 Molotov-Ribbentrop Pact divided Europe between Germany and the Soviet Union. Soviet occupation was interrupted by three years of Nazi occupation during which 94 percent of Lithuania's Jews were exterminated. Soviet troops pushed out the Nazis in 1944, and Lithuania was again merged into the Soviet Union on July 7, 1944. The Soviets deported a quarter of a million Lithuanians to Siberia and Polish Lithuanians were extradited to Poland.

Under Soviet occupation, industry (see Photo 6.30) catered to the needs of Russia. Although employees were poorly paid, necessities and transportation (see Photo 6.31) were subsidized. As was the case throughout the Soviet Union, automobiles were for the elite (see Photo 6.32). Most Lithuanians lived modestly (see Photo 6.33), and economic disadvantage was evident (see Photo 6.34).

On December 20, 1989, the Lithuanian Communist Party declared itself independent from that of the Soviet Union. On March 11, 1990, Lithuania declared its independence from the Soviet Union. This was the first splintering in the unity of the Soviet Union, and the Kremlin demanded a withdrawal of the declaration. On March 15, Soviet deputies in Moscow resolved that, "the decisions taken Sunday by the Lithuanian parliament—suspending the Soviet Constitution and re-establishing the Baltic republic's prewar independence—were not legally binding" (Fein, 1990, p. A1). President Mikhail Gorbachev set a deadline of March 19 for Lithuania to reverse its decision to secede. Premier Nikolai Ryzhkov ordered the KGB and other central government bodies to stop Lithuania from carrying out measures that would disengage Lithuania's economy from that of the Soviet Union. In addition, he told his ministers to take immediate direct management of all centrally owned businesses in Lithuania. The premier also instructed the Interior Ministry in Moscow to prevent Lithuania from establishing its own customs system. The Soviet president subse-

PHOTO 6.30. Industrial complex at Rokiškis near Lithuania's border with Belarus.

PHOTO 6.31. Local transport in Vilnius.

PHOTO 6.32. For the elite.

PHOTO 6.33. Typical home.

PHOTO 6.34. Traditional transport.

quently ordered Lithuanian citizens to surrender all their weapons. On April 17, 1990, Moscow imposed an economic blockade on Lithuania. In January 1991, thousands of pro-Soviet demonstrators protested against price increases implemented by the Lithuanian government.

On February 12, 1991, Iceland became the first country to recognize the independence of Lithuania; the United States did so on September 2. In June 1993, Lithuania replaced the ruble with the lita (LTL). A currency board arrangement has been in effect since April 1, 1994. On June 12, 1995, Lithuania signed an Association Agreement with the European Union. By August 1995, 5,700 formerly state-owned enterprises had been privatized. Established in 1995, the Lithuanian Privatization Agency took over functions previously administered by the Ministry for the Economy. A property restitution law, on July 1, 1997, allowed pre-WWII property owners and their descendants to reclaim property nationalized by the Soviets.

With Lithuanian corporate income tax at 25 percent, the Lithuanian Taxation Inspectorate became concerned when, in 2000, Estonia implemented new legislation making company income nontaxable until it is distributed.

Lithuania joined the WTO in 2001. That same year, the Law on Company Bankruptcy, the Law on Company Restructuring, and the Law on Cover Funds were passed. The Law on Cover Funds grants payments to a company with no assets.

In 2002, considerable debate ensued over joining the European Union. In March, 6,000 farmers complained to the Lithuanian prime minister. Tracevskis reported the statement of the chairman of the Association of Lithuanian Vegetable' Producers: "We'll lose Lithuania's freedom and traditions after joining the EU. . . . The EU needs our market. They don't need our farmers" (2002, p. 7). Nevertheless, in May 2003, with 62 percent of the electorate participating in the European Union referendum, 91 percent of voters opted for joining the union.

Promoting Entrepreneurship

Lithuania has been successful at creating an environment that supports local entrepreneurs. Under the authority of the Ministry of Economy, the Lithuanian Development Agency for Small and Medium Enterprises was established in 1996. Its purpose is to stimulate the birth rate of Lithuanian small and medium enterprises; to increase their competitiveness and their survival rate; to increase the level of IT literacy among them; and to promote job creation. It also promotes cooperation between small and medium enterprises and large corporations (see Dana, 2000c; Dana, Etemad, and Wright, 1999, 2000).

The Lithuanian Development Agency for Small and Medium Enterprises developed a Web site (http://www.svv.lt), which has been serving as an active portal of information for entrepreneurs. Topics include setting up a business, funding opportunities, investment, labor relations, exporting, importing and customs, and other taxes.

More recently, efforts have been focused on developing an entrepreneurship-friendly public policy. In July 2001, Resolution N° 887 provided for guarantees of loans extended to small and medium enterprises. With the aim of increasing the competitiveness and effectiveness of the sector, in July 2002, Resolution N° 1175 approved several development measures, including the enhancement of the legal and economic environment. A program called the Formation of a Favorable Service Infrastructure for Small and Medium Businesses implements development projects to stimulate and improve the skills of first-time entrepreneurs. Supported by the government, the program also provides entrepreneurs accessibility to information.

Resolution N° 1175 also called for an amendment Resolution N° 887, in order to increase the number of loan recipients. In addition, Resolution N° 1175 called for the provision of training and consultancy services for entrepreneurs in Lithuania, and for the encouragement of women in the sector.

Five independent chambers of commerce, industry, and crafts—in Kaunas, Klaipėda (formerly known in German, as Memel), Panevėžys, Šiauliai, and Vilnius—also attempt to stimulate enterprise development, supporting the initiatives of entrepreneurs and representing their interest in government structures. Likewise, the Association of Lithuanian Chambers of Commerce, Industry, and Crafts represents the interests of business. An umbrella, organization, it represents the interests of entrepreneurs at government ministries, the Customs Department, and the State Tax Inspectorate. The association awards the Lithuanian Exports Prize. Along similar lines, the Confederation of Lithuanian Industrialists organizes competitions to encourage entrepreneurship. Among these are competitions for Best Product and Successful Company.

Foreign Entrepreneurs

Rather than rely on foreign buyers to assist in the privatization process, Lithuania implemented a voucher program and made possible employee ownership. The European Commission expressed concern over Article N° 47 of the Lithuanian constitution, prohibiting non-Lithuanians from purchasing arable land, and also over the system of permits that limits purchases of nonarable land. This was said to hinder the climate for foreign entrepreneurs in Lithuania, and a 2003 law introduced a gradual phase-in process allowing citizens of selected countries to make some purchases in the medium-term future.

The State of Small Business and Entrepreneurship

The Law on Small and Medium Business Development was passed in 1998. It defined a microenterprise as a family business (see Photo 6.35); a small enterprise is an enterprise with the average number of people on payroll not in excess of nine; and a medium enterprise is one with the average number of people on payroll not in excess of

PHOTO 6.35. Family businesses.

forty-nine. On January 1, 2002, Lithuania had 53,228 enterprises with fewer than ten employees; 11,139 firms with ten to forty-nine employees; and 4,059 ventures with fifty to 249 employees.

The Law on Small and Medium Business Development was amended on October 22, 2002. This legislation redefined a medium enterprise as being an independent firm with fewer than 250 employees and annual income not exceeding LTL 138 million, or total assets with a book value not exceeding LTL 93 million. As well, a small enterprise was redefined as being an independent firm with fewer than fifty employees, and annual income not exceeding LTL 24 million, or the book value of its assets not exceeding LTL 17 million. The amendment redefined a microenterprise as an independent firm with fewer than ten employees and an annual income not exceeding LTL 7 million, or the book value of its assets not exceeding LTL 5 million (see Photo 6.36). The legislation provides small and medium enterprises with financial assistance, including tax relief, access to loans on favorable terms, provision of guarantees, credit insurance, reimbursement of certain cash outlays, and subsidies for job creation. In addition, it provides for advisory services, training, and the establishment of business centers and incubators. The law came into effect on January 1, 2003.

Entrepreneurs in Lithuania now benefit from a variety of incentives, along with assistance from numerous business incubators, credit

PHOTO 6.36. Microenterprise redefined.

unions, industrial parks, and science and technology parks. Assistance is also available from the Lithuanian Agricultural Agency for International Trade, the Lithuanian Development Agency for Small and Medium Enterprises, the Lithuanian Economic Development Agency, the Lithuanian Export Import Insurance, the Lithuanian Innovation Center, and the National Payment Agency.

Toward the Future

Resolution N° 1175, passed on July 19, 2002, states that the small- and medium-business sector constitutes one of the most important objectives of economic policy in Lithuania. The document predicts that unemployment will fall, and the number of new ventures will grow. However, the entrepreneurs I interviewed expressed concern about the long-term survival of their firms. They complained about increased bureaucratic procedures, rising labor costs, and the introduction of new taxes. In addition, many retailers (see Photo 6.37) perceive a threat from Western chains (see Photo 6.38) that could push them out of business.

PHOTO 6.37. Feeling threatened.

PHOTO 6.38. Young Lithuanians outside McDonald's.

Chapter 7

Toward the Future

Contrary to Marxist dogma, the nationalization of factories and farms did not increase motivation among workers. It did the opposite. Emmott's question is quite appropriate: "Why, then, did command economies take so long to fail?" (1999, p. 9).

Perhaps a more pressing question is: How can the continued success of transition be ensured? Behrman and Rondinelli (1999) observed,

> Despite the fact that many Central and Eastern European countries have made progress in restructuring their economies and increasing the economic output of the private sector, all countries in Central Europe, the Balkans, the Baltics, and the former Soviet Union face serious challenges. (p. 1)

One of these challenges is making a market economy work. According to McMillan (2002), there are five prerequisites for a market to work:

1. the smooth flow of information;
2. people may be assumed to live up to promises;
3. competition must be fostered;
4. property rights must be protected; and
5. the market must not have a negative impact on third parties.

The preceding chapters of this book have shown that successful transition to a market economy is possible. Poland's big-bang model of transition, the architect of which was Harvard University's Professor Jeffrey Sachs, is to be praised for having ended shortages and queues. Hungary's more cautious approach was also successful. One difference is that the small-business sector grew especially fast in

Hungary, providing mainly part-time employment. Lithuania cut government spending, resulting in a surplus. Estonia and Slovenia also shine among the success stories.

Yet the flow of information does not exhibit equal levels of smoothness across Eastern Europe and not all people are living up to promises. In some economies competition is weak in certain sectors, and property rights are not protected to the same degree across countries. The degree of work ethic also varies (see Photo 7.1).

Another serious problem facing several economies in transition is that social inequities may limit economic development in the future. Where transition has led to impoverishment, the underground economy is often perceived to be a means of survival. Although entrepreneurship is a positive force, problems can arise from an increased income gap between new entrepreneurs and the masses. The solution is to identify ways to broaden participation in economic development and to get young people involved (see Photo 7.2).

What is needed is a mutually reinforcing set of concerted actions, aimed at fostering conditions for start-ups and spin-offs; expansion of small and firms; and emergence from the parallel economy. The means to these aims could be facilitated by

1. promoting a strong work ethic and a culture of enterprise,[1] increasing the social desirability of becoming an entrepreneur such that entrepreneurs can be convinced of the rightness of their occupation, even in societies that traditionally frowned on entrepreneurship;
2. developing a program of education useful for entrepreneurs (see Kirby, 1989) while improving vocational education;
3. encouraging innovation, within the realm of legal activities;[2]
4. developing a facilitative environment by dismantling barriers such as excessive paperwork requirements;[3] and
5. maintaining a stable legal framework.

Transition to a market economy has often been prescribed as the means to national prosperity; it is important, however, to examine the broader picture. Variations in host environments, culture, infrastructure, and policy lead to unequal propensities toward entrepreneurship, and the phenomenon takes on different styles with local flavors.

PHOTO 7.1. Did not need to work so hard under communism.

PHOTO 7.2. Young and motivated.

IMPLICATIONS FOR POLICYMAKERS

Writing during the eighteenth century, Adam Smith discussed the importance of a stable legal framework (1892). This is crucial even today and is especially important in transitional economies. Even when governments strive for rapid reform, they can be seriously handicapped by the lack of established legal frameworks. O'Driscoll, Holmes, and Kirkpatrick (2001) found that in the absence of a firm commitment to a solidly established rule of law, even a decline in government intervention has not led to economic freedom. Where bureaucrats are insufficiently trained and where control techniques are lacking, vague laws provide opportunities for inconsistent discretionary treatment, and this opens the door to corruption. Much literature discusses the fact that the demand for bribes by government employees decreases the attractiveness of being an entrepreneur in the formal sector (Cornelius and Lenain, 1997; Johnson et al., 2000; Johnson, Kaufmann, and Zoido-Lobaton, 1998; Shleifer, 1997; Shleifer and Vishny, 1993b, 1994).

A priority for governments should be to determine the appropriate degree of regulation to enact and to enforce, such that the benefits to society exceed the costs of compliance. John Stuart Mill (1869) argued that the only purpose for which power can be rightfully exercised over a member of society against his or her will is to prevent harm onto others. Although some regulation is required to ensure order, excessive intervention is counterproductive; this was acknowledged in the Bologna Charter, the summary of the first OECD Ministerial Conference on SMEs, held June 13-15, 2000.

Experts are skeptical of targeted economic development programs because these often subsidize the wrong people, with no lasting benefits. Although microfinance programs and credit-guarantee schemes seem to be most appropriate for transitional economies, no funding should be distributed without postloan or postgrant training. Recipients should be familiarized with finance, tax, and payroll issues. Otherwise, of what use is capital unless there is knowledge to invest it?

It appears that the optimal level of regulation and government intervention is culture specific. Policymakers should keep in mind that the success of a policy or program in the West does not guarantee equal success elsewhere. For this reason, it is crucial to avoid translocating these from one environment to a different one. To be effective, policies and programs should be appropriate to the culture of a society. Policymakers should be aware of the cultural attributes of different ethnic groups, and policy should consider these differences. Keeping in mind that the key to economic growth is granting enterprises and consumers the economic freedom to respond to incentives, policy priorities should include

1. reduction of poverty, by accelerating agricultural development, and in some cases by controlling population growth;
2. improvement of property rights and the legal basis for commerce;
3. strengthening of the financial infrastructure;
4. further liberalization of trade;
5. revision of policies to attract foreign investment, with an understanding that investment takes place when there is expectation of adequate return;
6. improvement of the management of government expenditures; and
7. reform of tax policies such as to broaden the state's revenue base, in a fair manner, without creating disincentives to existing entrepreneurs (e.g., a tax holiday for new entrants could prompt existing firms to close and restart to benefit).

IMPLICATIONS FOR EDUCATORS

Where entrepreneurial spirit exists, new-venture programs may further enhance the environment for entrepreneurship, as is the case in the United States. However, in a transitional society with little experience of legitimate entrepreneurship, education should first focus on encouraging an entrepreneurship-friendly ideology. Where a vibrant entrepreneurial class is absent, this absence may be due to the public policy environment, or to the lack of to social norms that affect propensity for entrepreneurship and the nature of enterprise. Štulhofer (1999) discussed the distrust of the state, banks, and legal institutions, especially among the elderly (see Photo 7.3).

Due to the rationalization of jobs during transition, and in the absence of appropriate retraining, many people have become self-employed, often in informal or covert activities. After decades of central planning that considered entrepreneurship to be criminal, the concepts underlying entrepreneurship are not fully understood, and

PHOTO 7.3. Once burned, twice shy.

there is confusion as legitimate entrepreneurship is mixed with illegal transactions. It would be beneficial, therefore, for educators to promote acceptance of entrepreneurship as a legitimate, value-adding activity. As was said by Child and Czeglédy, "In the context of something as fundamental as the transformation of Eastern Europe, managerial learning extends to the redefinition of the tasks themselves and of the goals which they reflect" (1996, p. 176).

The problem is that much education in transitional economies has focused on managerial content and methods, while trainees are told the procedures to follow (Kenny and Trick, 1995). Emphasis should be placed on values as well as technical content. In the absence of the values related to sustainable long-term entrepreneurship—such as asceticism, frugality, thrift, and work ethic (Weber, 1904-1905)—managerial skills are not being put to optimal use.

Across Eastern Europe there is often a mismatch between market demand and skills available in the workforce. The workforce needs retraining in skills that are in demand. Consequently, the technical content of courses needs to be adapted to changes in the economy. As the economy of a nation becomes increasingly complex, marketing functions will mature and become more specialized. Training will be required to help managers solve new problems of planning distribution and transportation. A difficulty, however, is that educational initiatives are fragmented.

IMPLICATIONS FOR WESTERN MANAGERS AND INVESTORS

If one generalization can be made about doing business in the transitional economies of Europe, it is that across these vast countries transactions and profits are often a function of networks and relationships (see Photo 7.4). Preferential treatment—when reciprocal—reduces overall transaction costs, thus increasing efficiency, competitiveness, and profitability. This is generally true, regardless of the specifics of an environment. Nevertheless, one must be cautious in attempting to generalize across cultures.

In the West, where the firm-type sector prevails, societies tend to take a form specific to them (Geertz, 1963). They resemble one another in their value system, class structure, family organization, governance, and economic models. Parsons (1951) identified this

PHOTO 7.4. Networking.

over half a century ago. It is still true today, and we have come to refer to this as globalization, but generalizations can be deceiving. Modern economies in the Occident are democratic and their mainstream society is secular. In the transitional economies of Eastern Europe, there is substantially less uniformity than is the case in the West. Some societies are more religious than others, and there are important differences between religions. Attitudes toward business also vary greatly. As summarized by Lewis,

> If a religion lays stress upon material values, upon thrift and productive investment, upon honesty in commercial relations, upon experimentation and risk-bearing . . . it will be helpful to growth, whereas in so far as it is hostile to these things, it tends to inhibit growth. (1955, p. 105)

Perhaps the most valuable advice one can give to Westerners in Eastern Europe is that the importance of cultural differences must never be underestimated. There is *not* one East European model. There is not one standard approach to transition. This is further complicated in pluralistic societies, where unlike cultures each have their own implicit and explicit assumptions. Risk also varies with different types of pluralism. Melting-pot pluralism—the situation prevailing when minorities adapt to a secular mainstream society—is stable. In contrast, when ethnic groups do not share a mainstream society, polarization can result in violence.

Nor is there consistency across time, and managers should keep in mind that in many transitional economies, the newly emerging private sector lacks professional, financial, and economic structure. Rules change frequently. What is legal today may be banned tomorrow, and vice versa. Also, the ownership of property is not always very clearly documented, and the liquidity of immoveable assets is often delayed. Where acquisition is not practical, foreign investors may enter markets via networks. Given that communist planners traditionally emphasized vertical integration, managers might find it necessary to explain how, in a market economy, synergy often comes from horizontal integration.

Western managers have mastered the art and science of doing business in the firm-type sector. In transitional economies, many opportunities are to be found in the bazaar, where the movement of raw materials, processing, distribution, and sales are intertwined activities.

The focus on relationships supersedes that which is being sold. A sliding-price system results in prices that are negotiated, reflecting not only the cost or perceived value of a good or service, but also negotiating skills, the relationship between the buyer and the seller, and possibly the time, as well. Also important is an understanding of the parallel sector.

TOWARD FUTURE RESEARCH

Although economic growth has been prescribed as the remedy for poverty, experience shows that growth creates problems of its own. Of what good is rapid transition if its adverse effects are uncontrolled? It is useful to look not only at the creation of wealth, but also at its distribution.

It would be a fallacy to attempt to understand economic transition in isolation. The move toward market economics is invariably an element of greater changes taking place in society. From an economics perspective, transition involves an increase in the efficiency of the use of resources toward the achievement of measurable objectives. From a human perspective, there are additional issues to consider. One must be wary of transition for the sake of change; *transition should be viewed as the means to a better life for members of society.*

What must change and what need not? More research is needed here. Classic theories cannot simply be taken and injected into transitional economies, in neglect of the environment in which they are to be placed (see Photo 7.5). Even among the former Soviet republics, there are important differences. Historical, sociocultural, and economic contexts appear to be important factors affecting transition and the environment for business. Societies cannot all adopt legitimate entrepreneurial systems at an equal pace, nor should they be expected to.

Future research might focus on the parallel market and its causal factors, including

1. the low initial role of commerce and services;
2. the high degree of political liberalization;
3. the lack of macrostability in some countries; and
4. the lack of developed market institutions.

PHOTO 7.5. Where old meets new.

TOWARD THE FUTURE

Although the West has provided much funding to transitional economies and infrastructure has been greatly improved in recent years, complaints are often heard about the problems arising from transition. Outsiders often fail to realize that transition to a market economy requires more than funding and infrastructure. In the words of Behrman and Rondinelli, "Although financing is important, it is not the most critical bottleneck to private enterprise development" (1999, p. 11). In fact, transition also involves mind-set. Business takes place between people, and the interaction between the parties does not take place in a vacuum, but rather it is part of a social system.

Whether transition is taking place gradually or rapidly, alongside political reform or in its absence, the mind-set of people often holds on to perceptions of former times. Consequently, in order to gain an understanding of the behavior of entrepreneurs and of the nature of their enterprises, one must first become familiar with a variety of explanatory variables, including culture, historical experience, and government policy. Transition is a function of all of these causal variables.

The move to a market economy—transition—is process driven, and this necessitates the understanding of people and their culture. Entrepreneurship cannot and will not gain the same level of acceptability in different cultures, nor should reform take place at an even pace.

Notes

Chapter 1

1. For a survey of empirical studies on privatization, see Megginson and Netter (2001).
2. See also Sacks (1993).
3. See also Hisrich and Vecsenyi (1990) and Zapalska and Zapalska (1999).
4. For discussions of transaction costs, see Coase (1937); Williamson (1975); and Williamson and Masten (1999).
5. For discussions of corruption, see Glinkina (1998) and Shleifer and Vishny (1993a).
6. For discussions of entrepreneurship in the informal sector, see De Soto (1989); Morris and Pitt (1995); Peattie (1987); Portes, Castells, and Benton (1989); Rosser, Rosser, and Ahmed (2000); Sanders (1987); and Tokman (1978).
7. For a discussion of subsistence self-employment, see Cole and Fayissa (1991).
8. For discussions of entrepreneurship in the covert sector, see Fadahunsi and Rosa (2002) and Feige and Ott (1999).
9. For a discussion of the sex trade in Eastern Europe, see Jacobs (2002).

Chapter 2

1. This section contains information obtained during interviews conducted with representatives of several organizations in Tirana, including: the Ministry of Agriculture and Food; the Ministry of Finance; and the Ministry of Industry, Transport and Trade. Statistics were provided by the National Institute of Statistics. The section also draws extensively on Dana (1996a, 2000b).
2. The International Monetary Fund (IMF) and the World Bank were established in Bretton Woods, New Hampshire, in 1944.
3. The mandate of the IMF is international monetary stability.
4. The mandate of the World Bank is to promote economic and social development.

Chapter 3

1. This section draws extensively on Dana (1994c, 2002).
2. See Chater (1930) for a description of the times.
3. This section contains information obtained during interviews conducted with representatives of several organizations, including the Democratic circle in Tuzla; the Muslim Bosniak Organization in Sarajevo; and the Serb Civil Council in Sarajevo.

Statistics were provided by the Agency for Statistics. The section also draws extensively on Dana (1999b).

4. For a discussion of middleman minorities, see Bonacich (1973) and Cherry (1990).

5. Whereas the mandate of the World Bank is to promote economic and social development, the mandate of the UNDP is human development.

6. This section contains information obtained during interviews conducted with representatives of several organizations in Zagreb, including the Croatian Agency for Small Business; the Ministry of Agriculture and Forestry; the Ministry for Crafts, Small and Medium-Sized Enterprises; the Ministry of Economy; the Ministry of Finance; and the Institute of Public Finance. Statistics were provided by the Croatian Bureau of Statistics.

7. This section contains information obtained during interviews conducted with representatives of several organizations in Skopje, including the Ministry of Development; the Ministry of Economy; and the Ministry of Labor and Social Policy. Statistics were provided by the State Statistical Office. The section also draws extensively on Dana (1998c).

8. For discussions about the effects of sojourning on entrepreneurship, see Light and Bonacich (1988) and Posadas and Guyotte (1990).

9. This sections contains information obtained during interviews conducted with representatives of several organizations in Belgrade, including the Agency for the Development of Small and Medium-sized Enterprises and Entrepreneurship; the Ministry of Economy and Privatization; the Ministry of Education and Privatization; the Ministry of Finance and Economy; and the Ministry of Foreign Affairs in Podgorica. Statistics were provided by the Federal Statistical Office.

10. This section contains information obtained during interviews conducted with representatives of several organizations in Ljubljana, including the Bank of Slovenia; the Ministry of the Economy; the Ministry for Small Business and Tourism; and the Small Business Development Center. Statistics were provided by the Statistical Office of the Republic of Slovenia. The section also draws extensively on Dana (1994c).

Chapter 4

1. This section contains information obtained during interviews conducted with representatives of several organizations in Sofia, including the Agency for Small and Medium-Sized Enterprises; the Bulgarian Chamber of Commerce and Industry; the Bulgarian Foreign Investment Agency; the Bulgarian International Business Association; the Center for Mass Privatization; the Ministry of Culture; the Ministry of Economy; the Ministry of Education and Science; the Ministry of Finance; the Ministry of Foreign Affairs; the Ministry of Health; the Ministry of Industry; the Ministry of Trade and Tourism; and the Podkrepa Trade Union. Statistics were provided by the Bulgarian National Bank, the National Statistical Institute, and the World Bank. The section also draws extensively on Dana (1999a).

2. Other members are the Czech Republic, Hungary, Poland, Romania, Slovakia, Slovenia, and, since March 1, 2003, Croatia.

3. Based on roundtable discussions with Sephardic Jews in Bourgas, Pazardzik, Plovdiv, Ruse, Samokov, Sofia, Varna, and Vidin. In Bourgas, Mme. Ernesta Leon ben-Rae (née Confino)—born in 1912—was most helpful, agreeing to several lengthy interviews in her home. In Plovdiv, Josif Mitrani was very welcoming. In Samokov, entrepreneur Yosif Gavriel (glassmaker) and his daughter Violetta (owner of the biggest electronic store in the region) were most generous with their time and willingness to provide information. In Sofia, Lili Bourjeva was most co-operative.

4. This section contains information obtained during interviews conducted with representatives of several organizations in Prague, including the Business Development Agency; the Ministry of Agriculture; and the Ministry of Industry and Economy. Statistics were provided by the Statistical Office. The section also draws extensively on Dana (2000d).

5. A detailed account of the communist takeover appears in Lauret (1978).

6. For a discussion of the retail trade and consumer services, see Earle et al. (1994).

7. This section draws heavily on Dana (1994b).

8. This section contains information obtained during interviews conducted with representatives of several organizations in Budapest, including the Chamber of Commerce and Industry of Pest County; the Hungarian Chamber of Handicrafts; the Hungarian Foundation for Enterprise Promotion; the Hungarian Investment and Trade Development Agency; the Ministry of Economy and Transport; the Ministry of Foreign Affairs; and the National Union of Handicraftsmen. Statistics were provided by the Hungarian Central Statistical Office.

9. A colorful account of interwar Hungary is found in Patric (1938b).

10. For a discussion of the new constitution, see Popov (1989).

11. This section contains information obtained during interviews conducted with representatives of several organizations in Warsaw including the Industrial Development Agency; the Ministry of Economy; the Ministry of Finance; the Polish Agency for Enterprise Development; the Polish Agency for Foreign Investment; and the Polish Craft and Small Business Association. Statistics were provided by the Central Statistical Office.

12. Case studies of Poland show the importance of skills (Johnson and Loveman, 1995).

13. It should be noted that the nature of the retail sector is changing. The issue of the big growth of microfirms in retailing was a major feature of the 1990s, but low profits have since prompted a decline in the number of microretailers.

14. This section contains information obtained during interviews conducted with representatives of several organizations in Bucharest including the Academy of Economic Studies; the Authority for Privatization and Management of State Ownership; the Chamber of Commerce; the Chamber of Commerce and Industry of Romania; the Council for Economic Coordination, Strategy and Reform; the Ministry of Finance; the Ministry of Foreign Affairs; the Ministry for SMEs and Cooperatives; the National Agency for Privatization; the National Agency for Small and Medium Enterprises of Romania; the National Council of Small and Medium Sized Private Enterprises (CNIPMMR); the Romania Credit Guarantee Fund; the Romanian Bank for Development; the Romanian Commercial Bank in Piatra Neamt; and the Romanian Development Agency. Especially helpful was Mayor Lungu Serafim of

Targu Neamt. Statistics were provided by the National Bank of Romania and the National Commission for Statistics.

15. This section contains information obtained during interviews conducted with representatives of several organizations in Bratislava, including the Ministry of Economy; the Ministry of Finance; and the National Agency for Development of Small and Medium Enterprises. Statistics were provided by the Statistical Office. The section also draws extensively on Dana (2000d).

16. Slovakia uses the same definition as the European Union.

Chapter 5

1. Since the focus of this book is Eastern Europe, this chapter deals with the European members of the CIS. Chapter 6 discusses the Baltic Republics. For an analysis of the Central-Asian members of the CIS, see Dana (2002).

2. In Russia, World War II is known as the Great Patriotic War.

3. This section contains information obtained during interviews conducted with representatives of several organizations in Minsk, including the Ministry of Economy; the Ministry of Entrepreneurship and Investments; and the National Agency for SME Development. Statistics were provided by and the Ministry of Statistics and Analysis.

4. This section contains information obtained during interviews conducted with representatives of several organizations in Chişinău, including the Association of Small Business Entrepreneurs of Balti; the Ministry of the Economy; the National Association of the Small Private Enterprises of Moldova; and the Small Business Association of Moldova. Statistics were provided by the Department for Statistics and Sociology of the Republic of Moldova. The section also draws extensively on Dana (1997c).

5. This section contains information obtained during interviews conducted with representatives of several organizations in Moscow, including the Agricultural Ministry; the Central Committee of the Russian Union of Medium and Small Business Workers; the Economy Ministry; the Finance Ministry; and the Foreign Ministry. Statistics were provided by the State Committee of Statistics of Russia. The section also draws extensively on Robinson et al. (2001).

6. For a detailed account, see Graves (1939).

7. For a discussion of Uzbek entrepreneurs, see Dana (2002).

8. This section was assisted by Y. A. Kosarev, President, Central Committee of the Russian Union of Medium and Small Business Workers, thanks to funding from the United Nations Department of Economic and Social Development.

9. For a detailed discussion of corruption in Russia, see Glinkina (1998).

10. For an analysis of entrepreneurship in Kazakhstan, see Dana (2002).

11. For further discussion, see Bruton (1998).

12. This section contains information obtained during interviews conducted with representatives of several organizations in Kiev, including the Ministry for the Economy; the Ministry of Education; the Ministry of Press and Information; and the State Committee for Entrepreneurship Development. Statistics were provided by the Ukrainian State Committee of Statistics. The section also draws extensively on Ahmed et al. (1998).

Chapter 6

1. For a detailed account of this agreement, see DeVillemarest and Rutchenko (1975).

2. This section contains information obtained during interviews conducted with representatives of several organizations in Tallinn, including the Bank of Estonia; Enterprise Estonia; the Estonian Association of Small and Medium-Sized Enterprises; the Estonian Chamber of Commerce & Industry; the Estonian Export Agency; the Estonian Institute; the Estonian Investment Agency; the Estonian Investment and Trade Development Foundation; the European Bank for Reconstruction and Development; the Ministry of Agriculture; the Ministry of Economic Affairs and Communications; the Ministry of Finance; and the Press and Information Department of the Foreign Ministry. Statistics were provided by the Statistical Office of Estonia. Especially helpful was Margit Kottise, Specialist of the Information and Marketing Section.

3. This section contains information obtained during interviews conducted with representatives of several organizations in Riga, including the Bank of Latvia; the Latvian Chamber of Commerce and Industry; the Latvian Development Agency; the Ministry of Agriculture; the Ministry of Economics; and the Ministry of Foreign Affairs. Statistics were provided by the Central Statistical Bureau of Latvia.

4. Under German rule, Liepàja was known as Libau.

5. This section contains information obtained during interviews conducted with representatives of several organizations in Vilnius, including the Association of Lithuanian Chambers of Commerce, in Industry, and Crafts; the Confederation of Lithuanian Industrialists; the Lithuanian Development Agency for Small and Medium-Sized Enterprises; the Ministry for the Economy; and the Ministry of Finance. Statistics were provided by the Department of Statistics. Especially helpful were Audrone Mishkiniene and Birute Stolyte.

Chapter 7

1. For a discussion of enterprise culture, see Gibb (1987).

2. The encouragement of innovation is addressed by Drucker (1985).

3. For a discussion of the impact of paperwork requirements, see Peterson and Peterson (1981).

References

Abalkin, Leonid (1989). "To Understand Means to Help." *Moscow News* 44(3396), October 29, p. 8.

Adair, John G. (1984). "The Hawthorne Effect: A Reconsideration of the Methodological Artifact." *Journal of Applied Psychology* 69(2), 334-345.

Ahmed, Zafar U., Leo Paul Dana, Syed Aziz Anwar, and Peter Beidyuk (1998). "The Environment for Entrepreneurship and International Business in the Ukraine." *Journal of International Business and Entrepreneurship* 6(2), December, 113-130.

Ahmed, Zafar U., Peter B. Robinson, and Leo Paul Dana (2001). "A U.S. Entrepreneur in Moscow." *Entrepreneurship and Innovation* 2(1), February, 51-58.

Aldrich, Howard E., Ben Rosen, and William Woodward (1987). "The Impact of Social Networks on Business Foundings and Profit in a Longitudinal Study." In Neil C. Churchill, John A. Hornaday, Bruce A. Kirchhoff, O.J. Krasner, and Karl H. Vesper, eds., *Frontiers of Entrepreneurship Research* (pp. 154-168). Wellesley, MA: Babson College.

Aldrich, Howard E. and Catherine Zimmer (1986). "Entrepreneurship Through Social Networks." In Donald L. Sexton and Raymond W. Smilor, eds., *The Art and Science of Entrepreneurship* (pp. 3-24). Cambridge, MA: Ballinger.

Alon, Ilan and Moshe Banai (2001). "Franchising Opportunities and Threats in Russia." In Dianne H. B. Welsh and Ilan Alon, eds., *International Franchising in Emerging Markets: Central and Eastern Europe and Latin America* (pp. 131-148). Chicago, IL: CCH.

Alon, Ilan and David McKee (1999). "The Impact of Crime and Corruption on Russia's Potential for Global Economic Integration." In Jerry Biberman and Abbass Alkhafaji, eds., *Business Research Yearbook: Global Business Perspectives* (pp. 375-379). Chicago, IL: International Academy of Business Disciplines.

Anderson, Robert (2002). "Slovakia's Gypsies Look to EU for Hope." *Financial Times,* London, December 14, p. 6.

Anonymous (1989a). "The Hole in the Map." *The Economist,* August 12, p. 15.

Anonymous (1989b). "Survey: Eastern Europe." *The Economist,* August 12, supplement.

Anonymous (1990). "Yugoslavia." *The Economist,* June 23, p. 103.

Anonymous (1991). "Post-Communist Poverty." *The Economist,* January 12, p. 65.

Anonymous (2001). "Will Montenegro Go Independent?" *The Economist,* April 21, p. 47.

Anonymous (2003). "Russia's Economy: Spend, Spend, Spend." *The Economist,* June 21, pp. 66-67.

Aoki, Masahiko (1995). "Controlling Insider Control: Issues of Corporate Governance in Transition Economies." In Masahiko Aoki and Hyung-Ki Kim, eds., *Corporate Governance in Transitional Economies* (pp. 3-29). Washington, DC: The World Bank.

Arendarski, Andrzej, Tomasz Mroczkowski, and James Sood (1994). "A Study of the Redevelopment of Private Enterprise in Poland: Conditions and Policies for Country Growth." *Journal of Small Business Management* 32(3), July, 40-51.

Arnold, Hugh J. and Daniel C. Feldman (1981). "Social Desirability Response Bias in Self-Report Choice Situations." *Academy of Management Journal* 24, 377-385.

Arnold, Hugh J., Daniel C. Feldman, and May Purbhoo (1985). "The Role of Social Desirability Response Bias in Turnover Research." *Academy of Management Journal* 28, 955-966.

Barth, Frederik, ed. (1963). *The Role of the Entrepreneur in Social Change in Northern Norway*. Bergen: Norwegian Universities' Press.

Barth, Frederik (1966). *Models of Social Organization*. London: Royal Anthropological Institute.

Barth, Frederik (1967a). "Economic Spheres in Darfur." In Raymond Firth, ed., *Themes in Economic Anthropology* (pp. 149-174). London: Tavistock.

Barth, Frederik (1967b). "On the Study of Social Change." *American Anthropologist* 69(6), December, 661-669.

Barth, Frederik (1981). *Process and Form in Social Life*. London: Routledge.

Beamish, Paul (1993). "The Characteristics of Joint Ventures in the People's Republic of China." *Journal of International Marketing* 1(2), 29-48.

Behrman, Jack N. and Dennis A. Rondinelli (1999). "The Transition to Market-Oriented Economies in Central and Eastern Europe: Lessons for Private Enterprise Development." *Global Focus* 11(4), 1-13.

Belyanova, Elena and Ivan Rozinsky (1995). "Evolution of Commercial Banking in Russia and the Implications for Corporate Governance." In Masahiko Aoki and Hyung-Ki Kim, eds., *Corporate Governance in Transitional Economies* (pp. 185-214). Washington, DC: The World Bank.

Berliner, Joseph (1957). *Factory and Manager in the USSR*. Cambridge, MA: Harvard University Press.

Biljan, Maja and Ljiljana Lovric (1995). "Structural Significance of SMEs for the Economy of Croatia." *Zbornik Radova* 13(2), 49-60.

Bird, Maryann (2002) "No News Is Bad News: Ukraine's President Kuchma Is Under Fire for Muzzling The Press, Quashing Dissent and More." *Time,* December 23, 22-24.

Birley, Sue (1985). "The Role of Networks in the Entrepreneurial Process." *Journal of Business Venturing* 1, 107-118.

Birzulis, Philip (2002). "Go Directly to Sleaze, Do Not Pass Morality." *Baltic Times* 7(300), March 28, 20.

Blawatt, Ken R. (1995). "Entrepreneurship in Estonia: Profiles of Entrepreneurs." *Journal of Small Business Management* 3(2), April, 74-79.

Bohlen, Celestine (1994). "Criminals Strangling Russian Economy." *The Gazette,* Montreal, January 30, pp. A1-4.

Bolton, Patrick and Gérard Roland (1992). "Privatization in Central and Eastern Europe." *Economic Policy* 15, October, 276-309.

Bonacich, Edna (1973). "A Theory of Middleman Minorities." *American Sociological Review* 38(5), October, 583-594.

Boycko, Maxim and Andrei Shleifer (1994). "What's Next? Strategies for Enterprise Restructuring in Russia." *Transition* 5, November-December, 8-9.

Boycko, Maxim, Andrei Shleifer, and Robert Vishny (1995). *Privatizing Russia.* Cambridge, MA: MIT Press.

Boylan, Scott P. (1996). "Organized Crime and Corruption in Russia: Implications for U.S. and International Law." *Fordham International Law Journal* 19, June, 1999-2027.

Bruton, Garry D. (1998). "Incubators and Small Business Support in Russia." *Journal of Small Business Management* 36(1), January, 91-94.

Brzezinski, Zbigniew (1991). "The Final Gasp: Moscow Drama Spells End of Soviet Communism." *The Gazette,* Montreal, August 24, p. B3.

Cantillon, Richard (1755). *Essai sur la Nature du Commerce en Général* [Essay on the general nature of commerce]. London and Paris: R. Gyles. (Translated into English in 1931, by Henry Higgs. London: MacMillan and Co.)

Carroll, J. Douglas and Paul E. Green (1995). "Psychometric Methods in Marketing Research: Part I, Conjoint Analysis." *Journal of Marketing Research* 32, November, 385-391.

Castro, Janice (1989). "Joint Misadventures." *Time,* April 10, p. 55.

Chamard, John and Michael Christie (1996). "Entrepreneurship Education Programs: A Change in Paradigm is Needed." *Entrepreneurship, Innovation, and Change* 5(3), September, 217-226.

Chandler, Douglas (1938). "Flying Around the Baltic." *National Geographic* 73(6), June, 767-806.

Chandler, Douglas (1939). "Kaleidoscopic Land of Europe's Youngest King." *National Geographic* 75(6), June, 691-730.

Chater, Melville (1930). "Jugoslavia—Ten Years After." *National Geographic* 58(3), September, 257-309.

Chau, Sandy S. (1995). "The Development of China's Private Entrepreneurship." *Journal of Enterprising Culture* 3(3), September, 261-270.

Cheney, Alan Glenn (1990). "Western Accounting Arrives in Eastern Europe." *Journal of Accountancy,* January, 40-43.

Cherry, Robert (1990). "Middleman Minority Theories: Their Implications for Black-Jewish Relations." *The Journal of Ethnic Studies* 17(4), Winter, 117-138.

Child, John and Andre P. Czeglédy (1996). "Managerial Learning in the Transformation of Eastern Europe: Some Key Issues." *Organization Studies* 17(2), 167-179.

Chow, K.W. Clement and W. K. Eric Tsang (1995) "Entrepreneurs in China: Development, Functions and Problems." *International Small Business Journal* 1, 63-77.

Coase, Ronald H. (1937). "The Nature of the Firm." *Economica* 4, 386-405.

Cockburn, Andrew (2003). "Twenty-first Century Slaves." *National Geographic* 204(3), September, 2-24.

Cole, Williamson E. and Bichaka Fayissa (1991). "Urban Subsistence Labor Force: Towards a Policy-Oriented and Empirically Accessible Taxonomy." *World Development* 19(7), 779-789.

Condon, Christopher (2003). "Low and Behold!" *Eurobusiness* 5(3), August-September, 46-47.

Cornelius, Peter K. and Patrick Lenain, eds. (1997). *Ukraine: Accelerating the Transition to Market.* Washington, DC: International Monetary Fund.

Cottrell, Robert (2002). "The Economy: Higher Inflation Causes Concern." *Russia, Financial Times Survey,* April 15, p. 2.

Crook, Clive (1990). "A Survey of Perestroika." *The Economist,* April 28, 1-24.

Crowne, Doug P. and David Marlowe (1960). "A New Scale of Social Desirability Independent of Psychopathology." *Journal of Consulting Psychology* 24, 349-354.

Dana, Leo Paul (1992). "Entrepreneurship, Innovation and Change in Developing Countries." *Entrepreneurship, Innovation, and Change* 1(2), June, 231-242.

Dana, Leo Paul (1994a). "Economic Reform in the New Vietnam." *Current Affairs,* University of Sydney, Australia, 70(11), May, 19-25.

Dana, Leo Paul (1994b). "Entrepreneurship, Innovation and Change in Former East Germany: An Ethnographic Account." *Entrepreneurship, Innovation, and Change* 3(4), December, 393-401.

Dana, Leo Paul (1994c). "The Impact of Culture on Entrepreneurship, Innovation, and Change in the Balkans: The Yugopluralist Model." *Entrepreneurship, Innovation, and Change* 3(2), June, 177-190.

Dana, Leo Paul (1994d). "A Marxist Mini-Dragon? Entrepreneurship in Today's Vietnam." *Journal of Small Business Management* 32(2), April, 95-102.

Dana, Leo Paul (1995). "Entrepreneurship in a Remote Sub-Arctic Community: Nome, Alaska." *Entrepreneurship: Theory and Practice* 20(1), Fall, 57-72.

Dana, Leo Paul (1996a). "Albania in the Twilight Zone." *Journal of Small Business Management* 34(1), January, 64-70.

Dana, Leo Paul (1996b). "The Last Days of the Compañero Model in Cuba." *Entrepreneurship, Innovation, and Change* 5(2), June, 127-146.

Dana, Leo Paul (1996c). "Small Business in Mozambique After the War." *Journal of Small Business Management* 34(4), October, 67-71.

Dana, Leo Paul (1997a). "Change, Entrepreneurship and Innovation in the Republic of Kazakhstan." *Entrepreneurship, Innovation, and Change* 6(2), June, 167-174.

Dana, Leo Paul (1997b). "Cohon, Russia." *Management Case Quarterly* 2(3), Autumn, 20-22.

Dana, Leo Paul (1997c). "Stalemate in Moldova." *Entrepreneurship, Innovation, and Change* 6(3), September, 269-277.

Dana, Leo Paul (1998a). "Small Business in Xinjiang." *Asian Journal of Business and Information Systems* 3(1), Summer, 123-136.

Dana, Leo Paul (1998b). "Small but Not Independent: SMEs in Japan." *Journal of Small Business Management* 36(4), October, 73-76.

Dana, Leo Paul (1998c). "Waiting for Direction in the Former Yugoslav Republic of Macedonia." *Journal of Small Business Management* 36(2), April, 62-67.

Dana, Leo Paul (1999a). "Bulgaria at the Crossroads of Entrepreneurship." *Journal of Euromarketing* 8(4), December, 27-50.

Dana, Leo Paul (1999b). "Business and Entrepreneurship in Bosnia-Herzegovina." *Journal of Business and Entrepreneurship* 11(2), October, 105-118.

Dana, Leo Paul (1999c). "Entrepreneurship As a Supplement in the People's Republic of China." *Journal of Small Business Management* 37(3), July, 76-80.

Dana, Leo Paul (1999d). *Entrepreneurship in Pacific Asia: Past, Present and Future*. Singapore, London, and Hong Kong: World Scientific.

Dana, Leo Paul (2000a). "Change and Circumstance in Kyrgyz Markets." *Qualitative Market Research* 3(2), April, 62-73.

Dana, Leo Paul (2000b). *Economies of the Eastern Mediterranean Region: Economic Miracles in the Making*. Singapore, London, and Hong Kong: World Scientific.

Dana, Leo Paul, ed. (2000c). *Global Marketing Co-Operation and Networks*. Binghamton, NY: The Haworth Press.

Dana, Leo Paul (2000d). "The Hare and the Tortoise of Former Czechoslovakia: Small Business in the Czech and Slovak Republics." *European Business Review* 12(6), November, 337-343.

Dana, Leo Paul (2002). *When Economies Change Paths: Models of Transition in China, the Central Asian Republics, Myanmar, and the Nations of Former Indochine Française*. Singapore, London, and Hong Kong: World Scientific.

Dana, Leo Paul and Teresa E. Dana (1999). "Franchising." *British Food Journal* 101(5-6), May, 483-505.

Dana, Leo Paul, Hamid Etemad, and Richard W. Wright (1999). "Theoretical Foundations of International Entrepreneurship." In Richard W. Wright, ed., *International Entrepreneurship: Globalization of Emerging Businesses* (pp. 3-22). Stamford, CT: JAI Press.

Dana, Leo Paul, Hamid Etemad, and Richard W. Wright (2000). "The Global Reach of Symbiotic Networks." *Journal of Euromarketing* 9(2), June, 1-16.

Dandridge, Thomas C. and Ignacy Dziedziczak (1992). "New Private Enterprise in Poland: Heritage of the Past and Challenges of the Future." *Journal of Small Business Management* 30(2), April, 104-109.

Dandridge, Thomas C. and David M. Flynn (1988) "Entrepreneurship: Environmental Forces Which Are Creating Opportunities in China." *International Small Business Journal* 6(3), 34-41.

Danforth, Kenneth C. (1990). "A House Much Divided." *National Geographic* 178(2), August, 92-123.

Denuelle, Bernard (1973). "Le Ghetto de Varsovie." *Historia* 315, 86-99.

De Soto, Hernando (1989). *The Other Path: The Invisible Revolution in the Third World.* New York: Harper & Row.

DeVillemarest, P. F. and Nicholas Rutchenko (1975). "Les dessous de l'alliance de Staline avec Hitler." *Historama* 280, March, 97-102.

Dilts, Jeffrey C. (2000). "Volunteers Assisting SMEs in Russia: The Citizens Democracy Corp." *Journal of Small Business Management* 38(1), January, 108-114.

Djankov, Simeon, Rafael La Porta, Florencio Lopez-de-Silanes, and Andrei Shleifer (2002). "The Regulation of Entry." *Quarterly Journal of Econometrics* 117(1), 1-37.

Doder, Dusko (1996). "Albania Opens the Door." *National Geographic* 182(1), July, 66-93.

Drucker, Peter (1985). *Innovation and Entrepreneurship: Practice and Principles.* London: Heinemann.

Earle, John S., Roman Frydman, Andrzej Rapaczynski, and Joel Turkewitz (1994). *Small Privatization: The Transformations of Retail Trade and Consumer Services in the Czech Republic, Hungary and Poland.* Budapest: Central European University Press.

Edwards, Mike (1987). "Ukraine." *National Geographic* 171(5), May, 595-631.

Edwards, Mike (1991). "Mother Russia on a New Course." *National Geographic* 179(2), February, 2-37.

Elenurm, Tiit (2001). "Development Needs of Estonian Entrepreneurs and Managers for International Business." *4th McGill Conference on International Entrepreneurship*, University of Strathclyde, Volume 1, pp. 384-407.

Elenurm, Tiit (2004). "Estonian Perspectives of International Entrepreneurship." In Leo Paul Dana, ed., *The Handbook of Research in International Entrepreneurship* (pp. 370-382). Cheltenham, UK: Edward Elgar.

Ellis, William S. (1975). "Romania: Maverick on a Tightrope." *National Geographic* 148(5), November, 688-713.

Emmott, Bill (1999). "Freedoms' Journey: A Survey of the twentieth Century." *The Economist,* September 11 (36-page insert).

Engholm, Christopher (1994). *The Other Europe.* New York: McGraw-Hill.

Estrin, Saul, ed. (1994a). *Privatization in Central and Eastern Europe.* London: Longman.

Estrin, Saul (1994b). "Privatization in the Transitional Economies of Central and Eastern Europe: Issues and Progress." *Business Strategy Review* 5(4), 81-96.

Evans, Joel R. and Richard L. Laskin (1994). "The Relationship Marketing Process: A Conceptualization and Application." *Industrial Marketing Management* 23(5), 432-452.

Fadahunsi, Akin and Peter Rosa (2002). "Entrepreneurship and Illegality: Insights from the Nigerian Cross-Border Trade." *Journal of Business Venturing* 17(5), 397-429.

Fan, Ying, N. Chen, and David Kirby (1996). "Chinese Peasant Entrepreneurs: An Examination of Township and Village Enterprises in Rural China." *Journal of Small Business Management* 34(4), October, 72-76.

Fay, Doris and Michael Frese (2000). "Working in East German Socialism in 1980 and in Capitalism 15 Years Later: A Trend Analysis of a Transitional Economy's Working Conditions." *Applied Psychology: An International Review* 49(4), 636-657.

Feher, Margit (2003). "Hungary Rate Rise Prompts Currency Concerns." *The Wall Street Journal Europe,* June 11, p. M4.

Feige, Edgar L. and Katarina Ott, eds., (1999). *Underground Economies in Transition: Unrecorded Activity, Tax, Corruption and Organized Crime.* Aldershot, UK: Ashgate.

Fein, Esther (1989). "Lithuania's Communists Vote to Break with Moscow." *The Gazette,* Montreal, December 21, p. A9.

Fein, Esther (1990). "Soviets Reject Lithuanian Independence." *The Gazette,* Montreal, March 16, p. A1-A2.

Franičević, Vojmir (1999). "Political Economy of the Unofficial Economy: The State and Regulation." In Edgar L. Feige and Katarina Ott, eds., *Underground Economies in Transition: Unrecorded Activity, Tax, Corruption and Organized Crime* (pp. 117-137). Aldershot, UK: Ashgate.

Frese, Michael, Wolfgang Kring, Andrea Soose, and Jeanette Zempel (1996). "Personal Initiative at Work: Differences Between East and West Germany." *Academy of Management Journal* 39, 37-63.

Frydman, Roman, Andrzej Rapaczynski, and John S. Earle, eds. (1993). *The Privatization Process in Central Europe.* Budapest: Central European University Press.

Fulop, Gyula (1994). "Entrepreneurship, Small-and Medium-Sized Enterprises in Northern Hungary." *Entrepreneurship and Regional Development* 6, 15-28.

Gardner, Abbey (1990). "The Retrograde Ruble." *Awakening* (Riga), April 30, p. 5.

Geertz, Clifford (1963). *Peddlers and Princes: Social Development and Economic Change in Two Indonesian Towns.* Chicago, IL: University of Chicago Press.

Geib, Peter and Lucie Pfaff (1999). "Strategic Management in Central and Eastern Europe: Introduction." *Journal of East-West Business* 5(4), 1-4.

Gibb, Allan A. (1987). "Enterprise Culture: Its Meaning and Implications for Education and Training." *Journal of European Industrial Training* 11(2), 3-28.

Gilmore, Eddy (1944). "Liberated Ukraine." *National Geographic* 85(5), May, 513-536.

Glas, Miroslav (1997). "The Ethics of Business in Slovenia: Is It Really Bad?" In Luis Montanheiro, Bob Haigh, David Morris, and Zarjan Fabjancic, eds., *Public and Private Sector Partnerships: Learning for Growth* (pp. 101-114). Sheffield, UK: Sheffield Hallam University Press.

Glas, Miroslav (1998). "Eastern Europe: Slovenia." In Alison J. Morrison, ed., *Entrepreneurship—An International Perspective* (pp. 108-124). Oxford, UK.

Glas, Miroslav and Meta Cerar (1997). "The Self-Employment Programme in Slovenia: Evaluation of Results and an Agenda for Improvement." Paper presented at Babson–Kauffman Foundation Entrepreneurship Research Conference, Wellesley, MA: April 17-20.

Glas, Miroslav, Meta Cerar, and Vanja Hazl (1996). *Evaluation of the Self-Employment and Entrepreneurship Programme for the Unemployed*. Ljubljana: Gea Ventures.

Glas, Miroslav, Mateja Drnovšek, and Damjan Mirtic (2000). "Problems Faced by New Entrepreneurs: Slovenia and Croatia—A Comparison." Paper presented at the Thirtieth European Small Business Seminar, Entrepreneurship Under Difficult Circumstances, EFMD Vlerick Leuven Gent Management School, Gent Belgium, September 20-22.

Glas, Miroslav, Robert D. Hisrich, Ales Vahcic, and Bostjan Antoncic (1999). "The Internationalization of SMEs in Transition Economies: Evidence from Slovenia." *Global Focus* 11(4), 107-124.

Glas, Miroslav and Tea Petrin (1998). "Entrepreneurship: New Challenges for Slovene Women." Paper presented at the Babson–Kauffman Foundation Entrepreneurship Research Conference, Gent, Belgium, May 20-24.

Glinkina, Svetlana P. (1998). "The Ominous Landscape of Russian Corruption." *Transitions* 5(3), 16-23.

Glinkina, Svetlana P. (1999). "Russia's Underground Economy During the Transition." In Edgar L. Feige and Katarina Ott, eds., *Underground Economies in Transition: Unrecorded Activity, Tax, Corruption and Organised Crime* (pp. 101-116). Aldershot, UK: Ashgate.

Godwin, Peter (2001). "Gypsies: The Outsiders." *National Geographic* 199(4), April, 72-101.

Golembiewski, Robert T. and Robert Munzenrider (1975). "Social Desirability As an Intervening Variable in Interpreting OD Effects." *Journal of Applied Behavioral Science* 11, 317-332.

Goodale, Greg (2003). "Poland's Lisbon Strategy." *Eurobusiness* 5(3), August-September, 76-78.

Graves, Sally (1939). *A History of Socialism*. London: The Hogarth Press.

Gray, Karin and Mark Allison (1997). "Microenterprise in a Post-Emergency Environment." *Small Enterprise Development* 8(4), December, 34-40.

Greenwald, John (1989). "Turning Up the Power." *Time,* April 10, pp. 50-51.

Gronroos, Christian (1989). "Defining Marketing: A Market-Oriented Approach." *European Journal of Marketing* 23(1), 52-60.

Grossman, Gregory (1977). "The Second Economy of the USSR." *Problems of Communism* 26(5), 25-40.

Grosvenor, Gilbert M. (1962). "Yugoslavia's Window on the Adriatic." *National Geographic* 121(2), February, 219-247.

Gurevich, Vladimir (1989a). "Congratulations on Cost Accounting." *Moscow News* 32(3384), August 6, p. 1.

Gurevich, Vladimir (1989b). "Daunted by Unemployment: Effective Employment Must Replace Fictitious Employment." *Moscow News* 36(3388), September 3, p. 9.

Hagen, Everett E. (1962). *On the Theory of Social Change: How Economic Growth Begins.* Homewood, IL: Dorsey.

Hakansson, Hakan, ed. (1982). *International Marketing and Purchasing of Industrial Goods: An Interaction Approach.* Chicester, UK: John Wiley and Sons.

Hammond, Thomas T. (1966). "An American in Mockba: Russia's Capital." *National Geographic* 129(3), March, 297-351.

Haskell, Martin R. and Lewis Yablonsky (1974). *Crime and Delinquency.* Chicago: Rand McNally.

Hayek, Friedrich A. (1948). *Individualism and Economic Order.* Chicago: University of Chicago Press.

Henry, Stuart (1978). *The Hidden Economy: The Context and Control of Borderline Crime.* London: Martin Robertson.

Herbig, Paul A. and Cynthia McCarty (1995). "Lessons to Be Learned from the Soviet and Chinese Socialist Experiments: A Cross-Cultural Comparison of Innovative Capabilities." *Journal of East-West Business* 1(1), 47-67.

Hisrich, Robert D. and Guyula Fulop (1995). "Hungarian Entrepreneurs and Their Enterprises." *Journal of Small Business Management* 33(3), July, 88-94.

Hisrich, Robert D. and Mikhail V. Gratchev (1993). "The Russian Entrepreneur." *Journal of Business Venturing* 8(6), 487-497.

Hisrich, Robert D. and Mikhail V. Gratchev (1995). "The Russian Entrepreneur: Characteristics and Prescriptions for Success." *Journal of Managerial Psychology* 10, 3-9.

Hisrich, Robert D. and Janos Vecsenyi (1990). "Entrepreneurship and the Hungarian Transformation." *Journal of Managerial Psychology* 5(5), 11-16.

Hodgson, Bryan (1977). "Montenegro: Yugoslavia's 'Black Mountain'." *National Geographic* 152(5), November, 663-683.

Hosmer, Dorothy (1938). "An American Girl Cycles Across Romania." *National Geographic* 74(5), November, 557-588.

Hosmer, Dorothy (1939). "Pedaling Through Poland." *National Geographic* 75(6), June, 739-775.

Hosmer, Dorothy (1940). "Caviar Fishermen of Romania." *National Geographic* 77(3), March, 407-434.

Hough, Jerry F. (2001). *The Logic of Economic Reform in Russia.* Washington, DC: Brookings Institute Press.

Hughes, Gordon and Paul Hare (1992). "Industrial Restructuring in Eastern Europe." *European Economic Review* 36, 670-676.

Hull, Galen Spencer (1999). *Small Businesses Trickling Up in Central and Eastern Europe.* Hamden, CT: Garland.

Huntington, Samuel P. (1993). "The Clash of Civilization." *Foreign Affairs* 72(3), 22-49.

Huntington, Samuel P. (1996). *The Clash of Civilization and the Remaking of World Order.* New York: Simon & Schuster.

Illesh, Yelena (1988). "Cooperative Banker." *Moscow News* 43(3343), October 23, p. 8.

Ivanov, Vladimir (1989). "Buy a 'Guest Worker' from the Province!" *Moscow News* 31(3383), July 30, p. 14.

Ivy, Russell L. (1996). "Small Scale Entrepreneurs and Private Sector Development in the Slovak Republic." *Journal of Small Business Management* 34(4), October, 77-83.

Jacobs, Timothy (2002). "Sex Trade Scars Baltic Women." *Baltic Times* 7(302), April 11, pp. 1-2.

Jernsletten, Johnny-Leo L. and Konstantin Klokov (2002). *Sustainable Reindeer Husbandry.* Tromsø, Norway: Centre for Sami Studies, University of Tromsø.

Jerschina, Jan, and Jaroslaw Górniak (1997). "Leftism, Achievement Orientation, and Basis Dimensions of the Socioeconomic and Political Attitudes in Baltic Countries versus Other Central and Eastern European Countries." In Neil Hood, Robert Kilis, and Jan-Erik Vahlne, eds., *Transition in the Baltic States: Micro-Level Studies* (pp. 80-107). London and New York: Macmillan.

Johanson, Jan and Jan-Erik Vahlne (1977). "The Internationalization Process of the Firm—A Model of Knowledge Development and Increasing Foreign Market Commitments." *Journal of International Business Studies* 8(1), 23-32.

Johanson, Jan and Finn Wiedersheim-Paul (1975). "The Internationalization of the Firm: Four Swedish Cases." *Journal of International Management Studies* 12(3), 36-64.

Johnson, Marguerite (1989). "An Epochal Shift: Communism Yields As Jaruzelski Asks Solidarity to Head a Government." *Time,* August 28, pp. 16-18.

Johnson, Simon, Daniel Kaufmann, John McMillan, and Christopher Woodruff (2000). "Why Do Firms Hide? Bribes and Unofficial Activity After Communism." *Journal of Public Economics* 76, June, 495-520.

Johnson, Simon, Daniel Kaufmann, and Andrei Shleifer (1997). "The Unofficial Economy in Transition." *Brookings Papers on Economic Activity* 2, Fall, 159-239.

Johnson, Simon, Daniel Kaufmann, and Pablo Zoido-Lobaton (1998). "Regulatory Discretion and the Unofficial Economy." *American Economic Review* 88(2), 387-392.

Johnson, Simon, Heidi Kroll, and Mark Horton (1993). "New Banks in the Former Soviet Union: How Do They Operate?" In Anders Aslund and Richard Layard, eds., *Changing the Economic System in Russia* (pp. 183-209). London: St. Martin's Press.

Johnson, Simon and Gary W. Loveman (1995). *Starting Over in Eastern Europe: Entrepreneurship and Economic Renewal.* Boston, MA: Harvard University Press.

Johnson, Simon, John McMillan, and Christopher Woodruff (2002). "Courts and Relational Contracts." *Journal of Law, Economics, and Organization* 18(1), Spring, 221-265.

Jordan, Robert Paul (1970). "Yugoslavia: Six Republics in One." *National Geographic* 137(5), May, 589-633.

Keller, Bill (1988). "In the New Russia, New Greed: Growing Private Sector Brings Crime and Corruption." *International Herald Tribune,* July 26.

Kenny, Brian and Bob Trick (1995). "Reform and Management Education: A Case from the Czech Republic." *Journal of East-West Business* 1(1), 69-96.

Khamidulin, Eduard (1988). "It's Only the Beginning." *Moscow News* 27(3327), July 3, p. 5.

Kirby, David A. (1989). "Encouraging the Enterprise Graduate." *Education Training* 31(4), 9-10.

Kirzner, Israel M. (1973). *Competition and Entrepreneurship.* Chicago: University of Chicago Press.

Kirzner, Israel M. (1979). *Perception, Opportunity, and Profit.* Chicago: University of Chicago Press.

Kirzner, Israel M. (1982). *Method, Process and Austrian Economics.* Lexington, MA: Lexington Books.

Kirzner, Israel M. (1985). *Discovery and the Capitalist Process.* Chicago: University of Chicago Press.

Kiselev, Denis (1990). "New Forms of Entrepreneurship in the U.S.S.R." *Journal of Small Business Management* 28(3), July, 76-80.

Kmecl, Matjaz (1993). *Slovenija iz Zraka.* Ljubljana: Mladinska Knjiga.

Kohan, John (1991). "Russia: Unmerry Christmas." *Time,* December 30, pp. 16-17.

Kohan, John and Naberezhnye Chelny (1991). "Strategy for Survival." *Time,* December 9, p. 36.

Kosmala-MacLullich, Katarzyna, Marta Sikorska, and Jerzy Gierusz (2003). "The Historical and Cultural Contingency of Accountability Processes in Poland." In R.S. Olusegun Wallace, John M. Samuels, Richard J. Briston, and S.M. Saudagaran, eds., *Research in Accounting in Emerging Economies.* Oxford: Elsevier Science, pp. 503-528.

Kruft, Anton T. and Andrea Sofrova (1997). "The Need for Intermediate Support-Structures for Entrepreneurship in Transitional Economies." *Journal of Enterprising Culture* 5(1), March, 13-26.

Kuhn, Delia and Ferdinand Kuhn (1958). "Poland Opens Her Doors." *National Geographic* 114(3), September, 354-398.

Kuteinikov, Andrei (1989). "A Bad Word Makes Good." *Moscow News* 4(3356), January 22, p. 14.

Kuznetsov, Andrei, Frank McDonald, and Olga Kuznetsova (2000). "Entrepreneurial Qualities: A Case from Russia." *Journal of Small Business Management* 38(1), January, 101-107.

Kvint, Vladimir (1991). "Food for Peace? Or for Civil War?" *Forbes,* January 21, pp. 39-40.

Lauret, Jean-Claude (1978). "Il y a trente ans: Le Coup de Prague." *Historia* 375, 94-103.

Lechner, Michael and Friedhelm Pfeiffer (1993). "Planning for Self-Employment at the Beginning of a Market Economy: Evidence from Individual Data of East German Workers." *Small Business Economics* 5, 111-128.

Lewis, W. Arthur (1955). *The Theory of Economic Growth.* Homewood, IL: Richard D. Irwin.

Lieven, Dominic (1990). "Bleak Prospects." *International Management,* March, 52-53.

Light, Ivan and Edna Bonacich (1988). *Immigrant Entrepreneurs.* Berkeley, CA: University of California Press.

Linehan, Edward J. (1968). "Czechoslovakia: The Dream and the Reality." *National Geographic* 133(2), February, 151-194.

Litvack, Jennie I. and Dennis A. Rondinelli, eds. (1999). *Market Reform in Vietnam: Building Institutions for Development.* Westport, CT: Quorum.

Liuhto, Kari (1996). "The Transformation of the Enterprise Sector in Estonia." *Journal of Enterprising Culture* 4(3), September, 317-329.

Lombardo, Gary A. (1995). "Chinese Entrepreneurs: Strategic Adaptation in a Transitional Economy." *Journal of Enterprising Culture* 3(3), September, 277-292.

Lyles, Marjorie, Inga S. Baird, and J. Burdeane Orris (1995). "Entrepreneurship in a Transition Economy: An Examination of Venture Creation in Hungary." *Journal of Enterprising Culture* 3(1), March, 59-84.

MacIntyre, John (1991). "Figuratively Speaking." *Inside Guide,* October/November, p. 65.

Manrai, Lalita A., Dana-Nicoleta Lascu, and Ajay K. Manrai (1999). "How the Fall of the Iron Curtain Has Affected Consumers' Perceptions of Urban and Rural Quality of Life in Romania." *Journal of East-West Business* 5(1-2), 145-172.

Marinov, Marin Alexandrov, Svetla Trifonova Marinova, Lalita A. Manrai, and Ajay K. Manrai (2001). "Marketing Implications of Communist Ideological Legacy in Culture in the Context of Central and Eastern Europe: A Comparison of Bulgaria, Romania and Ukraine." *Journal of Euromarketing* 11(1), 7-35.

Marshall, Tyler (1990). "New Era Opens As East Germans Vote Today." *The Gazette,* Montreal, Sunday, March 18, p. B1.

Martin, James H. and Bruno Grbac (1998). "Smaller and Larger Firms' Marketing Activities As a Response to Economic Privatization: Marketing Is Alive and Well in Croatia." *Journal of Small Business Management* 36(1), January, 95-99.

Marx, Karl and Friedrich Engels (1848). *Manifest der Kommunisitischen Partei* [The Communist Manifesto]. London: J.E. Burghard.

Masterov, Valery (1989). "Poland: There Can Be No Government of National Accord Without Communists." *Moscow News* 36(3388), September 3, p. 1.

McClelland, David Clarence (1961). *The Achieving Society*. Princeton, NJ: D. Van Nostrand.

McDowell, Bart (1971). "Hungary." *National Geographic* 139(4), April, pp. 443-483.

McKinsey, Kitty (1992). "Top American Economist Says Yeltsin's Plan is Paying Off." *The Gazette,* Montreal, January 16, p. A8.

McMillan, John (2002). *Reinventing the Bazaar: The Natural History of Markets*. New York: Norton.

McMillan, John and Barry Naughton (1992). "How to Reform a Planned Economy: Lessons from China." *Oxford Review of Economic Policy* 8, Spring, 130-142.

Meager, Nigel (1992). "The Fall and Rise of Self-employment (Again): A Comment on Bögenhold and Staber." *Work, Employment and Society* 6(1), March, 127-134.

Megginson, William L. and Jeffry M. Netter (2001). "From State to Market: A Survey of Empirical Studies on Privatization." *Journal of Economic Literature* 39(2), 321-389.

Michaels, Daniel (1993). "In Poland the Spirit of Capitalism Begins to Take Root and Blossom." *The Journal of Wall Street* (Europe), February, p. 1.

Mill, John Stuart (1869). *On Liberty*. London: Longman, Roberts and Green.

Misiunas, Romuald J. and Rein Taagepera (1983). *The Baltic States: Years of Dependence, 1940-1980*. Berkeley: University of California Press.

Misiunas, Romuald J. and Rein Taagepera (1991). "Population Changes 1939-1989." *Awakening* (Riga), March 31, p. 3.

Mitchell, Jeannine (1989). "Soviet Summer." *Financial Post Moneywise,* April, pp. 69-81.

Morris, Michael H. and Leyland F. Pitt (1995). "Informal Sector Activity As Entrepreneurship: Insights from a South African Township." *Journal of Small Business Management* 33(1), January, 78-86.

Moskowitz, Howard R. and Samuel Rabino (2001). "International Product Concept Development—A Research Platform and Its Transfer to a Transitional Economy." *Journal of Euro-Marketing* 10(3), 45-63.

Murrell, Peter (1993). "Privatization's Harms: Economics in Eastern Europe." *Current* 349, 34-39.

Myalo, Xeniya (1988). "Inspired by the Flame: Consumerism and Spiritual Values." *Moscow News* 34(3334), August 21, p. 11.

Nedialkova, Aneta (2001). "Bulgaria: Economic Development and Franchising." In Dianne H. B. Welsh and Ilan Alon, eds., *International Franchising in Emerging Markets: Central and Eastern Europe and Latin America* (pp. 203-214). Chicago, IL: CCH.

Nixon, Richard M. (1959). "Russia As I Saw It." *National Geographic* 66(6), December, 715-750.

Noar, Jacob (1985). "Recent Small Business Reforms in Hungary." *Journal of Small Business Management* 23(1), January, 65-72.

North, Douglass (1990). *Institutions, Institutional Change, and Economic Performance.* Cambridge, MA: Harvard University Press.

Novikova, Svetlana I., Ludmila M. Petrovskaia, and Alexey V. Daniltchenko (1999). "Analysis of Small Business Development in the Countries in Transition: A Case of Belarus." Paper presented at the International Conference of the International Council for Small Business, Naples, June 20-23.

O'Driscoll, Gerald P., Kim R. Holmes, and Melanie Kirkpatrick (2001). *2001 Index of Economic Freedom.* New York: The Wall Street Journal.

Oliver, Katerina (1991). "Bribes and the Mafia Still Rule Moscow Life." *The European,* October 25-27, p. 5.

Overholt, William H. (1993). *The Rise of China: How Economic Reform Is Creating a New Superpower.* New York: Norton.

Parker, John (1990). "The Soviet Union: Survey." *The Economist,* October 20, pp. Survey 1-24.

Parsons, Talcott (1951). *The Social System.* Glencoe, IL: Free Press.

Parsons, Talcott and Neil Smelzer (1956). *Economy and Society.* Glencoe, IL: Free Press.

Patric, John (1938a). "Czechoslovaks, Yankees of Europe." *National Geographic* 74(2), August, 173-225.

Patric, John (1938b). "Magyar Mirth and Melancholy." *National Geographic* 73(1), January, 1-55.

Patton, Michael Quinn (1982). "Qualitative Methods and Approaches: What Are They?" In Eileen Kuhns and S. V. Martorana, eds., *Qualitative Methods for Institutional Research* (pp. 3-16). San Francisco: Jossey-Bass.

Patton, Michael Quinn (1987). *How to Use Qualitative Methods in Evaluation.* Newbury Park, CA: Sage.

Patton, Michael Quinn (1990). *Qualitative Evaluation and Research Methods.* Newbury Park, CA: Sage.

Pavlin, Igor (2001). "Central Europe: Franchising in Slovenia." In Dianne H. B. Welsh and Ilan Alon, eds., *International Franchising in Emerging Markets: Central and Eastern Europe and Latin America* (pp. 189-201). Chicago, IL: CCH.

Pavlovskis, Raimonds (1990). "Latvia Prepares to Open Doors for Foreign Investors." *Awakening* (Riga), July 31, p. 8.

Peattie, Lisa (1987). "An Idea in Good Currency and How It Grew: The Informal Sector." *World Development* 15(7), 851-860.

Peng, Michael W. (2000). *Business Strategies in Transition Economies.* Thousand Oaks, CA: Sage.

Peterson, Rein (1988). "Understanding and Encouraging Entrepreneurship Internationally." *Journal of Small Business Management* 26(2), April, 1-7.

Peterson, Rein and Mari A. Peterson (1981). "The Impact of Economic Regulation and Paperwork." Regulation Reference Working Paper Series. Ottawa: Economic Council of Canada.

Petrus, Marek (2003). "Czechs See Their Country As a High-tech Magnet." *International Herald Tribune,* April 5, p. 13.

Piaseski, Bogdan and Daniel S. Fogel (1995). *Regional Determinants of SME Development in the Central and Eastern European Countries.* Lodz: Lodz University Press.

Popov, Alexander (1989). "Hungary on the Road of Reform." *Moscow News* 44(3396), October 29, p. 2.

Popov, Vladimir (1991). "Comes the Revolution: A Top Soviet Economist Sizes Up the Hard Road Ahead." *Barron's,* August 26, pp. 8-12.

Porter, Ethel Chamberlain (1944). "The Clock Turns Back in Yugoslavia." *National Geographic* 85(4), April, 493-512.

Portes, Alejandro, Manuel Castells, and Lauren A. Benton, eds. (1989). *The Informal Economy: Studies in Advanced and Less Developed Countries.* Baltimore, MD: John Hopkins University Press.

Posadas, Barbara M. and Roland L. Guyotte (1990). *Unintentional Entrepreneurs.* Berkeley, CA: University of California Press.

Pozzi, Henri (1935). *Black Hand over Europe.* London: The Francis Mott Company.

Radaev, Vadim (1993). "Emerging Russian Entrepreneurship: As Viewed by the Experts." *Economic and Industrial Democracy* 14, 55-77.

Radyshevsky, Dmitry (1989). "Poland: Skyrocketing Prices and the Price of Freedom." *Moscow News* 44(3396), October 29, p. 6.

Rahim, M. Afzalur (1983). "A Measure of Styles of Handling Interpersonal Conflict." *Academy of Management Journal* 26, 368-376.

Range, Peter Ross (1996). "Reinventing Berlin." *National Geographic* 190(6), December, 96-117.

Raun, Toivo U. (1987). *Estonia and Estonians.* Stanford, CA: Hoover Press.

Rebernik, Miroslav (2003). "From Innovation to Entrepreneurship." In Erich Schwarz, ed., *Technologieorientiertes Innovations Management* (pp. 139-160). Wiesbaden: Gabler.

Rebernik, Miroslav, Dijana Močnik, Jozica Knez Riedl, Karin Širec Rantaša, Matej Rus, Polona Tominc, and Tadej Krošlin (2003). *Slovenian Entrepreneurship Observatory 2002,* translated by Igor Rizner and Michael Manske. Maribor: Faculty of Economics and Business, Institute for Entrepreneurship and Small Business Management.

Reichlin, Igor (1992). "International Business: Where Cutthroat Competition . . ." *Business Week,* March 2, p. 51.

Remnick, David (1997). "Moscow: The New Revolution." *National Geographic* 191(4), April, 78-103.

Robinson, Peter B., Zafar U. Ahmed, Leo Paul Dana, Gennady R. Latfullin, and Valentina Smirnova (2001). "Towards Entrepreneurship and Innovation in Russia." *International Journal of Entrepreneurship and Innovation Management* 1(2), 230-240.

Ronayne, Chris (2002). *Rudi Gopas: A Biography.* Auckland, New Zealand: David Ling Publishing.

Ronnås, Per (1996). "Private Entrepreneurship in the Nascent Market Economy of Vietnam." In John McMillan and Barry Naughton, eds., *Reforming Asian Socialism: The Growth of Market Institutions* (pp. 135-165). Ann Arbor: University of Michigan Press.

Rosefielde, Steven (1986). "Regulated Market Socialism: The Semi-Competitive Soviet Solution." *Soviet Union/Union Sovietique* 13, p. 13.

Rosenkrantz, Stuart A., Fred Luthans, and Harry W. Hennessey (1983). "Role Conflict and Ambiguity Scales: An Evaluation of Psychometric Properties and the Role of Social Desirability Response Bias." *Educational and Psychological Management* 43, 957-970.

Rosser, J. Barkley Jr., Marina Rosser, and Ehsan Ahmed (2000). "Income Inequality and the Informal Economy in Transition Economies." *Journal of Comparative Economics* 28, 156-171.

Sachs, Jeffrey (1993). *Poland's Jump to the Market Economy.* Cambridge, MA: MIT Press.

Sacks, Paul M. (1993). "Privatization in the Czech Republic." *Columbia Journal of World Business* 28, 188-194.

Sanders, Rickie (1987). "Toward a Geography of Informal Activity." *Socio-Economic Planning Sciences* 24(4), 229-237.

Schumpeter, Joseph Alois (1912). *Theorie der wirtschaftlichen Entwicklung: Eine Untersuchung über Unternehmergewinn, Kapial, Kredit, Zins und den Konjunkturzyklus.* Munich and Leipzig: Dunker und Humblat.

Schumpeter, Joseph Alois (1928). "The Instability of Capitalism." *Economic Journal* 38, 361-386.

Schumpeter, Joseph Alois (1934). *The Theory of Economic Development: An Inquiry into Profits, Capital, Credit, Interest, and the Business Cycle.* Cambridge, MA: Harvard University Press.

Schumpeter, Joseph Alois (1939). *Business Cycles: A Theoretical, Historical and Statistical Analysis of the Capitalist Process.* New York: McGraw-Hill.

Schumpeter, Joseph Alois (1942). *Capitalism, Socialism and Democracy.* New York: Harper and Brothers.

Schumpeter, Joseph Alois (1947). "The Creative Response in Economic History." *Journal of Economic History* 7(2), November, 149-159.

Schumpeter, Joseph Alois (1949). "Economic Theory and Entrepreneurial History." In Joseph Alois Schumpeter, ed., *Change and the Entrepreneur* (pp. 63-84). Cambridge, MA: Harvard University Press.

Seibert, Horst, ed. (1992). *Privatization.* Tübingen: Mohr.

Shaw, Bernard (1928). *The Intelligent Woman's Guide to Socialism, Capitalism, Sovietism and Fascism.* London: Constable and Company.

Shirk, Susan (1993). *The Political Logic of Economic Reform in China.* Berkeley: University of California Press.

Shleifer, Andrei (1997). "Joseph Schumpeter Lecture: Government in Transition." *European Economic Review* 41(3-5), April, 385-410.

Shleifer, Andrei and Robert W. Vishny (1993a). "Corruption." *Quarterly Journal of Economics* 108(3), August, 599-617.

Shleifer, Andrei and Robert W. Vishny (1993b). *The Grabbing Hand: Government Pathologies and Their Cures.* Cambridge, MA: Harvard University Press.

Shleifer, Andrei and Robert W. Vishny (1994). "Politicians and Firms." *Quarterly Journal of Economics* 109(4), November, 995-1025.

Simoneti, Marko (1993). "A Comparative Review of Privatization Strategies in Four Former Socialist Countries." *Europe-Asia Studies* 45, 79-102.

Siu, Wai-Sum and David A. Kirby (1995). "Marketing in Chinese Small Business: Tentative Theory." *Journal of Enterprising Culture* 3(3), September, 309-342.

Smith, Adam (1892). *Inquiry into the Nature and Causes of the Wealth of Nations,* Volumes I and II (reprinted from the sixth edition with an introduction by Ernest Belfort Bax). Covent Garden, London: George Bell and Sons, York Street.

Speier, Christa and Michael Frese (1997). "Generalized Self-efficacy As a Mediator and Moderator Between Control and Complexity at Work and Personal Initiative: A Longitudinal Field Study in East Germany." *Human Performance* 10(2), 171-192.

Stamp, L. Dudley (1936). *A Commercial Geography.* London: Longmans, Green and Co.

Stankevich, Sergei (1989). "Legal Strikes." *Moscow News* 44(3396), October 29, pp. 8-9.

Stead, Deborah, Rose Brady, Igor Reichlin, Patricia Kranz, and Walecia Konrad (1991). "Will Yeltsin's New Order Put Bread on the Table?" *Business Week,* December 23, pp. 42-46.

Stoever, William A. (1995). "The Role of Foreign Investment in Poland's Economic Restructuring: Some Polish Views." *Journal of East-West Business* 1(1), 97-115.

Stone, Eugene F., Daniel C. Ganster, Richard W. Woodman, and Marcelline R. Fusilier (1979). "Relationships Between Growth Need Strength and Selected Individual Difference Measures Employed in Job Design Research." *Journal of Vocational Behavior* 14, 329-340.

Štulhofer, Aleksandar (1999). "Between Opportunism and Distrust: Socio-Cultural Aspects of the Underground Economy in Croatia." In Edgar L. Feige and Katarina Ott, eds., *Underground Economies in Transition: Unrecorded Activity, Tax, Corruption and Organized Crime* (pp. 43-63). Aldershot, UK: Ashgate.

Tan, C. L. and T. S. Lim (1993). *Vietnam: Business and Investment Opportunities.* Singapore: Cassia.

Taubman, William (2003). *Khrushchev: The Man and His Era.* New York: Norton.

Thomas, Kenneth W. and Ralph H. Kilmann (1975). "The Social Desirability Variable in Organizational Research: An Alternative Explanation for Reported Findings." *Academy of Management Journal* 18, 741-752.

Thomas, Stephen (1993). "The Politics and Economics of Privatization in Central and Eastern Europe." *Columbia Journal of World Business* 28, Spring, 168-178.

Thompson, Jon (1991). "East Europe's Dark Dawn: The Iron Curtain Rises to Reveal a Land Tarnished by Pollution." *National Geographic* 179(6), June, 36-69.

Tokman, Victor E. (1978). "Competition Between the Informal Sectors in Retailing: The Case of Santiago." *World Development* 6(9), September, 1187-1198.

Tracevskis, Rokas M. (2002). "PM Tells Farmers Not to Fear EU." *Baltic Times* 7(300), March 28, p. 7.

Ungern-Sternberg, Irina (1939). "Estonia: At Russia's Baltic Gate." *National Geographic* 76(6), December, 803-834.

Utsch, Andreas, Andreas Rauch, Rainer Rothfuss, and Michael Frese (1999). "Who Becomes a Small Scale Entrepreneur in a Post-Socialist Environment: On the Differences Between Entrepreneurs and Managers in East Germany." *Journal of Small Business Management* 37(3), July, 31-42.

Vamosi, Tamas (2003). "The Role of Management Accounting in a Company in Transition from Command to Market Economy." *Journal of Small Business and Enterprise Development* 10(2), 194-209.

Vesilind, Priit J. (1980). "Return to Estonia." *National Geographic* 157(4), April, 485-511.

Vesilind, Priit J. (1982). "Two Berlins—A Generation Apart." *National Geographic* 161(1), January, 2-51.

Vesilind, Priit J. (1989). "The Baltics: Arena of Power." *National Geographic* 175(5), May, 602-635.

Vesilind, Priit J. (1990). "The Baltic Nations." *National Geographic* 178(5), November, 2-37.

Viducić, Ljiljana and Gordana Brcić (2001). "The Role of Franchising in the Establishment and Internationalization of Business with Special Reference to Croatia." In Dianne H. B. Welsh and Ilan Alon, eds., *International Franchising in Emerging Markets: Central and Eastern Europe and Latin America* (pp. 215-222). Chicago, IL: CCH.

Volin, Vladimir (1989). "Moldavia: 150,000 Unemployed People." *Moscow News* 36(3388), September 3, pp. 8-9.

Wagstyl, Stefan (2002). "EU Entry Deal." *Financial Times*, December 14, p. 6.

Wasilczuk, Julita (2000). "Advantageous Competence of Owner/Managers to Grow the Firm in Poland: Empirical Evidence." *Journal of Small Business Management* 38(2), 88-94.

Weber, Max (1904-1905). "Die protestantische Ethik und der Geist des Kapitalismus." *Archiv fur Sozialwissenschaft und Sozialpolitik* (20-21); translated, in 1930, by Talcott Parsons, *The Protestant Ethic and the Spirit of Capitalism.* New York: George Allen and Unwin.

Weber, Max (1924). *The Theory of Social and Economic Organization.* New York: The Free Press.

Webster, Frederick E. (1992). "The Changing Role of Marketing in the Corporation." *Journal of Marketing* 53, October, 1-17.

Wei, Liu (2001). "Incentive Systems for Technical Change: The Chinese System in Transition." *International Journal of Entrepreneurship and Innovation Management* 1(2), 157-177.

Williams, E. E. and Jing Li (1993). "Rural Entrepreneurship in the People's Republic of China." *Entrepreneurship, Innovation, and Change* 2(1), 41-54.

Williams, Maynard Owen (1932). "Bulgaria, Farm Land Without a Farmhouse." *National Geographic* 62(2), August, 184-201.

Williamson, Oliver E. (1975). *Markets and Hierarchies.* New York: Free Press.

Williamson, Oliver E. and Scott E. Masten, eds. (1999). *The Economics of Transaction Costs.* Northampton, MA: Edward Elgar.

Wilson, Paul (1992). "Czechoslovakia: The Pain of Divorce." *New York Review of Books* 39, 69-75.

Zapalska, Alina M. (1997a). "A Profile of Woman Entrepreneurs and Enterprises in Poland." *Journal of Small Business Management* 35(4), October, 76-82.

Zapalska, Alina M. (1997b). "Profiles of Polish Entrepreneurship." *Journal of Small Business Management* 35(2), April, 111-117.

Zapalska, Alina M. and Lucyna Zapalska (1999). "Small Business Ventures in Post-Communist Hungary." *Journal of East-West Business* 5(4), 5-22.

Zerbe, Wilfred J. and Delroy L. Paulhus (1987). "Socially Desirable Responding in Organizational Behavior: A Recognition." *Academy of Management Review* 12(2), 250-264.

Zhuplev, Anatoly V., Fred Kiesner, Asyleeck B. Kozhakmetov, Tan Wee Liang, and Alexander Konkov (1998). "Traits of Successful Business Owners: A Comparative Study of Entrepreneurs in Singapore, the USA, Russia and Kazakhstan." *Journal of Enterprising Culture* 6(3), 257-268.

Zineldin, Mosad Amin (1998). "Towards an Ecological Collaborative Relationship Management." *European Journal of Marketing* 32(11-12), 1138-1164.

Index

Page numbers followed by the letter "f" indicate figures; those followed by the letter "t" indicate tables.